Standards and Quality in Higher Education

Higher Education Policy Series

**The Use of Performance Indicators
in Higher Education, 3rd edition**
The Challenge of the Quality Movement
Martin Cave, Stephen Hanney, Mary Henkel
and Maurice Kogan
ISBN 1 85302 345 0
Higher Education Policy Series 3

Quantity and Quality in Higher Education
John Radford, Kjell Raaheim, Ruth Williams and Peter de Vries
ISBN 1 85302 433 3
Higher Education Policy Series 40

Are Professors Professional?
The Organisation of University Examinations
David Warren Piper
ISBN 1 85302 540 2
Higher Education Policy Series 25

**Goals and Purposes of Higher Education
in the 21st Century**
Edited by Arnold Burgen
ISBN 1 85302 547 X
Higher Education Policy Series 32

Improvement and Accountability
A. I. Vroeijenstijn
ISBN 1 85302 546 1
Higher Education Policy Series 30

Dimensions of Evaluation in Higher Education
Report of the IHME Study Group on Evaluation in Higher Education
Urban Dahllöff, John Harris, Michael Shattock,
André Staropoli and Roland in't Veld
ISBN 1 85302 526 7
Higher Education Policy Series 13

Higher Education Policy Series 37

Standards and Quality in Higher Education

Edited by John Brennan, Peter de Vries and Ruth Williams

Jessica Kingsley Publishers
London and Bristol, Pennsylvania

First published in the United Kingdom in 1997 by
Jessica Kingsley Publishers Ltd
116 Pentonville Road
London N1 9JB, England
and
1900 Frost Road, Suite 101
Bristol, PA 19007, U S A

Library of Congress Cataloging in Publication Data
A CIP catalogue record for this book is available from the
Library of Congress

British Library Cataloguing in Publication Data
A CIP catalogue record for this book is available from the British Library

ISBN 1 85302 423 6

Printed and Bound in Great Britain by
Athenæum Press, Gateshead, Tyne and Wear

Contents

List of Figures

List of Tables

Preface

The origins of the majority of the chapters in this book lie in papers contributed to two conferences which took place in Paris and London in December 1995 and February 1996. The Paris conference, entitled 'Institutional Responses to Quality Assessment', was organised by the programme for Institutional Management in Higher Education (IMHE) of the Organisation for Economic Co-operation and Development (OECD). The chapters by Dill, Massaro, Woodhouse, Ottenwaelter, Thune, Barblan, Engwall, Rasmussen and Baldwin are from this source.

The London conference, entitled 'Changing Conceptions of Academic Standards', was organised by the UK Open University's Quality Support Centre (QSC) and the chapters by Brown, Watson, Finch and Becher are based on papers presented there. The chapters by Williams, Thune and Staropoli, and Shah were written specially for this volume.

Finally, the editors acknowledge the considerable help provided by Deana Parker of the Quality Support Centre in bringing together the various articles which form the present volume.

John Brennan, Peter de Vries, Ruth Williams
October, 1996

Chapter 1

Introduction

John Brennan

How has something so self-evidently desirable as quality become so controversial? Who can fail to be in favour of quality in higher education? Who can argue with the proposition that we should strive continuously to improve it? Yet debates about quality in higher education have indeed provoked controversy in many countries. The purpose of this book is to shed light on these controversies by providing a range of perspectives from a number of different countries on developments in the assessment of quality in higher education.[1]

The controversy about quality in higher education is partly about *language*, many of the terms used embracing values which some people find inappropriate and potentially threatening to higher education's traditions. The controversy is also partly about *power*, about the relative autonomy of higher education from other institutions of society, most importantly the state, and about the relative autonomy of individual academic staff within the institutions in which they work. The controversy is also about *change*, about the many external social and economic changes which are requiring change in higher education, and about the managerial and other mechanisms with which higher education institutions seek to steer this change. In this introductory chapter, each of these potential sources of controversy will be considered in turn. In addition, the so far distinctively British debate about standards

---

1 The term 'quality assessment' is used here in a generic sense to refer to any systematic review, evaluation or assessment of educational provision in institutions of higher education.

will be introduced and some reasons for it suggested. Finally, the chapter will attempt to identify the main interests which are represented in these debates about quality and standards and which will figure to a greater or lesser extent in the chapters which follow.

A controversy about language

Part of the problem lies with the term itself. 'Quality' has become all pervasive in modern society, almost a totem of post-modernism and mass culture. As a prefix, it attaches itself to everything: from automobiles to baked beans, from plumbing to lager. The adjectival use of the term evokes the marketplace, the advertising hoarding, the 'ad' in Yellow Pages. It is part of the none-too-subtle 'hard sell'. It is noticeable that its use has not, on the whole, been adopted by the more elite professions and social institutions: there appear to be relatively few 'quality' solicitors, priests and doctors. Thus, its adoption by higher education might suggest to some the invasion of the marketplace, and a particularly 'down market' invasion at that, bringing with it alien concepts and practices which take no account of higher education's special characteristics.

Much of the language of quality reflects contemporary management theory as developed in manufacturing and service industries. It is a language which can turn students into customers, academic staff into producers/providers, universities into businesses and their departments into profit centres. Of course, many of these trends have less to do with quality initiatives and much to do with cuts in funding, competitiveness and the need to secure new sources of income. But for many academics, quality initiatives are implicated in these broader trends which they see as threatening to undermine higher education's 'special' characteristics and status.

The language of quality has, of course, acquired its own experts, experts who know the difference between quality assurance and quality control, between quality improvement and quality enhancement, between assessment and audit, between evaluation and appraisal. But this is a language which exists outside of the specialist discourses of academic staff, socialised into and owing a primary loyalty to specialist disciplines. To them, the language of quality can appear imperialistic, a spurious quasi-discipline with suspicious links to management.

Of course, higher education has its traditional language of quality reflecting notions of standards, of academic coherence and progression, of attainment and understanding. But the meaning of such terms is frequently implicit, perhaps even fuzzy, not readily communicable to people outside the discourse of the specialist discipline. The outsider might feel: never mind the coherence, are the customers happy?

Much of the language of quality appears to have been imported into higher education from elsewhere and, as such, emphasises and strengthens what have been termed higher education's extrinsic functions over its intrinsic functions, for example, servicing the economy over the creation and transmission of new knowledge. Some of the language of quality requires us to change the way we think about higher education: the controversy about language is about more than words.

A controversy about power

Systems of higher education in different countries vary in the extent to which things are decided by the state, by individual institutions, by faculties and departments, by individual academic staff (with considerable additional variation in the power of seniority and professorial status), by students and by various external stakeholders. These different sources of power reflect respectively the state, the academic profession and markets. Notwithstanding a near universal emphasis on 'autonomy', in practice higher education institutions are subject to all sorts of controls – political, economic and cultural – from many different sources. In some higher education systems, the complex balance of powers is such as seemingly to reinforce the *status quo* forever. In particular, the power of interest groups to block rather than to initiate change is an important source of either stability or inertia, depending on your point of view.

Quite a lot of the controversy about quality assessment in higher education has been about who should 'own' it. Where ownership reflects the existing balance of power – e.g. a state-sponsored agency in a system where the ministry has traditionally decided most things – controversy over ownership may be limited. But where ownership suggests a significant change in the balance of power – e.g. the introduction of a state-sponsored agency in a system where there have been relatively few mechanisms of state control – controversy over ownership is likely to be high. In some cases, it may be resolved by the creation of a symbolically 'independent' agency, balance secured through the composition of its governing body.

The controversy about power is reflected not only in questions of ownership; it also embraces questions of method. Thus, a preference for self-evaluation is expressed by representatives of institutions while representatives of government emphasise a need for externality in the assessment process. These preferences may have less to do with the proven efficacy of any particular assessment method and have everything to do with the exercise of power.

The controversy about power can sometimes appear to be between only two interest groups: higher education institutions and the state. But a rather different kind of controversy exists at the institutional level: the controversy of so-called managerialism. From the perspective of the individual staff member, local controls and constraints can appear to be far more powerful than anything that exists at the system level. Thus, approaches to quality assessment which emphasise institution-level responsibility tend to be accompanied by the introduction of institution-wide procedures and policies which have the effect of shifting power away from the basic unit or department towards the institutional centre.

Power at the institutional level also impacts on attitudes to method. On the whole, an assessment method which focuses on the institutional level is likely to reinforce the power of institutional management. It does so by concentrating on matters which are largely management preserves: resources, policies, procedures. Conversely, an assessment method which focuses on the subject level will tend to reinforce the importance of subject values and academic work, thereby enhancing the power of the subject group.

Thus, much of the debate about quality assessment at both system and institutional levels is a debate about power. All parties to the debate are in favour of quality but each feels that it, better than the others, knows best how to achieve it (and what it is); and, at least in some systems and institutions, each mistrusts the motives and agendas of the others.

A controversy about change

Much of the mistrust reflects the scale of the changes occurring in higher education, changes which themselves have relatively little to do with quality assessment directly. The changes have involved expansion – new institutions, the growth of existing ones, larger class sizes; they have involved diversification – different kinds of students, different kinds of courses and new ways of teaching and assessing them; they have placed greater emphasis on higher education's extrinsic functions – to do with training people for jobs, greater relevance in research; they have been accompanied by declining resource levels and greater accountability for the use of them. All of these changes are interconnected and, in the eyes of many academic staff, are linked to the most painful change of all: a decline in the status, remuneration and conditions of work associated with academic life.

Quality assessment is associated with these changes in a variety of ways. First, its introduction is a reflection of the greater costs, visibility and assumed social and economic importance of higher education. Governments want to know what they are getting for the resources invested in higher education. Relatedly, in some countries at least, governments have relaxed other forms of control which they have traditionally exercised over higher education. In large part, they have done so to encourage the process of change, freeing institutions to respond more rapidly and effectively to new demands. This movement towards greater autonomy of higher education institutions has brought with it requirements of greater accountability. The introduction of quality assessment has been an important part of this. (There are some notable exceptions to this trend: the introduction of quality assessment in the UK was part of a much larger process of greater centralisation and state control.)

Second, quality assessment has been associated with institutional issues raised as a result of expansion and diversity. Are institutions – and the staff within them – sufficiently equipped to deal with new kinds of students with new kinds of wants and needs? Developments such as credit systems, modularity, greater interdisciplinarity, calls for teacher training for academics, are all responses to a perceived need to change in order to meet new kinds of demand. The process of quality assessment can contribute by questioning the appropriateness of existing practice to changing circumstances; it can provide a forum for the exchange of practice and experience across institutions; it can provide a reference point for change in a single institution by disseminating system-wide information and recommended good practice; in short, quality assessment can contribute towards the maintenance and improvement of quality in changing circumstances.

Third, quality assessment can contribute to institutional problem-solving. Although a lot of the debate about quality has focused on the work of national agencies, this neglects the volume of internal assessment activity generated within higher education institutions quite independently of the requirements of external agencies. Institutions are having to review their activities and practices for all of the reasons cited above. They are faced with hard decisions and with a need for better information to inform them, and perhaps also to legitimise them. Thus, many institutions have undertaken evaluations or internal reviews of specific aspects of their work – sometimes concerning individual departments, sometimes concerning cross-institutional functions, sometimes concerning organisation and management – in order to inform those involved in decision-making and institutional change. Sometimes these reviews are instituted on a regular basis, more often they are *ad hoc*. They are perhaps rarely regarded as being about the assessment of quality as such, but the processes involved are hardly distinguishable from many of the processes of quality assessment.

Quality assessment is both a response to change and a mechanism for managing it at both institutional and system levels. Controversy can therefore arise from the substance of change – many current changes are unwelcome ones to large numbers of the academic profession – and from the question of steerage: whose hands are on the steering wheel?

Conflict of interests?

Quality, therefore, is controversial and recognising the controversy is perhaps a first step towards resolving it. The assessment of quality is called upon to perform different functions by different interest groups. Not all interests may be reconcilable. Choices may need to be made.

It is worth recording some of the main interest groups involved in these debates. First, there is government, within which politicians and civil servants may have different perspectives. Second, there are intermediary bodies, including quality agencies, which have their own professional staff, their own constituencies or sponsors and their own co-opted 'members' from other institutions; each will have its own interests and perspectives. Third, there are the higher education institutions within which senior managers, academics and administrators can be distinguished as representing distinctive interests and concerns. Fourth, there are interest groups within institutions which also have influential system-wide representation: staff developers are important in some countries in this respect. There is every reason to expect these various groupings, representing different interests, values and experiences, to find things to disagree about. It is these disagreements which provide the basis for the debates about quality and standards.

This book provides several perspectives on these debates. Contributors write both from the perspectives of different kinds of organisations and their roles within them, and from the contexts of countries with different traditions of higher education. Several contributors are writing about national systems which are changing rapidly, often in response to the sorts of controversies and debates referred to above. The details of particular approaches to quality assessment may be less significant than the national and institutional circumstances which have given rise to them. These circumstances both frame the assessment systems and methods that are introduced and mediate their impact.

From quality to standards

Within the United Kingdom debates about quality have recently been extended to address questions of standards. Is this a semantic distinction or a distinction of substance? In its UK context, concern about standards draws attention to outcomes of higher education: it focuses upon the characteristics of graduates rather than the processes of teaching and learning which they experienced as students. This concern reflects both the greater expansion of higher education and its conversion into a unified, predominantly university system, raising questions of comparability and, for some people, the possibility of deterioration of standards.

There are two additional distinctly British features to the concern about standards. The first is a reflection of the high degree of autonomy over curricula possessed by UK institutions. In many countries, governments could assume that they knew what students were being taught because they exercised control over curricula. In the UK, they cannot be sure. A second feature is that, in large part to appease institutional sensitivities over threats to their autonomy, the assessment of quality in UK institutions placed great emphasis on relating assessment to institutional mission and goals. This could be regarded as adopting a relativistic approach to the assessment of quality and representing a failure to address questions about comparability of standards across the expanded university system.

Although the debate about standards does not appear to have spread to other countries, the concerns which it reflects are present in many of the systems for the assessment of quality. Thus, the Evaluation Centre in Denmark places considerable emphasis on the characteristics and experiences of graduates and it commissions extensive surveys of graduates and their employers. Many national quality agencies use foreign experts as part of their peer review teams in order to reference local 'standards' of education against international norms. It seems likely, therefore, that a concern about standards is taken for granted in the approaches to quality assessment of other countries.

Impact

The question of impact of quality assessment is perhaps the most difficult one to attempt to answer. When so much is changing, the impact of any single change becomes almost impossible to discern. Impact can be upon the structure and policies of whole institutions, on their organisational form and administrative procedures, on the incentives and constraints which are placed on the work of academic staff. The nature of academic work itself allows plenty of scope for resistance and subversion, for the creation of a gap between appearance and reality. At subject and department level, attitudes and behaviour may be influenced by processes of self assessment and dialogue with peers in ways not readily apparent to managers and administrators. For these reasons, there are large differences in perception according to where people are located within the system. The perceptions of people working for national quality agencies, of institutional leaders and administrators, of individual academic staff are all legitimate but will frequently not coincide, each perceiving a different aspect of quality assessment and placing it within a different agenda and context.

An absence of definition

Some readers may be disturbed by the absence so far of any attempt to define key terms of 'quality' and 'standards'. As far as 'quality' is concerned, usage permits of no single definition. Many have been attempted and several will be offered in the following chapters. To an extent, the absence of an agreed definition is another source of controversy. Is the quality of a lecture to be assessed in terms of the importance of its ideas or the clarity of their exposition? Of course, the answer has to be both but the balance between the two will be emphasised differently by different people. The student who is looking for intellectual stimulation and excitement may have a quite different view about quality from the student who is anxious to obtain a qualification without undue exertion. How might we assess the 'quality' of a whole institution? One university leader might wish to emphasise research productivity; another might look to the scores achieved in the assessment of teaching quality; yet another might refer to the culture of the institution, the quality of the relationships existing between institutional members, both staff and students. Academic staff, students and administrators will all see and emphasise different things. And there is no more reason to expect consensus within groups than there is to expect it between them. Quality in higher education is a multi-dimensional concept and any attempt to legislate a single definition seems bound to end in failure.

A similar situation exists with regards to 'standards'. Although the term has had a longer and more accepted usage in higher education – referring primarily to levels of academic achievement – to such usage must now be added the applications of standards terminology from manufacturing and service industry and, in the United Kingdom at least, the intrusion of political conceptions of standards. As with quality, dispute over terminology concerning standards is also a dispute about values, and the power of one interest group to impose its values on others.

The organisation of this book

This book is arranged in four parts. Part One, *National Developments in Quality Assessment*, describes recent developments in six national higher education systems. The focus is on the role of quality assessment agencies of various kinds. Three of the authors work for agencies and three of the authors are university-based researchers who have studied the workings of such agencies. Part Two, *A UK Debate about Standards*, explores further particular national developments in the United Kingdom, again from various perspectives: of national agencies, institutional managers, and higher education researchers. Part Three, *International Initiatives on Quality in Higher Education*, looks at the work of three international organisations which have recently undertaken projects on aspects of quality assessment. These projects provide a comparative perspective on quality debates and relate them to broader trends of internationalisation of higher education. In Part Four, *Institutional Experiences of External Quality Assessment*, the impact upon institutions of quality assessment is explored through the experiences of three very different universities, each subject to quite different systems of quality assessment. Each part of the book contains a brief introduction by the editors.

The book contains perspectives on standards and quality in higher education from nine countries and from contrasting vantage points within them. It is not the purpose of this book to advocate any one approach to quality in higher education but to attempt to shed some light onto the various debates that are involved and to clarify some of the choices which will have to be made in resolving them.

PART ONE

National Developments in Quality Assessment

This section examines national developments in the assessment of higher education quality in six countries. Common to all of them is the establishment of national agencies (or state level initiatives in the case of the US) to assess quality and ensure accountability. The mechanisms developed by each country to achieve these purposes will vary in detail as shown by the case studies presented here which cover Australia, Denmark, France, New Zealand, the United Kingdom (specifically the English processes) and the US.

The case of the US, as described by David Dill, reveals an attempt by the federal government to establish a national body for accreditation standards. The proposals were rejected because they were seen as intrusive and as a possible platform for future federal government intervention. This development might be seen to 'portend a loosening of standards, a drift to academic anarchy', but Dill maintains that this is an oversimplification. Given that US higher education is a decentralised, complex and mass system with many players and processes contributing to the assurance of quality, experiences of certain states could well offer insights and inform practice elsewhere in the world where it is being recognised that mass higher education cannot always be centrally controlled. Dill offers a number of insights which include the notion of universities as self-developing organisations, the use of quality ratings and consumer information, the relationship between the concept of 'social capital' (networking) and academic quality, and the negotiation of standards.

Vin Massaro, on the other hand, argues in his chapter that the move from what was once a highly regulated Australian higher education system to one which is now unregulated has compromised diversity. This compromise has been reached because the quality assessment processes exercised by the federal government were seen to be rewarding the traditional norm of university and creating 'upward status drift' in the new universities. Massaro provides an overview of the development of Australian higher education which echoes similar developments in the UK: the growing role of the federal government in higher education funding and planning, expansion of the system, economic downturn, cuts to funding, a clearly differentiated binary system, an ending of the binary system and the redesignation of the colleges as universities, and the emergence of quality as a major issue which coincided with a period of consolidation in order to ensure that quality and standards were not further damaged. He goes on to document the establishment of quality assessment to make recommendations on funding and to reward diversity. The outcome, however, was league tables which demonstrated that diversity was not being rewarded, with the consequent move towards a more uniform higher education system. Massaro asks whether other processes might promote diversity more successfully and proposes some possible solutions.

In New Zealand's case, as presented by David Woodhouse, recent legislation has created a complex set of agencies which are developing in the separate sectors of higher education for programme approval and accreditation. These agencies are still evolving and attempting to understand each other's roles. The two sectors comprise the non-university institutions and the universities, both of which through the recent legislation are treated equally in relation to institutional autonomy, funding, governance and reporting requirements. Woodhouse describes the educational and cultural contexts, the funding process and allocation of student numbers, the demands for greater accountability which have been the price for increased institutional autonomy, and the external checks on quality assurance. In respect of the latter he describes the complex arrangements which govern both sectors. He also discusses the role of the New Zealand Qualifications Authority's National Qualification Framework which recognises competencies of qualifications, and the current issue of whether or not to register degrees on the Framework.

In France, the national agency – the Comité National d'Évaluation (CNE) – was set up in 1984, much earlier than any of the other national agencies described in this section. And unlike some of those agencies, the CNE has no authority to regulate or manage French institutions of higher education. As Marie-Odile Ottenwaelter states in her chapter, it is up to the institutions whether or not they implement the CNE's recommendations. Ottenwaelter describes the type of evaluations undertaken by CNE which comprise institution-wide evaluations, comparative evaluations of subject disciplines (as a means of providing national analyses of issues and as a comparator with the rest of Europe), and studies of university missions. She describes the way in which evaluations have so far taken place and how they are being developed for the second round. The revised method will take account of the closer relationships universities are developing with industry and business; it will emphasise the internal evaluation phase; and it will look at an institution's implementation of the initial round recommendations and changes that have taken place since that time.

Christian Thune takes a slightly different approach from the other authors in this section by discussing the virtues of accountability and improvement, and the tensions between the two. He does so in the context of the establishment and development of the Danish Centre for Quality Assurance and Evaluation in Higher Education. He claims that the tension lies in whoever owns the evaluation process; if it is government, then evaluation tends to be focused on accountability; if it is university self-regulation, then it tends towards improvement. He claims that the Danish Centre, although government-owned, focuses on both accountability and improvement with the emphasis on the latter. He discusses the Danish context in the light of the government reforms of higher education which decentralised the system and gave autonomy and freedom to institutions, and the mandate and operation of the Danish Centre. Thune claims that the Danish model has proved acceptable to institutions. The reasons are discussed together with the mechanisms that have been developed to ensure both accountability and improvement.

Finally, Ruth Williams describes the developments which have taken place in the UK since the abolition of the binary line in 1992, and the establishment of quality audit as operated by the Higher Education Quality Council and quality assessment as conducted by the funding councils, in particular the Higher Education Funding Council for England. She looks at the outcomes of the first rounds of quality assessment and quality audit, and the system-wide implications of those outcomes. She describes the problems that the dual processes have presented institutions, and the emergence of the current debate about academic standards and the outcomes of that debate. She concludes with the measures that have been taken by the government to bring quality audit and assessment together.

Chapter 2

Accreditation, Assessment, Anarchy?
The Evolution of Academic Quality Assurance Policies in the United States

David D. Dill

Introduction

The United States system of higher education, similar to the systems of most other countries of the world, is undergoing major reform. These reforms include declines in the amount of public financial support per student, changing social demands as to the types and mix of public services provided by higher education, alterations in the traditional forms of federal and state regulation, and challenges to existing forms of quality assurance (Dill and Sporn 1995a).

Historically quality assurance in the US system of higher education had been associated with a process of voluntary self-regulation carried out by professional accrediting organisations and regional accrediting agencies independent of government control. In the 1980s, in addition to the traditional process of voluntary accreditation, a new mechanism for quality assurance emerged under the rubric of 'assessment'. By 1990 over two-thirds of the states passed regulations encouraging public institutions of higher education to implement various forms of 'student assessment' programs designed to place greater institutional attention on the improvement of student learning (Ewell 1997). Ultimately, all five regional accrediting bodies also adopted an assessment criterion as one of their criteria for reviewing institutions of higher education. The amendments to the Higher Education Act of 1992 led to an even more dramatic change, the direct involvement for the first time of the federal government in quality assurance. The new legislation required that the states create State Postsecondary Review Entities (SPREs) with responsibility for reviewing the quality of all postsecondary institutions and their eligibility for federal student financial aid. In addition, under pressure from the federal Department of Education, the various accreditation agencies formed a National Policy Board on Academic Accreditation, which proposed more rigorous and national standards for academic accreditation with particular emphasis on measures of student learning. These changes were widely expected, both by observers within and without the United States, to lead to a national system of academic quality assurance more consistent with the models of other developed countries (Dill and Sporn 1995a).

The congressional elections of 1994, however, led to the most significant political changes at the federal level in over 60 years. As a result, federal solutions to educational and social problems were strongly attacked by the 104th Congress. As a consequence federal funding for the SPRE initiative has been eliminated, before it was fully implemented, and neither the Congress nor the administration plan to seek re-authorisation of the SPRE legislation when the Higher Education Act is next renewed. In this new political climate the proposals of the National Policy Board on Academic Accreditation, which would have led for the first time to national standards for academic accreditation and for public dissemination of accreditation reviews, was soundly rejected by public and private institutions of higher education in the summer of 1995. Instead of moving closer to the quality assurance policies of other countries, the sudden changes in the United States seem to portend a loosening of standards, a drift toward academic anarchy. Under these conditions it would appear that the quality assurance policies of the United States offer little guidance to those countries now seeking effective means of regulating academic quality in their rapidly changing systems of higher education.

A major purpose of this chapter is to suggest that this interpretation of events in the United States markedly oversimplifies developments in its quality assurance practices. Given the size, complexity and decentralisation of the US higher education system, and given the current political rhetoric about the supposed failures of national or centralised forms of government (a view not exclusive to the United States, but perhaps most vociferously expressed there), this mis-perception is understandable. But the policies evolving in a number of the American states as well as the experiences of numerous colleges and universities as they seek to improve their academic quality in a new context of diminishing resources and increasing competition, could be informative to developments in other countries. In particular the decentralisation and complexity of quality assurance practices in the United States suggests that in modern mass systems of higher education an effective system of quality assurance and accountability cannot be centrally determined, but must consist of different players – levels of government, professional associations, institutions – and processes – accreditation, assessment and audit – acting together (Romer 1995).

It is also important to stress that quality assurance policies in all countries are evolving in an active environment. Recent research on the evolution of higher education policies in different countries (Goedegebuure *et al.* 1994) confirms both a dynamism of change in all systems, including the United States, and increasing convergence among different countries in government policies and forms of control and co-ordination. As other nations rapidly expand access to higher education, 'off-load' operational responsibility to academic institutions, and encourage competition within their systems through deregulation and increased opportunity for private colleges and universities, their higher education context will become increasingly similar to that now confronting the United States (Dill and Sporn 1995b). Thus while current approaches to quality assurance in the United States may not appear to offer the most innovative models or policies, the scope and complexity of the US academic system may better portend the future challenges that quality assurance policies in all countries will have to address than do the current conditions in those countries that have implemented more cohesive and co-ordinated systems of quality assurance.

In the arguments that follow the traditional forms of quality assurance in the United States – federal, state and voluntary self-regulation – will be reviewed and recent developments will be introduced (note that the discussion focuses on quality assurance for teaching and learning, primarily in undergraduate programs). Of particular importance are the evolution of accountability measures at the state level, which have been reinforced by the SPRE legislation, and are unlikely to disappear even if this federal requirement is ended. As reviewed, these policy changes are having some effects on the behaviour of individual institutions, but I will argue that of even greater significance for college and university practices on quality assurance is the academic restructuring now being undertaken in the face of government cost-cutting and increasing competition. Finally, some possible implications of the United States experience for other countries are outlined.

The US system of higher education

The US system of higher education is the largest and most diverse in the world. Although the number of new entrants to the higher education system as a proportion of the relevant population expanded rapidly in all OECD countries between 1975–1990, the US proportion was still the highest at 50.6% (Dill and Sporn 1995b). This enrolment, however, is distributed across an extremely diverse system of postsecondary institutions, with a substantial private sector (see Table 2.1).

As Table 2.1 illustrates, US higher education has a number of different sectors. These include:

1. doctorate-granting universities that offer a full range of baccalaureate (first level) programs, are committed to graduate education through the doctorate (third level), and give high priority to research (the Research Universities I grouping of 88 institutions includes the US's best known universities – private institutions such as Harvard, The University of Chicago, Stanford, and public institutions such as The University of North Carolina at Chapel Hill, The University of Michigan and the University of California at Berkeley)

2. masters colleges and universities that offer a full range of baccalaureate programs and are committed to graduate education through the masters degree (second level)

3. baccalaureate colleges that are primarily undergraduate institutions with an emphasis on baccalaureate degree programs

Table 2.1 Enrolment in US institutions of higher education and number of institutions, by type and control: 1994

Type of Institution	Enrolment (thousands)			per cent		Number of Institutions			per cent	
	Total	Public	Private	Public	of total	Total	Public	Private	Public	of total
Total	**15263**	**12072**	**3191**	**79.1**	**100.0**	**3595**	**1576**	**2019**	**43.8**	**100.0**
Doctorate-Granting Institutions	**3981**	**3111**	**869**	**78.2**	**26.1**	**236**	**151**	**85**	**64.0**	**6.6**
Research Universities I	2030	1652	379	81.3	13.3	88	59	29	67.0	2.5
Research Universities II	641	488	153	76.2	4.2	37	26	11	70.3	1.0
Doctoral Universities I	658	467	191	70.9	4.3	51	28	23	54.9	1.4
Doctoral Universities II	651	505	147	77.5	4.3	60	38	22	63.3	1.7
Master's Colleges and Universities	**3139**	**2291**	**848**	**73.0**	**20.6**	**529**	**275**	**254**	**52.0**	**14.7**
Master's Colleges and Universities I	2896	2177	719	75.2	19.0	435	249	186	57.2	12.1
Master's Colleges and Universities II	243	114	129	46.9	1.6	94	26	68	27.7	2.6
Baccalaureate Colleges	**1053**	**275**	**777**	**26.2**	**6.9**	**637**	**86**	**551**	**13.5**	**17.7**
Baccalaureate Colleges I	268	20	248	7.5	1.8	166	7	159	4.2	4.6
Baccalaureate Colleges II	784	255	529	32.5	5.1	471	79	392	16.8	13.1
Associate of Arts Colleges	**6527**	**6234**	**292**	**95.5**	**42.8**	**1471**	**963**	**508**	**65.5**	**40.9**
Specialised Institutions	**563**	**160**	**404**	**28.4**	**3.7**	**722**	**101**	**621**	**13.9**	**20.1**

Note: This classification includes all colleges and universities in the United States that are degree-granting and accredited by an agency recognised by the US Secretary of Education. Note that the categories within institutional types refer to relative standing (i.e. 'I' indicating highest) on various measures: the categories within doctorate-granting institutions refer to relative activity in research, doctoral education, and federal research grants received; the categories within masters colleges and universities refer to the relative number of masters degrees produced; and the categories within baccalaureate colleges refer to relative selectivity in admissions.

Source: Carnegie Foundation 1994

4. associate of arts colleges (i.e. two-year colleges, the public sector form of which are called community colleges) that offer the associate of arts degree and usually offer no baccalaureate degrees

5. specialised institutions including theological schools, medical schools and medical centres, other separate professional schools, and tribal colleges and universities.

As noted in Table 2.1 while private colleges constitute a majority of the institutions, almost 80 per cent of enrolment is in public colleges and universities. The table also illustrates the diverse sectors of the US higher education system in terms of institutional missions and functions.

Over the last 25 years there has been a distinct 'research drift' in the US system. This is reflected in the increase in the proportion of the system that consists of doctorate-granting institutions and specialised institutions between 1970 and 1994, from 21 per cent to 25.9 per cent (Carnegie Foundation 1994), but is perhaps better represented in changes in faculty activity. Geiger and Feller (1995) have noted that the proportion of competitive federal research funds won by the top research universities has declined as research activity has become more dispersed across the system as a whole. More significantly, national surveys of faculty activity reveal that since the 1980s, with the singular exception of associate of arts colleges, the proportion of time faculty members report to be engaged in research has increased in all categories of colleges and universities, and the proportion of time spent teaching has declined (Fairweather 1996). Because prestige in the US system is highly correlated with faculty research productivity and visibility, all types of colleges and universities – even liberal arts colleges traditionally committed to undergraduate teaching – are now recruiting productive scholars, often by means of reduced teaching loads, and are placing increasing weight on faculty research as a criterion for achieving tenure and promotion (Winston 1994). A recent survey by Feller (1995) has also indicated that major research universities, now confronting heightened competition for a limited pool of federal research grants, are increasingly subsidising their research activities with internal funds that in previous decades might have been invested in improving the quality of undergraduate instruction. This observed research drift, and its potential negative impact on teaching and learning, has been one of the frequently voiced rationales for public policies at the state level designed to influence the quality of undergraduate education (Romer 1995).

Within the US system academic quality was traditionally assured by a 'triad' composed of the federal government, regional accrediting agencies, and state governments, all acting collectively to maintain the quality of the system of higher education (McGuinness 1995). The federal role has historically included providing direct subsidies to individual students to assist them in attending institutions of higher education, and to faculty members and institutions participating in federal programs. For example, federal agencies (Teich 1994) currently provide over two-thirds of the funding for university-based research and development, a proportion that has been slowly declining from a post-war high of 74 per cent in 1966 (the three other primary sources of academic R&D funding are: (1) internal institutional support, and (2) industry, the relative proportions of which have both been rising, and (3) 'other sources' such as foundations and state and local governments, the relative proportion of which has remained constant). Quality assurance in federally-funded academic research has been achieved by a peer review process for individual competitive grants, as well as by external peer reviews of university-based research centres, which often receive longer term, renewable, federal research support (for a discussion of the US quality assurance process in research, see Chubin and Hackett 1990). Because of the limited direct involvement of the federal government in supporting academic programs, its primary concern has been with ensuring that institutions act as trustworthy stewards of public funds and provide students with that for which they are in fact paying. Thus the federal government approach to quality assurance has been the enforcement of set standards governing eligibility for federal funds. Historically, these standards were tied to institutional accreditation conducted by regional accrediting agencies representative of colleges and universities themselves.

The institutional accreditation role in the United States is performed by six regional accrediting agencies responsible for determining whether institutional missions and objectives are appropriate for the institutional or degree level, whether sufficient resources are available to meet the objectives, and whether the resources are being effectively applied to produce the desired outcomes. Accreditation is criterion-referenced in that it compares observed performance against pre-set threshold standards usually determined by the accrediting agency. The accreditation process generally utilises a combination of performance indicators, self-study, and peer review. Performance indicators provide quantitative data on resources and performance. They might include: funding levels; facilities, equipment, and libraries; student profile and admissions selectivity indices; and student retention and completion rates. Self-studies represent an institution's evaluation of its own performance in relation to the standards and its own particular aspirations, based on both performance indicators and subjective factors. Peer review relies on the experience of outside experts who visit the campus and form their own opinions about performance in relation to threshold standards. Program level accreditations are also conducted using a similar process, but by independent professional associations in areas such as accounting, business, chemistry, law, and engineering.

The state role has historically included licensing or authorising institutions to operate within the state, although state licensing standards vary substantially, particularly for private institutions. Unlike the federal government, the states also directly operate public universities and in this capacity define the mission of each public college or university in terms of the degrees to be awarded, the programs to be offered, and the clientele to be served. Most states also review proposals from public institutions for new academic programs. Since the late 1970s, many states have also instituted periodic reviews of existing academic programs. The form of these reviews varies. During recent periods of severe financial stringency, many states have conducted 'paper' reviews of the productivity of programs as a means of identifying programs to be selected for termination or performance improvements.

This traditional 'triad' is now being altered by the changing political context of the United States as well as the changing context of higher education. In particular, the quality assurance polices and practices of the states are becoming stronger and more complex.

The changing context of academic quality assurance

The rise of international economic competition over the last quarter of a century is having a profound effect on the higher education systems of all countries (Dill and Sporn 1995a). Contemporary social demands about individual employment opportunities, standards of living, and industrial competitiveness have raised expectations regarding rates of student participation in higher education, have made academic credentials essential for success in a 'work force lottery', and have increased employer concerns about the preparation and productivity of the work force. Government financial resources for social and educational programs are being constrained by related social demands regarding governmental 'efficiency'. The increasing scope and complexity of higher education providers, the evolution of information technology as a viable mechanism for teaching and learning, and the emergence of 'entrepreneurial' colleges and universities in many countries are also drastically changing the traditional academic context upon which previous quality assurance policies and practices were based.

While the United States has had a diverse system of mass higher education for many decades, these new economic and social realities brought new attention to its quality assurance practices by both state and federal policy makers. At the state level growing concerns about the quality of college graduates entering the work force first led, in the 1980s, to policies on student assessment designed to improve the quality of undergraduate education. In 1992, for the first time since World War II, state support for higher education declined in real terms, and most prognosticators project that future economic conditions will require states to pursue policies designed to increase productivity from their public higher education expenditures (Breneman 1993). At the federal level, concerns in the late 1980s about growing federal budget deficits led first to declines in real terms in federal support for research, and second, in the Higher Education Amendments of 1992, to policies designed to lessen financial losses due to student defaults on federally-financed student loans. Substantial further cuts in research support and cuts in federally-provided student loan funds are widely expected outcomes of the continuing efforts to balance the federal budget. The net effect of these new forces in the United States has been to add to existing policies on academic improvement new policies on academic accountability. This is a shift from assuring threshold standards of academic quality to increasing, in Bruce Johnstone's useful phrase, 'learning productivity' (1995), in which government at all levels seeks to improve the quality of academic outcomes, while at the same time to lower costs to taxpayers and to students.

Federal developments

From its initial founding in sectarian institutions during the colonial period, US higher education has had a strong tradition of institutional independence and autonomy. The decision by the US Supreme Court in 1819 to confirm the independence of Dartmouth College from the state of New Hampshire became the cornerstone of corporate law in the United States. With regard to higher education, the case led to the tradition of a strong private sector. Federal control over US higher education has subsequently always been quite limited, but even state control and co-ordination has been weak until recently. The federal Higher Education Act Amendments of 1972, and subsequent amendments in the late 1970s, extended eligibility for federal student financial aid programs to students attending proprietary schools, thereby expanding the definition of 'institutions of higher education' to a broader term encompassing 'postsecondary education' (McGuinness, Epper and Arredondo 1994). Because the federal eligibility process depended in part on state licensure, the new requirements placed greater responsibility for oversight, co-ordination, and regulation of institutions of higher education on state governments. The amendments explicitly linked eligibility for certain federal categorical programs to the state's commitment to undertake comprehensive planning of postsecondary education. Because few states had a mechanism for co-ordinating higher education of this broad a scope, and because most college and university leaders – public and private – resisted this imposition on their autonomy, the federal law was subsequently amended to nullify the earlier requirements.

The 1992 re-authorisation of the Higher Education Act, which required the creation of State Postsecondary Review Entities (SPREs), again created incentives for state-based regulation of higher education, and added for the first time highly prescriptive new regulations for accrediting bodies (Longanecker 1994). These changes were specifically motivated by charges of fraud and abuse with regard to federal student financial aid funds, and built upon consumer-based accountability measures previously implemented under federal 'Student Right-to-Know' legislation. Each SPRE was charged with developing quantified performance standards for postsecondary institutions in five basic areas: graduation rates; withdrawal rates; occupational placement rates for vocational and professional programs; licensure and certification pass rates for applicable programs; and the degree to which tuition and fee charges in vocational programs were 'excessive'.

In all five areas, the SPREs were directed both to develop measures and to establish minimum thresholds of performance. These indicators ultimately were to be used as 'triggers' for reviewing all postsecondary institutions in a state for continued eligibility for participation in federal student aid programs. While these federal demands for accountability again have been rolled back in legislation approved by the 104th Congress, largely because of concern over federal intrusion into state affairs, the view that colleges and universities have 'won' the accountability battle is likely to be premature. As Peter Ewell (1995) has argued, while 'regulatory relief' has become a basic belief at both the federal and state level in the United States, deregulation is traditionally extended to the private sector and the tax-paying public, not to the recipients of public funds. There is evidence at both the federal and state level of increased emphasis on performance-based forms of funding, and of policy instruments designed to focus public programs by producing more clearly defined and largely utilitarian public benefits. The longer term impact of the apparently failed federal SPRE initiative may be to develop the capacity of each state better to carry out the quality assurance function.

Among the discernible effects of the SPRE experiment at the state level to date have been the following (McGuinness, Epper and Arredondo 1994): a greater familiarity of state authorities with the range of postsecondary providers in the state; a re-examination of the state licensure function; improved state information systems especially in educational outcomes and work force-related issues; direct experience at the state level in the development and application of performance reviews utilising explicit performance standards on academic programs and institutions; successful experience in developing collective policy approaches to educational standards; and successful experience with interstate collaboration. It is probable, therefore, as discussed below, that these experiences and capacities will continue to evolve into more systemic policies and practices on quality assurance within and between states. In sum, while it is unlikely in the current political context of the United States that federal standards for academic quality assurance will rapidly emerge, it is likely that state level and regional standards for academic quality assurance and accountability will continue to prosper.

Accreditation developments

Concerned that the credibility of academic accreditation was threatened by potential government regulation, conflict among the accrediting bodies themselves, and public confusion about the purposes of academic accreditation, the higher education community formed a National Policy Board on Higher Education Institutional Accreditation (NPB) in 1994 to pursue significant changes in 'institutional accreditation', the traditional means for certifying and enhancing quality through voluntary self-regulation among colleges and universities. The NPB subsequently proposed in 1995 the formation of a new accrediting agency whose mission would have included (National Policy Board 1994): promoting understanding and support among the public for voluntary self-regulation of colleges and universities through accreditation; facilitating co-ordination and collaboration among accrediting agencies; certifying accrediting agencies in conformance with stated common standards; assuring that rigorous standards for the assessment of institutional quality were applied consistently in the evaluation of colleges and universities, with particular attention to measuring institutional effectiveness through student achievement; and ensuring public disclosure of relevant information on the effectiveness of affiliated institutions and certified accrediting agencies.

The political rationale for these recommended reforms was well understood by the accrediting community. The 1992 amendments to the Higher Education Act sought to federalise academic accreditation; Congress subsequently authorised and states were establishing new State Postsecondary Review Entities (SPREs) with authority to conduct comprehensive reviews of institutions that violated certain standards embodied in the law; college presidents voiced growing dissatisfaction with the increasing numbers of professional accrediting agencies and the demands they place on institutions; and the national body attempting to speak for accreditation, the Council on Postsecondary Accreditation (COPA), dissolved at the end of 1993, at least in part because of continuing disagreements among its members.

The NPB proposals for reform, however, generated considerable opposition and criticism within the higher education community and, despite several attempts to modify the proposals, they were essentially abandoned in the summer of 1995. Many colleges and universities, particularly private institutions, were concerned that the NPB's call for uniform institutional eligibility requirements and for core standards for student learning that would be common among accrediting agencies, would infringe on institutional autonomy. There was particular concern that the creation of a centralised regulatory body might prove as intrusive as a government agency, and might provide a better forum for future government intervention. In the well-chosen words of Robert II. Atwell, President of the American Council on Education, 'people saw this thing as national, Washington, bad'. With the legislative changes in Washington following the 1994 elections, the national political climate appeared less supportive of government regulation and the leadership of colleges and universities felt confident in opposing the proposed changes in accreditation.

Following the rejection of the NPB proposals, a Presidents' Work Group on Accreditation continued in search of a workable proposal for reform. Their report (Presidents' Work Group on Accreditation 1995) proposed a Council for Higher Education Accreditation (CHEA), a board designed to recognise and co-ordinate accrediting bodies. Establishment of the CHEA was overwhelmingly endorsed in a special referendum of college and university presidents in the spring of 1996. The new Council will be similar to the previous co-ordinating organisation, COPA, in that it will provide information services, and advocate and preserve non-governmental higher education accreditation. The mission of the new Council does not explicitly include or discuss any of the substantive reforms proposed by the NPB. A contrasting report by an independent team of leaders in higher education, Accountability of Colleges and Universities: An Essay (Graham, Lyman and Trow 1995), recognises many of the problems of traditional accreditation outlined by the NPB, but suggests a very different function for regional accreditation agencies. The report essentially advocates the adoption by US regional accrediting bodies of the process of 'academic audit' as developed in the UK. Individual institutions would be responsible for implementing faculty-led internal reviews of the quality of teaching and learning in each academic unit, as well as institution-wide systems of internal accountability overseen by administrators and senior academic leaders. The proposed audits would build upon the existing system of private, voluntary regional accrediting agencies utilising peers to conduct institution-wide reviews. The existing process would shift from an assessment of the quality of the overall institution to an audit of the internal quality control mechanism of the institution. The concept of an institutional self-study would be maintained, but would now focus on teaching and learning, on identifying weaknesses, and on the effectiveness of the actions needed to address those weaknesses.

Precisely how or whether voluntary accreditation will change in the US is unclear as of this writing. Although there is continued general agreement that the current accreditation system is an ineffective instrument for academic quality control (Atwell 1994), it is likely in the current political climate that there will be increased sympathy for private solutions to public problems and efforts to restore some of the balance characteristic of the traditional 'triad' of federal, state, and regional accreditation quality assurance mechanisms. In the meantime, however, the primary activity of quality assurance in the US system is at the state level.

State developments

As noted above, an early effort in the area of academic quality assurance policies was state-mandated assessment programs designed to improve instruction at the undergraduate level and to demonstrate accountability on a state-wide basis (Ewell 1994). Developed in the relatively resource rich 1980s, these state policies emphasised curricular renewal and experimentation, improvement rather than accountability. This was underscored by the nature of assessment mandates, which generally adopted a campus-centred improvement approach, allowing each institution to develop its own statements of expected outcomes and its own means of gathering evidence of their achievement. With some notable exceptions, such as the state of Florida's testing program,

inter-institutional comparisons were avoided. Assessment activities were often separately funded through addition-to-base incentive grants and rarely directly connected to state-level planning
and budgeting processes. By 1990 over two-thirds of the states had
adopted assessment requirements for colleges and universities
and, stimulated in part by new Department of Education requirements, all six regional accrediting agencies also implemented similar criteria, requiring the development of institutionally defined
assessment programs by both private and public institutions.
While the proportion of colleges and universities reporting involvement in assessment in annual surveys by the American
Council on Education rose significantly between 1988 and 1995,
from 55 per cent to 94 per cent, by 1990 there were increasing
questions as to whether existing state policies on assessment were
leading to credible improvement in undergraduate education –
assessment efforts appeared widespread but marginal to academic
quality assurance (Ewell 1991).

In the 1990s state policies have taken a dramatic turn. Con-
fronted with new fiscal realities, the states made major cuts in
higher education funding and began to press for new policy
instruments designed to increase academic accountability. Table
2.2 reviews this changing pattern in ten states heavily engaged in
academic quality assurance activities and illustrates the transition
in state policy from improvement to accountability. In every state
where institutional assessment was first introduced, some form of
performance indicators is now also required. While State Higher
Education Agencies in Colorado, Illinois, New York, and Wisconsin made successful pre-emptory efforts to develop indicator initiatives before such policies were politically mandated, in the
majority of the states the indicators have been imposed by legislative action. As noted in Table 2.2, earlier assessment policies were
often nominally connected to state budgets in that, in states such
as Colorado, Virginia, and South Carolina, failure to implement an
assessment program might eventually lead to some budget sanc-
tion. In no state, save Tennessee, were the actual results of assessment tied to funding. The new policies in these ten states, however,
exhibit more interest in eventually linking reported performance
with budgeting and academic program planning and review processes. In Texas, the 1992 legislature considered performance-based
aid for institutions of higher education, with discretionary alloca-

tions set at 10 per cent of base, but political pressures and implementation problems have thus far delayed this initiative. Other direct linkages have been proposed in Wisconsin and Kentucky. More typical is the experience in Illinois, where indicators are related to program rather than institutional funding, or the proposals in Colorado, Virginia, and New York, where indicators will be utilised to identify areas of potential state investment.

Table 2.2 Improvement to accountability: the evolution of quality assurance policies in ten states

State	Initiative	Who initiated	When initiated	Link to budget	Link to planning
Colorado	Assessment	Legislature	1985	Sanction	Low
	State Indicators	SHEA*	1991	Low	Low
Florida	Assessment	Legislature	1991	Unknown	Unknown
	State Indicators	Legislature	1991	Unknown	Unknown
Illinois	Assessment	SHEA	1986	Moderate	High
	State Indicators	SHEA	1991	Moderate	Moderate
Kentucky	Assessment	SHEA	1990	Low	Low
	State Indicators	Legislature	1991	Low/ planned	Low
New York	Assessment	SHEA	1987	None	Low
	State Indicators	SHEA	1993	Low	Low/ planned
South Carolina	Assessment	Legislature	1988	Sanctions	Low
	State Indicators	Legislature	1992	Low	Low
Tennessee	Assessment	SHEA	1979	High	Moderate
	State Indicators	Legislature	1989	Low	Moderate
Texas	Assessment	SHEA/Leg.	1987	Moderate	Low
	State Indicators	Legislature	1992	High	Low/ planned
Virginia	Assessment	SHEA	1986	Sanctions	Moderate
	State Indicators	Legislature	1993	Unknown	Unknown
Wisconsin	Assessment	Gov./SHEA	1987	Low	Low
	State Indicators	Blue Ribbon /SHEA	1992	Low/ planned	Low/ planned

*State Higher Education Agency

Source: Adapted from Ewell, 1994

The type of measures included in these performance indicator policies represent a change from the conventional input, or efficiency measures that have traditionally been collected for analysis at the state level or considered as criteria in institutional accreditation reviews. The overall focus of attention suggested by the array of indicators used in these ten states, despite an intent to be comprehensive, suggests concern with instructional processes and outcomes at the undergraduate level. Typical measures of instructional processes, in order of frequency, include: time to degree and credits required for graduation; faculty workload; average class size; student persistence and retention; course demand analyses; total number of student-contact hours; and total number of credits produced. An unusual inclusion in Virginia, which reflects research on factors that enhance student learning, is the number of small class/seminar experiences, and number of integrative learning experiences. Typical measures of instructional outcomes, again in order of frequency, include: graduation rates; performance of graduates on licensure exams; job placement rates of graduates; results on standardised exams; total number of degrees awarded by discipline; graduate and employer satisfaction; and graduate and employer surveys. These measures reflect growing state concern that existing institutional quality assurance and assessment processes were too focused on internally-established academic goals. The mandate to include measures of employer and student satisfaction was intended to ensure that higher education addresses larger societal or client-driven goals in the design and improvement of academic programs.

These changes represent a more active state policy agenda on quality assurance with an emphasis on accountability for public colleges and universities. The implementation of performance indicator systems, the increased interest in performance funding, and the encouragement of institutions to collect and use data on student performance after graduation, all suggest a growing desire to bring state and institutional objectives into greater alignment – to make public higher education more of a public resource. With the information and experience the states have developed with private and postsecondary education as part of the early implementation of the federal SPRE initiative, the states are likely to be the primary locus of quality assurance activities for the foreseeable future.

Institutional developments

To this point, the focus of the discussion on quality assurance has been on federal and state policies. Ewell (1997) has argued that the changing context of higher education in the United States, particularly the competitive necessity for institutions to hold down expenditures while maintaining quality and increasing output, will also have an effect on assessment practices within colleges and universities.

One practical example of this is the need for colleges and universities in the new competitive environment to engage in internal program review and restructuring. Traditionally these internal institutional reviews have considered programs for reduction, closure, or expansion by evaluating them against criteria such as academic quality, cost, and demand (Dill 1996). These quality judgements, however, have in the past been highly subjective because of the lack of well-developed institutional data on program performance. State mandates for performance indicators are now making available to colleges and universities reliable student outcomes data including graduation rates, occupational placement rates, and pass rates on established licensure or certification procedures. Assessment information is thus becoming more valuable to institutions as they confront strategic choices among their academic programs.

A related example of institutional change is the growing realisation within colleges and universities of the financial and educational costs caused by a decline in 'educational cohesion' (Dill 1995). That is, there has been an increasing 'destructuring' of the baccalaureate curriculum due to academic specialisation and the dominance of elective or modular forms of course organisation in colleges and universities. Systematic research in the United States on teaching and learning has consistently revealed that while what students learn is related to the quality of teaching they receive, it is also closely associated with the nature and cohesiveness of their curricular experiences, their course-taking patterns, and the extent to which institutional structures promote cohesive environments that value the life of the mind (Terenzeni and Pascarella 1994). Therefore more systematic efforts to improve the efficiency and quality of learning outcomes often involve attempts to 'restructure' the curriculum, to redesign course sequences and requirements in order to identify instances where greater academic coherence can be achieved. Consequently the US assessment movement has evolved from an initial focus on standardised tests, to increased appreciation of the contribution that authentic, instructionally-embedded assessment techniques can make to improving curricula and student learning. Capstone courses (i.e. courses taught at the conclusion of an academic program, which are designed to help students integrate the knowledge, skills, and values taught throughout the curriculum), senior seminars, and major field comprehensive examinations (once a common component of undergraduate curricula, but largely abandoned in the 1960s and 1970s) have begun to re-appear as colleges and universities take more seriously academic planning and pedagogical design.

The new competitive environment of higher education in the United States, in contrast to the period of the 1980s when the academic assessment movement was born, now provides clear incentives for using assessment information to improve academic performance and productivity. Assessment information can thereby become a powerful force for academic improvement, but only if it is systematically linked with curricular design, academic planning, and budgeting processes.

Secondary markets

Finally, while not normally considered a part of a system of quality assurance, a secondary market of information on academic quality has developed within the United States over the last decade. This includes quality ratings of colleges and universities, as well as ratings of specialised programs within institutions, by commercial publications such as *US News and World Report* and *Money Magazine*. These 'league tables' are based upon subjective peer ratings by institutional representatives polled by the magazines, on data from publicly available sources, and on institutional surveys specially conducted by the magazines. These data include program costs as well as data on academic inputs such as faculty salaries, institutional financial support per student, library expenditures, proportion of faculty members with a doctorate, student/faculty ratios, average scores on entrance examinations (e.g. the Scholastic Aptitude test – note that the US has no national examination for college and university entrance, so 'aptitude' tests are frequently but not universally used by colleges and universities to assess applicants), and the institution's acceptance rate of incoming students. Several process and output measures are also included, notably the rate of 'retention' and graduation of admitted students (i.e. the extent to which they successfully progress through and complete their program). In rankings of professional programs, additional measures of outputs include rankings of the programs by significant individuals in the profession, and the median starting salaries of graduates. The validity and reliability of these magazine quality rankings are controversial; recently charges have been made that certain institutions are manipulating or misrepresenting the data they provide to the publications. As a result, a number of colleges and universities have refused to supply information to the magazines.

A related source of information on academic quality, in the more limited sector of research-doctorate programs, are the quality surveys sponsored by the National Research Council (Goldberger, Maher and Flattau 1995). Quality rankings of doctoral programs based upon peer surveys were initiated in the US in 1925 by Raymond Hughes, and were subsequently replicated and extended in the 1960s in separate studies by Hayward Keniston and Alan Carter, and in the 1970s by Kenneth Roose and Charles Anderson (Webster 1992). These early studies based their rankings entirely upon reputational measures and were consequently heavily criticised. In the 1980s, the Conference Board of Associated Research Councils, consisting of representatives of leading academic professional societies, developed a national study of research-doctorate programs explicitly designed to correct the limitations of previous studies based solely on reputational ratings. This study surveyed knowledgeable faculty members in each field, provided them with selected information about each of the programs to be evaluated, and asked for ratings on multi-dimensional measures of academic quality. The resulting publication (Jones, Lindzey and Coggeshall 1982) evaluated 2699 research-doctorate programs in 32 fields of study including the arts and humanities, biological sciences, engineering, physical sciences and mathematics, and social and behavioural sciences. Because of the rigour of the study and the respect accorded its sponsors and authors, these rankings have been seriously considered by both academic institutions and policy makers (Webster 1992). In a well-known study of successful leadership and change in higher education, Martin Trow (1983) illustrated how the quality rankings from the 1982 National Research Council study eventually led to the reorganisation of the biological sciences at Berkeley.

A recent replication of this study of research doctorate programs (Goldberger *et al.* 1995), examined 3600 programs in 270 universities, in 41 fields of study. The 1995 study again surveyed faculty members participating in research-doctorate programs and asked them to rate randomly selected programs on scholarly quality of the faculty, effectiveness of the program in educating research scholars/scientists, and change in program quality in the last five years. In addition to the faculty surveys, the study utilised information from institutions and federal agencies on the total number of faculty and percentage of full professors participating in the program, the percentage of program faculty with research support, the number of full- and part-time graduate students enrolled, the number of PhDs produced by the program, the percentage of PhDs who reported their primary support to be teaching or research assistantships, the median time lapse from student entry to graduate school to receipt of the PhD, and information on the proportions of women, minority and US citizens among the doctoral students. Data were also collected on faculty publications and publication citations for fields in engineering and the sciences using data from the Institute of Scientific Information (because these publication and citation sources do not include books and monographs, these ratings were not utilised for the arts and humanities). It is worth noting that one explicit goal of this most recent study of research-doctorate programs by the National Research Council is to stimulate the long-term development of data and research essential to understanding the nature and causes of academic quality.

This review of the evolution of quality assurance practices at the federal and state level, in the accreditation process, within institutions of higher education, and in the secondary markets that provide information to the public, suggests both the complexity and dynamism of the US system. It also suggests that the US system can provide some insights into the types of challenges to academic quality assurance that will be faced by other countries as they move to mass systems of higher education. In the next section, some of the implications of the US experience for the development of quality assurance policies in other countries are explored.

Implications of the American experience

A superficial analysis of academic quality assurance practices in the United States would suggest that the cancellation of the federal SPRE initiative and the failure to reform academic accreditation have produced a system with no coherent policy. While it is clear that a federal or national system of quality assurance is not imminent in the United States, a more systematic look at developments in the US system suggests the complexity of players and processes that together contribute to assuring academic quality. It is likely that as other countries adopt mass systems of higher education featuring increasing deregulation and competition they will also need to consider co-ordinating multiple actors (e.g. regional governments) and processes (e.g. professional accreditation) to secure academic quality. The US system offers, therefore, potential insights into the types of quality assurance challenges that will confront other countries in the future. These include: designing quality assurance policies that encourage colleges and universities to become 'self-developing' organisations; attending to the difference between quality ratings and consumer information; comprehending the relationship between academic 'social capital' and academic quality; and seeking means for negotiating academic standards.

Universities as self-developing organisations

The initial US experiment with assessment programs as a means of institutional quality improvement was relatively ineffective. These programs were not tied to any tangible incentives or sanctions, and thus were readily ignored by the academic community. Recent experience has suggested several policy instruments for encouraging colleges and universities to become 'self-developing' organisations – institutions continually seeking improvement in their teaching and learning processes. Performance funding, limited in scope and tied to demonstrated implementation of institution-based quality assurance mechanisms, can provide a continuing incentive for institutional improvement as has been demonstrated in Tennessee's experience. Categorical funding, if it directs institutions toward demonstrably effective teaching and learning practices, can also enhance educational improvement. Florida and Texas, for example, provide funds to institutions that reduce lower-division English class sizes to promote writing achievement. Minnesota directs state funding toward the development of senior 'capstone experiences' (e.g. a senior research thesis or individual project) in undergraduate curricula. Technical assistance also may be helpful for disseminating information on good practice as, for example, in the implementation of university-based program review procedures. Common performance measures, such as those required in New York and Tennessee, can introduce into universities data on student attainment after college and employer satisfaction that are consequently more likely to be utilised in the internal assessment and program review process, better relating academic programs to social needs. Finally, an external audit of an institution's internal quality assurance process (Massy, Wilger and Colbeck 1994), even if carried out by a voluntary body, could make a useful contribution to academic improvement, especially if such an audit addresses the connection of these quality assurance activities with institutional planning and budgeting processes.

Quality ratings versus consumer information

Many contemporary academic quality assurance policies rest directly or indirectly upon the 'market failures' assumption of insufficient information (Dill 1995). That is, it is assumed that the student has insufficient information about the quality of academic institutions or programs to make discriminating choices. If such information were to be provided, either by institutions under government mandate, or by independent quality assurance agencies, it is assumed that subsequent student choices would provide incentives for institutions to improve their academic quality. This simple logic lies behind the development and publication of academic quality ratings in many countries. However, this logic rests upon a long and complicated causal chain, which assumes that reliable and valid measures of academic quality readily exist and that students will base their enrolment choices on this type of information. Research in the United States (Dill 1995) suggests that even in this most market-oriented system of higher education, quality ratings do not decisively influence student undergraduate college choices. Furthermore, the public use of such rating schemes, unless they are highly correlated with student learning (which is rarely established), could lead to ineffective (and from the society's perspective, inefficient) investments by institutions seeking to improve their ratings. Policies directed toward providing quality ratings may thus paradoxically lead to lower quality education.

An alternative approach, being experimented with in several US states, is the provision of consumer information to students, which could help the student in evaluating whether a particular program or institution is best for them (Romer 1995). These data might include: characteristics of the student body; typical educational experiences the student will encounter; immediate employment opportunity outcomes for vocational and professional programs; and indicators of previous student and graduate satisfaction, including perceptions of program specific strengths and weaknesses.

The relationship between 'social capital' and academic quality

In many countries, including the US, academic quality assurance policies have been influenced by traditional theories about regulation, including the respective logics of hierarchical control through government inspection and performance funding, and reliance on enhancing market competition through deregulation and information provision. Recent social science research, however, has begun to emphasise the role that 'social capital' can play as an alternative to hierarchy and markets in solving problems of collective action (Putnam 1995). By social capital is meant the horizontal networks of social interaction that facilitate co-ordination, communication, and the sharing of community norms, and which promote individual engagement in a community. While international research in higher education has consistently confirmed the importance of disciplinary and professional networks to the life and work of faculty members (Becher 1989), it is striking how little attention has been given to promoting or sustaining academic social capital in the design and development of academic quality assurance policies.

In the United States, the effect that market competition among institutions of higher education has on the quality of teaching and learning is becoming more discernible. In a national system which features competitive funding for academic research, but has no clear, valid, or reliable measures of academic program quality, research reputation becomes a proxy for academic quality. Conse-

quently there is increasing competition among all four-year institutions of higher education in the US for faculty members of high
research reputation, which has the further effect of lessening professorial commitment to teaching. When this pattern is coupled
with the growing specialisation of knowledge and academic traditions of individual academic autonomy, there is an observed
decrease in communication and contact among faculty members
of different disciplines and programs and a decline of individual
involvement in the collective quality assurance activities of academic program planning and co-ordination, which has been aptly
termed 'hollowed collegiality' (Massy *et al.* 1994). There is good
reason to believe that this tendency toward the 'privatisation' of
academic work is a major contributor to the declining cohesion and
quality of academic programs in the United States. Therefore,
quality assurance policies that emphasise program reviews managed by individuals external to an institution may do little to
re-weave the bonds of collective accountability for academic programs within an institution that are essential for quality education
to occur. Institutionally administered quality reviews, such as
those developed collectively and managed by the faculty at North-
western University (Dill 1996), are likely to be both more valid and
reliable than reviews conducted by external agencies, but also are
more likely to promote the collegial connections and communication of academic norms that will lead to quality academic programs. In this sense, the true total costs of external quality
assessment systems include not only their direct and indirect costs,
but the opportunity costs of foregone academic social capital that
may have been developed through an emphasis on building an
institutional-level quality assurance system. The concept of social
capital, therefore, poses the following challenge for academic quality assurance policies – how can we design mechanisms of external
academic accountability that will reinforce and enhance mechanisms of internal academic accountability?

Similarly, the existing networks of professional associations
could be a possible valuable resource for conducting and enhancing quality assurance activities. The studies of the National Research Council in the United States have led to the development,
without government involvement, of quite sophisticated quality
information on US research doctorate programs. This information
is highly respected within the academic profession, in comparison

to the ratings by commercial magazines, and is often used as a basis for institutional quality evaluations and strategic planning. The National Research Council studies have also led to the development of a valuable research base on academic program quality, and to an ongoing effort by the Council to develop future public data bases, including graduate career information, that could be a useful resource for future program evaluations. On balance, the academic professional societies represent an untapped potential source of social capital for quality assurance in higher education, but appropriate quality assurance policies must be crafted with this potential in mind.

The negotiation of academic standards

Quality assurance in higher education confronts some of the same problems as environmental regulation. Both academic programs and students, like air and water, are becoming mobile resources. Entrepreneurial universities offer programs through subsidiary institutions around the world; the world-wide web permits electronic learning anywhere; and students seek to earn or apply their academic credentials in countries other than their nation of origin. In this new context quality assurance policies predicated upon geographic boundaries quickly become obsolete. This is as true within the United States as it is across the world. Similar to environmental policies, therefore, the future development of academic quality assurance policies will likely depend upon discovering means of achieving integration of standards and indicators, across states, across nations, across regions. Within the United States this type of co-operation is already occurring, without the involvement of the national government. The governors of the western states are exploring the development of regional standards for a new 'virtual' university. Internationally, the European Rectors are experimenting with a system of institutional audits, and international professional associations, in fields such as engineering and architecture, are moving to international licensure. These few examples illustrate the importance of conceptualising quality assurance as multiple processes and multiple players, and reinforce the previous point about building upon existing networks and social capital in the development of quality assurance systems. As with the establishment of environmental standards, negotiation of regional and international policies on academic quality assurance will likely be protracted and complex, but an essential task nonetheless.

In closing, it is worth noting that as higher education systems throughout the world evolve into forms less reliant on central government control, competition will become an increasingly powerful force for assuring academic quality. As Clark Kerr noted in a statement intended for university leaders in both developing and advanced societies:

> For the first time, a really international world of learning, highly competitive, is emerging. If you want to get into that orbit, you have to do so on merit. You cannot rely on politics or anything else. You have to give a good deal of autonomy to institutions for them to be dynamic and to move fast in international competition. You have to develop entrepreneurial leadership to go along with institutional autonomy (as quoted in Clark 1995, p.168).

References

Atwell, R.H. (1994) 'Putting our house in order.' *Academe 80*, 4, 9–12.

Becher, T. (1989) *Academic Tribes and Territories: Intellectual Enquiry and the Cultures of Disciplines.* Milton Keynes: SRHE and Open University Press.

Breneman, D. (1993) *Higher Education: On a Collision Course with New Realities.* Washington, DC: American Student Assistance.

Bruce Johnstone, D. (1995) 'Learning productivity: a new imperative for American higher education.' In W.C. Barba (ed) *Higher Education in Crisis: New York in National Perspective.* New York: Garland Publishing.

Carnegie Foundation for the Advancement of Teaching (1994) *A Classification of Institutions of Higher Education.* Princeton: Carnegie Foundation for the Advancement of Teaching.

Chubin, D.E. and Hackett, E.J. (1990) *Peerless Science: Peer Review in US Science Policy.* Albany, NY: SUNY Press.

Clark, B.R. (1995) 'Complexity and differentiation: the deepening problem of university integration.' In D.D. Dill and B. Sporn (eds) *Emerging Patterns of Social Demand and University Reform: Through a Glass Darkly.* Oxford: Pergamon Press.

Dill, D.D. (1995) 'Through Deming's eyes: a cross-national analysis of quality assurance policies in higher education.' *Quality in Higher Education 1*, 2, 95–110.

Dill, D.D. and Sporn, B. (eds) (1995a) *Emerging Patterns of Social Demand and University Reform: Through a Glass Darkly.* Oxford: Pergamon Press.

Dill, D.D. and Sporn, B. (1995b) 'The implications of a postindustrial environment for the university: an introduction.' In D.D. Dill and B. Sporn (eds) *Emerging Patterns of Social Demand and University Reform: Through a Glass Darkly*. Oxford: Pergamon Press.

Dill, D.D. (1996) 'Academic planning and organizational design: lessons from leading American universities.' *Higher Education Quarterly 50*, 1, 35–53.

Ewell, P.T. (1991) 'Assessment and public accountability: back to the future.' *Change 23*, 6, 12–17.

Ewell, P.T. (1994) 'Developing statewide performance indicators for higher education: policy themes and variations.' In S.R. Ruppert (ed) *Charting Higher Education Accountability: A Sourcebook on State-Level Performance Indicators*. Denver: Education Commission of the States.

Ewell, P.T. (1995) 'From the States: so, are they really going away?' *Assessment Update 7*, 4, 8.

Ewell, P.T. (1997) 'Accountability and assessment: recycling quality and performance data.' In M.W. Peterson, D.D. Dill and L. Mets (eds) *Planning Strategies for the New Millennium: Redirecting, Reorganizing, and Renewing Postsecondary Education*. San Francisco: Jossey-Bass.

Fairweather, J. (1996) *Faculty Work and Public Trust: Restoring the Value of Teaching and Public Service in Academic Life*. Boston: Allyn Bacon.

Feller, I. (1995) *The Changing Academic Research Market*. Paper presented at the National Bureau of Economic Research, Science and Technology Policy Meeting, August.

Geiger, R. and Feller, I. (1995) 'The dispersion of academic research in the 1980s.' *Journal of Higher Education 66*, 3, 336–360.

Goedegebuure, L., Kaiser, F., Maassen, P., Meek, L., van Vught, F. and de Weert, E. (1994) *Higher Education Policy: An International Comparative Perspective*. Oxford: Pergamon Press.

Goldberger, M.L., Maher, B.A. and Flattau, P.E. (1995) *Research Doctorate Programs in the United States: Continuity and Change*. Washington, DC: National Academy Press.

Graham, P.A., Lyman, R.W. and Trow, M. (1995) *Accountability of Colleges and Universities: An Essay*. New York: Columbia University, Office of the Provost.

Jones, L.V., Lindzey, G. and Coggeshall, P.E. (1982) *An Assessment of Research-Doctorate Programs in the United States*. Five Volumes. Washington, DC: National Academy Press.

Longanecker, D.A. (1994) 'The new federal focus on accreditation.' *Academe 80*, 4, 13–17.

McGuinness, A.C. Jr. (1995) *State/Federal Partnerships for Quality Assurance: Recent History and Emerging Potential*. Paper presented at the American Association for Policy Analysis and Management, Annual Research Conference, Washington, DC, November.

McGuinness, A.C. Jr., Epper and R.M., Arredondo, S. (1994) *State Postsecondary Education Structures Handbook.* Denver: Education Commission of the States.

Massy, W.F., Wilger, A.K. and Colbeck, C. (1994) 'Overcoming hollowed collegiality.' *Change 26,* 4, 10–20.

National Policy Board (1994) *Independence, Accreditation and the Public Trust.* Washington, DC: National Policy Board on Higher Education Institutional Accreditation.

Presidents' Work Group on Accreditation (1995) *The Council for Higher Education Accreditation.* Urbana, IL.: University of Illinois.

Putnam, R.D. (1995) 'Bowling alone: America's declining social capital.' *Journal of Democracy 6,* 1, 65–78.

Romer, R. (1995) *Making Quality Count in Undergraduate Education.* Denver: Education Commission of the States.

Teich, A.H. (1994) 'Priority-setting and economic payoffs in basic research: an American perspective.' *Higher Education 28,* 95–107.

Terenzeni, P.T. and Pascarella, E.T. (1994) 'Living with myths: undergraduate education in America.' *Change 26,* 1, 28–32.

Trow, M.A. (1983) 'Organizing the biological sciences at Berkeley.' *Change 15,* 28–53.

Webster, D. (1992) 'Reputational ratings of colleges and universities and individual disciplines and fields of study from their beginnings to the present.' In J.C. Smart (ed) *Higher Education: Handbook of Theory and Research.* New York: Agathon Press.

Winston, G.C. (1994) 'The decline in undergraduate teaching: moral failure or market pressure?' *Change 26,* 5, 9–15.

Chapter 3

Institutional Responses to Quality Assessment in Australia[1]

Vin Massaro

Introduction

The aim of this chapter is to address whether external quality assurance processes have helped to create diversity in university systems. The method adopted for assessing quality in Australia entailed an assessment of performance against a university's mission, explicitly to ensure that diversity was both maintained and encouraged. The chapter examines, therefore, whether this aim has been achieved in the Australian system before drawing more general conclusions about the quality of the quality process. To understand the Australian situation one must examine the degree of diversity which existed before the quality assurance process began, and the extent of institutional sovereignty, to see whether universities can decide to be different and not fear that they will suffer as a consequence. To begin with, an overview of the Australian higher education system is provided.

The Australian higher education system

The Australian Federation of States is governed by a Constitution which defines the powers of the Commonwealth (the Federal government) in the governance of the country. The Constitution

---

1   This paper was first published in *The Journal of Higher Education and Management 18*, 1, 35–44.

gives the Commonwealth power over foreign trade, foreign affairs, defence, taxation, etc., but it is silent on the question of education. Therefore, the Commonwealth has no power over education matters. Before federation in 1901 Australia was a collection of independent colonies administered by the British Government. (In fact, the Australian Constitution is an Act of the British Parliament.) Each state had a constitution and each had developed a parliament, a form of government and, among other things, an education system. The process of federation involved a negotiation among independent states about the powers they would cede to a national parliament in return for creating a nation.

Education was deemed to be a matter for the states, and so it has remained. As each state developed its first university it looked to Britain for guidance and, like Britain, gave its universities a significant degree of independence. The maintenance of quality was assured by writing into the Act of Establishment that the university could award degrees, provided that they were of similar standard to those awarded by the universities of Oxford or Cambridge. (New universities were often referred to their older counterparts for this quality standard. This idea of referral to antecedent institutions was not uniquely Australian, as can be seen from the charters of most of the older European universities – Uppsala was referred to Bologna, for example (Hermans and Nelissen 1994).

Universities are established as bodies corporate by individual Acts of Parliament. They are given control over their governance and management and are able to decide within their budgets what they will teach; what research they will pursue; whom they employ as lecturers, professors and administrators, including the Vice-Chancellor; whom they admit to courses; and the conditions upon which they will award degrees. Universities may own and manage property and may invest funds at the discretion of their Councils. Professor Malcolm Frazer (Frazer 1995) has developed a very useful taxonomy of how autonomy in universities can be defined as shown in Table 3.1. If Australian universities were judged by that taxonomy, it would be apparent that they have the greatest possible level of autonomy.

Table 3.1 Perceptions of autonomy

Property	Questions revealing the extent of autonomy	Relation to external evaluation
Legal status	Is the institution recognised in law as a separate entity? Is the institution free to own property? Can it enter into contracts with others, without reference to higher authority?	No direct relation
Academic authority	How does the institution obtain its authority to operate and to make academic awards? Is this authority subject to review and renewal?	In some countries, institutional accreditation (sometimes periodic)
Mission	Does the institution determine its own mission (goals)?	In most countries, the mission is not subject to external evaluation but is the starting point for it
Governance	Is the body which governs the institution appointed by some other authority? Is the governance of the institution independent from any higher authority? Is the institution responsible for quality control and assurance?	Likely to be subject of external evaluation
Financial	Is the institution free to make decisions about expenditure, subject to the financial laws of the country, and any financial contractual conditions?	Subject to external financial audit
As an employer	Can the institution appoint, employ, promote and dismiss its own staff without reference to others?	Yes

Table 3.1 Perceptions of autonomy (continued)

Property	Questions revealing the extent of autonomy	Relation to external evaluation
Academic	Does the institution determine the admission of students?	Yes
	Does the institution have to seek approval to establish each programme of study – once only, or periodically?	In some countries, programme accreditation
	Does the institution determine the curriculum – goals, content, teaching and assessment methods?	Yes
	Is there freedom to pursue research in any area?	Yes

Source: Frazer 1995

Despite its lack of specific powers, the Commonwealth has been playing an ever greater role in higher education as well as in general education. It has taken an increasing role in the funding of higher education, and an increasing level of control over its planning. The Commonwealth now spends over $8 billion annually on education, most of it on tertiary education, even though the Constitution has not been amended. Universities are still established under state Acts of Parliament and are accountable to state Ministers. While the Commonwealth had established a Universities Commission as early as 1946 to advise it on university policies and funding, it was only in 1964 that it appointed a Minister Assisting the Prime Minister in matters affecting education and research, and only in 1966 that it appointed its first full Minister for Education and Science.

The early stages of the Commonwealth's involvement in higher education can be defined as benign. The federal government was interested in having internationally recognised universities, in increasing the country's independence in research, and wanted to improve the educational opportunities of its growing population. The arrival at university age of the post-war baby boomers and the children of post-war immigrants, coupled with a period of considerable economic growth and stability, meant that the government could be generous in its support of higher education. Furthermore, reading the reports of the two major Committees (Martin 1964–65; Murray 1957) which led, respectively, to the creation of an advanced education sector and an expansion in the number of universities, one is left with the impression that the government was listening to enlightened advisers who spoke in their reports about the creation of excellence. The joint Commonwealth/state funding of universities, which resulted from recommendations in the Murray Report, was extended to the advanced education sector in 1966, following the Martin Report. The arrangement entailed the Commonwealth providing $1 of recurrent funding for every $1.85 of state recurrent funding, and capital funding was shared equally. Because the states still provided the bulk of funding, the major negatives in the system at this time were those state governments who could not see with sufficient clarity the vision being accepted by the Commonwealth.

The result of these funding interventions by the Commonwealth in the 1960s was a significant expansion of higher education. Given this growth, and funding which accompanied it, the period from the mid-1960s to the mid-1970s was probably the closest Australian higher education will come to a Golden Era. The Commonwealth assumed complete funding responsibility for higher education in 1974, in return for the states abolishing tuition fees. It created a new body, the Tertiary Education Commission, to provide planning and funding advice for both sectors. While nothing had changed constitutionally, the Commonwealth could now influence the higher education system through its granting mechanisms, while the states acted as post-boxes for the funds. Unfortunately, the completion of this federal avenue to the land of milk and honey coincided with an economic downturn, leading to funding reductions which have yet to be recovered.

The binary system which had emerged consisted of universities and an advanced education sector, the latter consisting of former teacher training colleges and institutes of technology. Modelled as it was on the United Kingdom and Californian systems, the responsibilities and missions of the two sectors were clearly differentiated. The university sector continued to have the traditional university mission to create, preserve and transmit knowledge, with research and doctoral studies being concentrated there. The college sector was to cater for students who were less interested in academic pursuits and more in the acquisition of applied skills.

The college system was to be 'equal to but different from' the university system, and could award the degree of Bachelor (later extended to include the degree of Master). A significant feature of this system, which lasted from 1965 until 1988, was the degree of external mission regulation from both state and Federal authorities.

The university sector continued to have independence over its academic affairs and could offer new courses or change its courses on the advice of its Academic Board and governing Council. The government decided whether a university would be funded to enter a new field of study, but once it had agreed to this, the university was assumed to have the capacity to determine the academic standards of the degrees it awarded. In practice, because the essence of a university was recognised to be its capacity to teach across the full spectrum of disciplines, medical training was the only major field which was controlled by the funding authorities. Universities could undertake research in any field provided funding was available from government or non-government sources. Funding for universities, while passing through the states, was specifically earmarked for each university in a federal Act of Appropriation.

The colleges were not so free to determine their destinies. They could not offer doctoral programmes, nor could they compete for government research funds. No infrastructure was provided for the pursuit of research, so they were funded at a different base level. Recurrent funding came from the Commonwealth through state co-ordinating bodies, which determined how each college would be funded. They were subject to a rigorous level of external course accreditation and were required to submit to a review by an accreditation committee before they were permitted to offer any new course. Having obtained agreement and funding for the new course, they were then required to undergo quinquennial re-accreditation. Accreditation committees were generally made up of university academics, and they examined every aspect of the organisation and management of the new development to ensure that it met appropriate standards and would be backed by appropriate resources. The courses were also scrutinised to ensure that they did not replicate the 'pure' aspects of their university counterparts.

The Australian system before 1988 was therefore highly regulated, albeit not as government-directed as some of the European ones. The Tertiary Education Commission was able to ensure that the level of diversity in the system was maintained because it determined what could be done. It kept the binary system intact through its funding mechanisms and a strict adherence to the concept of mission differentiation. When the very first merger between a university and a college took place in 1986/87, the Commonwealth took great interest in the extent to which this might blur the binary divide and require the merged university to be funded at a different level to account for its larger research role. The merger had been promoted as the only means by which a specialist health sciences institution could move into research, and the change to university status and funding was explicit in all negotiations with the Commonwealth. The corollary that the new institution would be entitled to research funding was seen as axiomatic.

By 1987, the two sides of the binary system were enrolling about equal numbers of students. The college sector was becoming increasingly frustrated by what it perceived as its second class status, and particularly its inability to pursue applied research. It wanted a new brief and had been lobbying skilfully to gain a new status. At the same time, the lobbying was being conducted on different perceptions of the likely result. As late as 1987 there was an assumption that if a college became a university its funding would be increased. However, when the Western Australian government tested this by passing legislation to transform the Western Australian Institute of Technology into the Curtin University of Technology, the Commonwealth was forced to act. Because it had not agreed to the change it refused to change its funding assumptions and continued to treat the new university as a college. However, even this left open the implication that university level funding would follow if the Commonwealth agreed to a change in status. It seemed that the question was more one of semantics and product labelling than about the academic assumptions which accompanied university status. Nevertheless, at this point Australian institutions had a system with significant internal autonomy, but a firm guiding hand which ensured that diversity was maintained through the rigorous insistence on defined missions.

A new Minister for Employment, Education and Training in 1987 (the Hon. John Dawkins) issued a policy discussion paper on higher education which proposed massive changes to the system. The Paper proposed an end to the binary system; a 40 per cent increase in graduates by the year 2001; a deregulation of the system to allow institutions greater freedom from central control; confirming the policy of allowing the enrolment of full-fee paying overseas students; and concentrating educational efforts to meet national priorities.

The government made it clear that it could not find the $1.2 billion required for this task, so a contribution from the beneficiaries of education would have to be sought. A special committee was given the task of finding a politically acceptable mechanism for re-introducing fees, and subsequently recommended the attractive idea of charging fees at 20 per cent of the average cost of courses, but allowing payment either in advance or through the taxation system. Students repay their fees only when they can afford to, because repayments begin when the graduate earns above a certain level. The scheme is equitable because it does not prevent a student from entering university merely on the grounds that he or she cannot afford the fees. A proposal to levy a special tax on industries which employed graduates (and were therefore also beneficiaries of higher education) was not pursued, although the idea has remained on the agenda.

The Tertiary Education Commission was abolished and control over the system was passed to the Department of Employment, Education and Training. The government set up a new National Board of Employment, Education and Training, with a Higher Education Council and an Australian Research Council to advise it on higher education matters, but neither the Board nor the Councils were given staff in sufficient numbers to be able to undertake the analyses which had been possible under the Commission. Another significant change was to increase the power of the Minister to determine funding allocations to institutions. Previously, the Commission advised the Minister and an Appropriation Act would be passed by Parliament embodying the Minister's decisions. From 1989, Parliament allocated a total budget to the Minister which he could then distribute without reference back to Parliament.

The promise of deregulation, at least as far as the advanced education sector was concerned, was kept to the extent that apart from the annual negotiations on profiles, institutions could offer any courses they wanted and all could compete for research funds. College staff could now apply for research funds in competition with their university counterparts, but research funding did not increase to take account of the higher demand. However, the colleges were able to persuade the government to transfer some research funds from the universities to the colleges to enable the latter to survive in the new competitive world. (A subsequent change saw the removal from university funding of the imputed research infrastructure component of their grants, so that infra-structure funding is now based on success in gaining research grants and research performance.)

The colleges then argued that there was no significant difference between what they were doing and what universities were ex-pected to do – indeed universities were probably not serving the current government agenda very well because they were doing pure rather than applied research and they were not giving enough importance to teaching. It was clear that the binary system should be dismantled if the government was serious about creating a competitive unified national system. The government eventually agreed, although it stopped short of allowing colleges to re-desig-nate themselves as universities without some prior examination of their worthiness. By mid-1989 even this position had become difficult to defend and it was agreed that any college could be re-designated as a university provided that no financial changes resulted from the re-designation. Within a short space of time, every tertiary institution in the country had become a university. Because these decisions were made for political and economic reasons, none of the new universities has been exhorted to main-tain minimum standards of academic performance. While earlier attempts might have been quaint and while it might be argued that some of the older universities being emulated were less than perfect (see, for example, Wilson 1995a), there are nevertheless benefits to be gained from being encouraged to examine what one does within a broader context.

Nevertheless, the most astounding result of these changes in Australia has been the degree of uniformity of mission which has developed. No sooner had the new universities gained their new titles than they began to copy their older university counterparts. All wanted to enter the research arena; all wanted to enrol doctoral students irrespective of their infrastructure (there has been a 90% increase in the number of PhD student enrolments since 1988, and a similar increase in masters by research enrolments; masters by coursework have increased by 150%); all wanted to introduce law faculties, and most did. The fears of commentators, who predicted that instead of creating a unified national system, a uniform national system (or 'uniform national mediocrity') was about to be created, were realised. The arguments which the college sector had mounted to demonstrate that, while it might be different from universities, it was certainly superior to them, and all the avowed emphasis on teaching and diversity disappeared.

The quality process

Quality became an issue because vice-chancellors and other commentators began to express concern that the reforms and the reductions in funding had led to a reduction in quality. The Minister asked the Higher Education Council in June 1991 to investigate the characteristics of quality in higher education; how quality might be monitored; and what strategies might be used to encourage, maintain and improve quality. The Council concluded that quality had suffered as a result of trying to spread too little money too thinly, and creating false expectations in the former colleges which had recently moved into postgraduate education at a rate which could not be supported by the available infrastructure (HEC/NBEET 1992). In October 1991 the Minister issued a policy statement, Higher Education: Quality and Diversity in the 1990s (Australia 1991), in which he announced that after a period of significant change there was to be a period of consolidation. It was therefore necessary to assure the community that the quality of higher education was of a high standard. The same statement announced an allocation of $70m (or 2% of Federal recurrent grants) to institutions which could demonstrate better than adequate quality of higher education provision; and the Higher Education Council was asked for advice on how quality assessment might be carried out.

In October 1992, the Council reported on the mechanisms to be used for measuring quality. In November of that year an inde-

pendent Committee for Quality Assurance in Higher Education
was established to undertake quality assessments and make recommendations to the Minister on the distribution of funds. Because of the fear that diversity might also have been reduced as a
result of deregulation, the quality assessment process was given
the specific encouragement to reward diversity by ensuring that
quality was not measured against some abstract notion, but against
the university's mission statement and a self-assessment of the
effectiveness of its quality assurance. The overall quality of outcomes would also be taken into account, although how this would
be done was not made explicit.

The results of the first round of quality assurance have been
reported elsewhere (Massaro 1994a, 1994b). The first report of the
quality committee asserted that it had found both quality and
diversity in the system. (It seems the Higher Education Council
had got it wrong when it expressed the concerns which led to the
creation of the Committee.) However, because the Committee
chose to report its findings in the form of rankings, and because of
the inevitable league tables which this produced, it sent a clear
message about its perceptions of quality. The first round had no
post-1987 universities in the top tier, and the second round included only three. It seemed that to be considered a quality institution you had to be as much like the traditional universities as
possible. The reaction of the University of Sydney (Australia's
oldest university), when it was placed in the second band after
Melbourne in the first round, was that it would strive to become
more like Melbourne. It is not yet known what the third round will
produce, but if one looks at the mission statements and quality
portfolios of Australian universities it would be difficult to tell
which university was being discussed – they see no merit in being
different.

Reflecting on the quality assurance processes for the first three
years, the Chairman of the Quality Committee, Professor Brian
Wilson (Wilson 1995a, 1995b), concluded that the process had not
produced diversity and complained that the focus on ensuring that
the funds were won, and the university was placed in the highest
band had led to a 'game mentality' in which those who were to
meet the reviewers were carefully coached, and overseas experts
were engaged to prepare the portfolios. He further stated that
ultimately it was not the additional funds that mattered, but where

the university was ranked. Nevertheless, he believed that this was acceptable provided the outcome was an improvement in quality. It is arguable whether, in the limited time (one day) available to the reviewers, they would have found it possible to discern the difference between the gloss and reality. It has been argued previously (Massaro 1994a) that 'we spend as much time devising structures and procedures which will impress the visiting group as we do ensuring that we are actually improving the quality of what we do. We are...forced into manufacturing the semblance of quality rather than effecting quality assurance'. This mendicant approach impedes the development of diversity because we try to please the assessing group by making assumptions about what it will find pleasing.

Achieving diversity

The quality assessment process in Australia has produced a tendency towards uniformity rather than diversity. Diversity was first reduced by the process of deregulation and the granting of greater institutional autonomy and then further depleted by the quality assessment process that was adopted. It is paradoxical in these times of greater devolution of authority and deregulation in both government and non-government sectors that diversity in higher education can apparently only be guaranteed through strong central regulation.

There is no question that participating in the quality process enabled institutions to do things which they could not otherwise have done. Management was often able to bring about major change on the grounds that it would demonstrate a commitment to quality. In one university, compulsory student evaluation of teaching was introduced, for example. However, the majority of the changes which might have led to diversity and innovation were being brought about by the process of deregulation. Even as institutions became more like each other, faced for the first time with the prospect of recruiting fee-paying students, they had to deal with the question of marketing and differentiation in the market-place. That meant that they had to concentrate far more on their image to persuade the market that the university in question would offer a better degree than one of its competitors. The results of the quality rounds may actually have reined in the more creative attempts to be different by reminding institutions that quality was still seen to reside in the old and traditional types of university. While it might have 'released the reformers' (Wilson 1995a), it is not convincing that an improvement culture in the universities was created. Part of the reason for this is that it is still seen as an externally imposed process and the reformers which it has released are largely to be found in the academic management ranks rather than among the academic community itself.

If the quality process adopted in Australia did not succeed in promoting diversity, are there different processes which might achieve that objective? The answers to this question revolve around the necessity for diversity and whether there are quality assurance mechanisms which might help to promote it. Diversity in higher education is needed because otherwise institutions will be driven by upward status drift to reduce student choice and to endanger the capacity to undertake significant research or to provide a trained workforce. It may be that institutions will be driven by the market to create diversity, but that has not been the case in Australia so far. In fact Australian surveys of student preferences demonstrate that they would prefer to enter university rather than technical and further education. There is still a significant level of unmet demand for university places, and the reality of student choice, as demonstrated by student admission preferences, is that they prefer overwhelmingly to enter the older universities. Irrespective of any claims of over-supply, it is also the case that the best students are still overwhelmingly seeking places in law and medicine. So the market is confirming and entrenching the notion that diversification does not pay dividends.

System diversity was affected by a number of factors which were likely to lead to uniformity because the system appeared to be rewarding particular types of behaviour. It seemed that the universities were being treated differentially and better than the colleges, and it seemed that the role played by the universities was being given a higher status than that played by the colleges. Predictions (Massaro 1992a, 1992b, 1992c) that the technical and further education sector would replace the colleges and ultimately seek degree granting status is also becoming true, with legislation having been passed in some states which enables technical and further education colleges to award degrees. The system risks becoming a uniformly mediocre one because no part of it will be funded adequately to perform its proper role. The tendency towards homogenisation was inherent in the removal of regulation and it was over-ambitious to expect quality assurance mechanisms to arrest it.

It may be that a level of broad planning is needed to promote diversity after all. While it is difficult to accept that workforce matters can be effectively regulated centrally, it is becoming increasingly apparent that in a publicly funded system the government has an obligation to ensure that there is clear mission differentiation between its sectors. It should be possible for governments to negotiate individual mission statements with each publicly funded institution to ensure that diversity is built into the system and that institutions are adequately funded for what they are expected to do. This does not necessarily lead to a new binary system, but it should be possible to plan at a more global level by determining the maximum number of students the government wishes to fund in each of the university and training sectors. Such figures must be capable of revision, but it should be more difficult to change an institution's mission.

Alternative quality strategies

If quality assessment has not created diversity, is there a quality assessment process which might encourage more of it? It has been argued previously (Massaro 1992b, 1992c, 1994a, 1994b) that the whole institution approach to quality assurance is flawed because it attempts to do too much, too precisely and in too short a time. In a paper delivered to the IMHE General Conference in 1994, the proposal was put forward for a process involving periodic peer review or self-assessment (Massaro 1994a). This was not a position which won support from the Australian Quality Committee. But as consideration is being given to what to do next, following the end of the current phase of three rounds, this approach is finding favour with both the Higher Education Council and the Quality Committee. The Quality Committee has argued that in this new phase, there should be a move away from a holistic approach to more focused annual reviews in which experts review a different aspect of a university's activities and, perhaps every three years, the institution as a whole. The Higher Education Council has suggested that universities be asked to produce a quality improvement portfolio, with performance assessed against that portfolio after three years. In the meantime, quality funds would be distributed to universities on the basis of enrolments. The funds would be in jeopardy if the university was found not to have performed well against its stated plan.

Quality assurance in universities should be about the quality of their academic pursuits rather than about their levels of efficiency. Their management practices and the way they use their resources are important issues, but it does not follow that a well-managed institution will produce good academic outcomes – that will depend on the quality of its staff and the quality of its offerings. Quality assurance processes should therefore be owned by the staff; they should involve academic assessments by people whose academic judgements are respected by staff; and they should concentrate on the core business of universities – teaching and research. The system proposed by this chapter involves each institution being given a share of quality funds, based on student load, to be used for quality assurance purposes. Quality control and assurance measures as well as assessments would be public. Quality visits might be conducted every three years, with each institution having provided and negotiated at the commencement of the process a quality improvement plan. The purpose of the visits would be to assess whether the institution had achieved what it had planned. If an institution had neither implemented quality measures nor acted on negative reports from independent assessors, funding would be withdrawn and closures of areas might be effected. This system would enable an institution to bring good judges of academic excellence to assess the quality of departments and programmes. It would also show whether poorer and younger institutions are capable of improving their position.

This system would also encourage universities who wish to be different to make their case during the planning stage and to defend their position at the time of the assessment. And at least they would know what the measuring standard would be in advance. While not suggesting that this will automatically lead to an increase in diversity, it will force institutions which have unrealistic aspirations in the context of their resources to recognise their limitations. The smart ones may opt to be different in order to survive.

Finally, a system involving an assessment of programme quality would move us away from an examination of process to one measuring the worth of what universities exist primarily to do – teaching and research. The results would be of more value to prospective students and the community. And the process itself, because it would be seen as owned by academics rather than imposed and conducted by 'quality experts' from outside, would be more likely to lead to a culture of continuous improvement.

References

Australia (1991) *Higher Education Quality and Diversity in the 1990s*. Policy Statement by the Hon. P. Baldwin MP, Minister for Higher Education and Employment Services. Canberra: Australian Government Publishing Service.

Frazer, M. (1995) *Academic Quality Assessment: A Survey by the European Centre for Higher Education*. Address to the OECD/IMHE Seminar on Institutional Responses to Quality Assessment, Paris, 4–6 December.

Hermans, J.M.M. and Nelissen, M. (eds) (1994) *Charters of Foundation and Early Documents of the Universities of the Coimbra Group*. Groningen: Groningen University Press.

Higher Education Council/National Board of Employment, Education and Training (HEC/NBEET) (1992) *Higher Education: Achieving Quality*. Canberra: Australian Government Publishing Service.

Martin, Sir L. (Committee Chairman) (1964–65) *Tertiary Education in Australia*. Report of the Committee on the Future of Tertiary Education in Australia (The Martin Report). Canberra: Australian Government Publishing Service.

Massaro, V. (1992a) 'Financing higher education.' In N. Marshall and C. Walsh (eds) *The Governance and Funding of Australian Higher Education*. Canberra: Australian National University.

Massaro, V. (1992b) *From Dawkins to Where?* Keynote address to the 1992 Australasian Institute of Tertiary Education Administrators Conference, Ballarat, 1 October.

Massaro, V. (1992c) 'Quality not quantity the key to excellence.' *The Australian*, 30 September.

Massaro, V. (1994a) *Quality Measurement in Australia – An Assessment of the Holistic Approach*. Address to the OECD Institutional Management in Higher Education Program, Twelfth General Conference, Paris, 5–7 September (published in Higher Education Management 7, 1).

Massaro, V. (1994b) *Measuring the Quality of the Australian Quality Process*. Keynote address to the 1994 Australasian Institute of Tertiary Education Administrators Conference, Adelaide, 29 September.

Murray, Sir K. (Committee Chairman) (1957) *Report of the Committee on Australian Universities* (The Murray Report). Canberra: Australian Government Publishing Service.

Wilson, B.G. (1995a) *Quality in Universities.* The Sir Robert Menzies Oration delivered at The University of Melbourne on 4 October.

Wilson, B.G. (1995b) *Campus Review*, 26 October-1 November. Interview with G. Maslen.

Further reading

Australia (1987) *Higher Education: A Policy Discussion Paper.* The Hon. J. S. Dawkins MP, Minister for Employment, Education and Training. Canberra: Australian Government Publishing Service.

Australia (1988) *Higher Education: A Policy Statement.* The Hon J. S. Dawkins MP, Minister for Employment, Education and Training. Canberra: Australian Government Publishing Service.

Australia (1993) *National Report on Australia's Higher Education Sector.* Department of Employment, Education and Training. Canberra: Australian Government Publishing Service.

Barnett, R. *et al.* (1994) *Assessment of the Quality of Higher Education: A Review and an Evaluation.* London: University of London, Institute of Education.

Commonwealth Tertiary Education Commission (1986) *Review of Efficiency and Effectiveness in Higher Education: Report of the Committee of Inquiry.* Canberra: Australian Government Publishing Service.

Department of Employment, Education and Training (1994) *Diversity and Performance of Australian Universities.* Report No 22 in the Higher Education Series. Canberra: Australian Government Publishing Service.

Linke, R.D. (1993) *Improving Quality Assurance in Australian Higher Education.* Paper presented at an IMHE Seminar on Quality Management and Quality Assurance in Higher Education, Paris, 6–8 December (published in Higher Education Management 7, 1).

Moses, I. (1994) 'The ranking game.' *Campus Review*, 9–15 June, pp.9–10.

National Board of Employment, Education and Training (NBEET) (1989) *Report of the Task Force on Amalgamations in Higher Education.* Canberra: Australian Government Publishing Service.

Chapter 4

Qualifications and Quality in New Zealand

David Woodhouse

Preamble

New Zealand has a population of 3.5 million, and its state higher education sector comprises seven universities, 25 polytechnics, four colleges of education, three *wananga* (Maori language institutions), in addition to a few small, special-purpose private institutions. It is difficult to separate the effects of external quality assurance from the effects of the other radical, structural changes in society over the last ten years. During that period, governments of both the right and left have pursued policies of corporatisation and privatisation, and contestability of funding. Quality assurance and quality assessment in higher education are affected by several pieces of legislation introduced during the last decade, and involve interaction between several different agencies. This gives rise to a high level of complexity because these agencies are still developing an understanding of each other's roles, and these roles are changing as the understandings develop.

The context

The reform process

A transition from elite to mass higher education over the last decade is taking place in a context of major social and economic change, including (Preddy 1993): financial market deregulation and reform, with reporting of financial performance (Public Finance Act 1989); public sector reform (State Sector Act 1988); and reform in education at all levels (Education Act 1989 as amended in 1990; Industry Skills Training Act 1992). These Acts affect the higher education institutions (HEIs) and other bodies as shown in Figure 4.1.

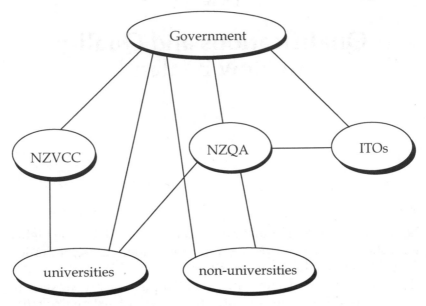

Source: Preddy 1993

Figure 4.1 Impact and reporting links

A central element in the process of economic reform in New Zealand has been the extensive restructuring of the state sector to increase the efficiency and accountability of public sector managers and the transparency of government spending. Many state-owned trading enterprises have been restructured into corporate form to emphasise clear commercial goals and managerial autonomy and accountability; while a radical overhaul of government departments has included making public sector chief executives responsible for the performance of their departments, the introduction of a capital charging regime to make departments recognise the cost of capital in delivering their services, and the separation of the policy and operations roles in departments.

The education, health and science sectors have also undergone considerable reform, although the restructuring in the higher education sector has not been as extensive as in health and science. Nonetheless, the general principles underlying the higher education reforms have mirrored those in the rest of the state sector.

These include self-management by individual entities within a strengthened reporting and accountability regime, a focus on output-based funding, greater targeting of expenditure, more contestability in supply, and greater distinction between the ownership and purchase roles of the Crown (i.e. the government).

Reform in the higher education sector has occurred largely in two discrete steps: first, the reforms incorporated into the Education Amendment Act 1990 (e.g. greater self-management of HEIs, fees introduced) (New Zealand Government 1990); and second the reforms announced in the July 1991 Budget (e.g. deregulation of tuition fees, the income contingent student loan scheme, proposed capital charging regime for HEIs). The deregulation of fee setting has seen varying responses by HEIs. The majority of institutions have adopted differential fees that vary with the cost of delivering the course, whereas others (mainly large urban institutions) have adopted a flat fee for all programmes. The proposed capital charging regime for HEIs would require them to recognise the cost of capital invested in them by the Crown, and is intended to encourage them to use their capital resources (more) efficiently (Blackmore 1995).

HEIs are statutory public corporations, controlled by their own councils, and have maximum autonomy consistent with the requirements of accountability for their public funding. Each university determines its own programmes, generally through an academic programmes sub-committee of Council. The Council is also responsible for approving course regulations and for maintaining the equivalencies of courses for degrees and other qualifications. Councils include Crown appointees, the Chief Executive of the institution, academic staff, general staff, students, alumni, nominees from the central employer, and worker organisations and others. Councils therefore represent business, industry, local authorities, universities, women's and ethnic groups, as well as wider education and community interests. The government is considering legislation to reduce the size of councils to four or five members, nominated by the Minister of Education from the business sector.

The educational context

The Education Act defines the particular characteristics of the various types of HEI. Before 1990, each type of state HEI was funded and regulated differently; since 1990 all have been treated consistently in terms of autonomy, funding, governance, and reporting requirements. For the non-university institutions, which were formerly part of the former government Department of Education, the autonomy has had a big impact. This, together with their new powers to award degrees (see below) has meant, *inter alia*, that they have had to improve their internal course approval processes, and that the largest polytechnics aspire to become universities (and a formal application from one polytechnic is currently – 1996 – being considered).

Besides restructuring aspects of education, the Education Act of 1990 reinforced facets of the role of HEIs. The Act gives 'tertiary institutions as much independence and freedom to make academic, operational and management decisions as is consistent with the nature of the services they provide, the efficient use of national resources, the national interests and demands of accountability'. This is a very positive statement (although, since it is impossible ever to prove that an educational institution is operating as efficiently as possible, the government could at any time reduce funding on the grounds of inefficiency). Furthermore, although the Act later guarantees *academic freedom* in very strong and comprehensive terms, the reference to the 'national interest' raises a possible area of conflict, especially since the exercise of this academic freedom is to be 'consistent with...the proper use by institutions of resources allocated to them'. Another significant feature is that universities are expected to 'accept a role as critic and conscience of society', which is a very positive statement.

Cultural context

A treaty was signed in 1840 at Waitangi between Maori chiefs and representatives of the British government, setting out an agreement on sovereignty and government. Five principles have been identified within this Treaty, as follows (Woodhouse 1994):

- government (*kawanatanga*): the government has the right to govern and make laws
- self-management (*rangatiratanga*): the *iwi* (clans) have the right to organise as *iwi* and, under the law, to control the resources they own
- equality: all New Zealanders are equal under the law

- reasonable co-operation: both the government and the *iwi* are obliged to accord each other reasonable co-operation on major issues of common concern
- redress: the government is responsible for providing effective processes for the resolution of grievances in the expectation that reconciliation can occur.

In 1975, a standing Tribunal was established by Act of Parliament to consider any claims brought by Maori against the Crown for redress of inequities occasioned by breaches of the Treaty. More positively, all institutions (such as educational institutions) are required by law to take account of the principles of the Treaty of Waitangi in their planning and actions. Maori and English are both official languages, and the government has established a principle of biculturalism.

The allocation process

Each year, the government determines the aggregate number of Effective Full-Time Student (EFTS) places it wishes to subsidise in the following year. (For the 1995 academic year, the number is just under 140,000.) Without knowing this aggregate number, individual institutions submit 'bids' to the Ministry of Education to offer the subsidised EFTS places that are available. Bids from institutions are based on the number of EFTS they expect to attract during the year. The Ministry assesses these bids and advises the Minister of Education on the allocation of EFTS places to individual institutions (La Rocque 1995).

Additional funded EFTS places are allocated on the basis of each institution's performance, including past enrolment trends, an institution's achievement of previous EFTS targets, and the Ministry's assessment of its ability to enrol further students, but taking into account Ministerial priorities (e.g. in 1993, some funding priority was accorded marginal growth in courses in science and technology in preference to courses in commerce, and the arts and humanities). The annual nature of this bidding and allocation process means that tuition subsidies paid to HEIs reflect current, not past, enrolments. As a result, shifts in student demand across courses and institutions can be reflected reasonably quickly in shifts in funding. Institutions that do not achieve their EFTS target for the year must either repay the government for the EFTS places they were unable to deliver or take in extra students the next year to make up for the shortfall (Preddy 1993).

A feature of the funding system is that the funding follows the student. State HEIs are funded on the basis of the number of EFTS that they attract, and in principle: (i) the system is student driven, and (ii) competition will encourage tertiary institutions to examine their costs so as to minimise the tuition fees that they are required to charge. Of relevance to a potential mismatch between the expectations of the university teachers and the knowledge of entering students is the debate, now taking place within several universities, of the balance between maximising growth in student numbers (by implication linked to lowering entry standards) and the achievement of academic excellence. The concern with student numbers arises from the dependence of the annual funding allocation on student numbers.

A central theme to the reforms since 1990 is that higher education students, who are likely to derive private benefit from higher education, should contribute to its cost. Although the government is putting more money into higher education, the amount per student is falling. The student contribution has increased from approximately 3 per cent of the cost of provision in 1989 to approximately 15 per cent in 1993, and will increase to 25 per cent by 2000.

There is currently no intention to introduce any system of ranking institutions on the basis of comparative performance based on performance indicators or any other device.

Quality assurance

Although the reform of tertiary education and training has given HEIs greater autonomy, the requirements for financial reporting and accountability for the use of state funding have also been strengthened. HEIs are subject to the legislatively-prescribed financial management reforms which focus on the government's specification of outcomes, and on selecting outputs that contribute to those outcomes. Every state HEI is required to produce a charter, setting out the institution's mission (purpose), values (philosophy), broad goals and operational objectives. The charter is then submitted to the Ministry of Education for approval by the Minister of Education. The Minister may suggest an amendment to an institution's charter, but is required to approve it unless satisfied on reasonable grounds that there is reason to withhold approval. The charter is to be valid for at least five years.

Every year, each HEI must develop a triennial statement of objectives, the achievement of which would fulfil, or make progress towards fulfilling, the goals set out in the charter. The statement of objectives must be approved by the Minister of Education as being adequate for this purpose. It must also specify the set of outputs the HEI can deliver, including projections of the number of EFTS places for which an institution is seeking EFTS funding in various cost categories. The HEI then becomes responsible for delivering those outputs agreed with the Minister of Education. The statement of objectives must also include performance measures or indicators (PIs) that will allow for the achievement of the objectives to be verified.

Each year institutions must produce a report which is tabled in Parliament. This annual report includes both the financial report and a statement of service performance, which reports on the PIs agreed with the Minister of Education. Unfortunately, this report is not checked by the Minister of Education, but is audited by the financial auditors, who had no part in agreeing the statement of objectives, and who operate under a different arm of government, which has rather different interpretations of the reporting requirements pertaining to tertiary education. Consequent negotiations between the institutions and the auditors on whether the objectives have been met may take a direction different to that which occurred in the earlier negotiations between the institution and the Minister of Education when the measures were agreed, and consequently inconsistencies may occur. The Ministry of Education monitors statements of service performance for the purpose of ascertaining whether the outputs achieved by institutions match the outputs for which they have been funded in both quantitative and qualitative terms. Each institution is also subject to further external checks, either by the New Zealand Qualifications Authority or the Academic Audit Unit (see below).

New Zealand Qualifications Authority

In the late 1980s, concerns emerged that higher education focused on the young; gaining credit for partial qualifications was not easy;

and recognition of certificates gained elsewhere in the country was not automatic. One purpose of the Education Act was therefore to reform educational administration so as to establish 'a consistent approach to the recognition of qualifications in academic and vocational areas', and it established the New Zealand Qualifications Authority (NZQA) for this purpose. The NZQA is in the process of implementing a National Qualifications Framework (see below), which is intended to be consistent, coherent and comprehensive (Barker 1993).

The NZQA's functions include: overseeing the setting of standards for qualifications in secondary schools and in post-secondary education and training; developing a framework for national qualifications in secondary schools and post-secondary education in which there is a flexible system for the gaining of qualifications, with recognition of competency already achieved; promoting and monitoring inter-institutional course approval and moderation procedures; and registering private training establishments. As originally proposed, the legislation would have given the NZQA jurisdiction to approve and accredit universities and their degree qualifications but, following strong arguments from the universities, the New Zealand Vice-Chancellors' Committee (NZVCC) was constituted as a legal entity with the jurisdiction to approve university degree qualifications and to accredit university institutions to offer those qualifications (Malcolm 1993).

The university entry standard for school leavers is based on performance in a national examination taken at the end of schooling, and under legislation is prescribed by the NZQA in consultation with the NZVCC. The colleges and the polytechnics set their own standards for entry, which for the polytechnics range widely, dependent on the level of the particular course.

The National Qualifications Framework

The National Qualifications Framework (NQF) recognises competencies acquired either in the senior secondary school, through courses offered by polytechnics and private tertiary establishments, from systematic training offered by accredited industry providers, or through previous work experience. The NQF is intended to apply to all post-compulsory learning, including secondary, post-secondary, vocational, and experiential. The building blocks of the NQF are *unit standards*, which are assigned to one of eight *levels* (Figure 4.2). There are detailed definitions of the nature and scope of the learning appropriate to each level. Each unit carries a *credit-rating* of between one and 120, determined on the basis that 120 credits represent the normal outcomes or 'educational gain' for a student undertaking a full-time, full-year course in a typical state institution (NZQA 1993b).

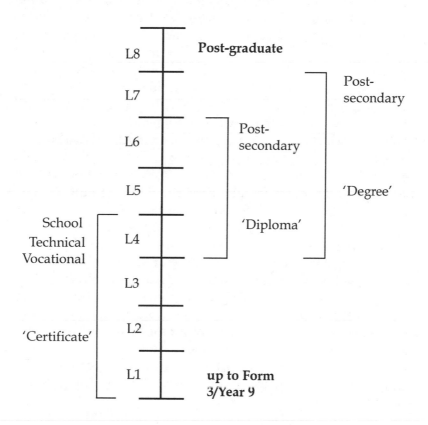

Figure 4.2 National Qualifications Framework (NQF)

The NZQA proposes to establish National Standards Bodies (NSBs) to represent all major user groups connected with a particular area of education or training. An NSB will be responsible for analysing the skills and knowledge in its area for the development of units and qualifications. For each unit, it will set standards for learners to achieve (i.e. statements of outcomes and associated performance criteria), and establish quality management systems and standards (including moderation to achieve national consistency, criteria and procedures for accrediting assessors, provision for regular review to maintain currency, etc.). When the NZQA has confidence in these, they are entered on the NQF as a unit standard. Combinations of these units into *qualifications* are registered in a similar way (NZQA 1993a). If an educational provider wishes to deliver one or more of the registered unit standards, it applies to the NZQA for *accreditation* to do so. A particularly contentious issue is that some secondary schools are being permitted to teach degree-level courses. The delivery of a unit standard, unlike the unit standard itself, is the responsibility of the provider.

The NQF is underpinned by a number of quality systems, including the registration and accreditation procedures already mentioned, but including also ongoing moderation and audit (NZQA 1994). This structure has provoked much debate. There are clear benefits, in terms of the purposes for which the NQF is intended. Critics say that, first, the sheer size of the undertaking is far too great (there are already many thousands of unit standards registered, and only a fraction of the possible scope has been covered). Second, this will straightjacket the whole educational endeavour by fitting all knowledge into the same framework. Third, despite the name, only in some of the more skill-oriented subjects, at lower levels, do unit standards have anything to do with standards: otherwise, they are just detailed outcomes. Fourth, because of this, an extensive network of moderation procedures will be needed. Fifth, there is no room for excellence (although a gradation of results is now being addressed); and finally, if the unit standards were as tightly specified as claimed, they would be inappropriate as a vehicle for embodying higher learning, particularly degrees.

Degrees on the NQF

Prior to the education reforms, universities were the only HEIs that could offer degree programmes. Other institutions are now able to offer degrees, subject to accreditation and approval being obtained from the NZQA, and over 100 degree programmes have been approved in the non-university sector. However, approval by NZQA does not guarantee an allocation of EFTS funding, which is a separate responsibility of the Ministry of Education. Also, these degree programmes have not yet been registered on the NQF, pending a decision as to how this can be done.

The relationship of the universities, and in fact all degree programmes, to the NQF is a very live issue, and a major initiative was begun in mid-1994 to resolve it. The working group reported recently (NZQA 1996), and the outlines of the likely agreement are that: all degrees will be registered on the NQF; at the option of the institution, the degree need not be expressed in terms of unit standards; the various sub-sectors may use different paths for degree approval; there will be a co-ordinating committee to ensure consistency of degrees approved through the different paths and expressed in different ways; and academic audit activity will be extended across the higher education sector in some way. Given the whole concept and structure of the NQF, however, it is not entirely clear what 'registration on the NQF' can mean for a qualification not split into unit standards. There is some concern that the requirements for 'registering a whole degree' might in practice require all component courses of the degree to be described in unit standard-like terms. Nevertheless, if an alternative specification is agreed, it is certain that all universities and most polytechnics will choose to use it. In the case of the polytechnics, a contrary pressure may come from the Industry Training Organisations (see below) insisting that they prefer unit standardised courses.

The higher education sector

The universities

Functions of the New Zealand Vice Chancellors' Committee set out in the 1990 Education Amendment Act include: setting up inter-university course approval and moderation procedures; exercising in relation to universities the powers of the NZQA to approve courses and to accredit institutions to provide them; and making recommendations to the NZQA on criteria for entrance to universities. It will be noticed that the first function interlocks with the third function of the NZQA as outlined above. It was clearly expected that the NZQA would not itself, in the long term, carry out such procedures. The universities have explicitly been given the responsibility for this task in their sector, while the NZQA has authorised the New Zealand Polytechnic Programmes Committee

(NZPPC) in relation to the polytechnic sector (see below). The pattern that is developing, therefore, is of separate bodies with responsibility for course approval and accreditation in the various sectors of tertiary education, each of which must be consulted by the NZQA on the policies and criteria it should establish for approval and accreditation. Each of these sectoral bodies must then apply the relevant criteria established by the NZQA. In the non-university sectors, the NZQA *delegates* the powers of approval and accreditation, while in the university sector, the NZVCC *has* these powers by virtue of the legislation. The extent to which the NZQA is willing to delegate authority is unclear, and statements on the matter sometimes differ from the actions.

The NZVCC set up a sub-committee (Committee on University Academic Programmes – CUAP) to carry out its course approval functions under the 1990 Education Amendment Act, and all university proposals for new degree courses must be put to, and approved by, CUAP before they can be introduced (NZVCC 1996). The CUAP also acts more generally for the NZVCC in consulting with the NZQA on policies and criteria for the approval of courses of study and accreditation. In this way the NZVCC and NZQA have agreed on the criteria for approving new degree courses and also, from time to time, they jointly determine university admission requirements. Notwithstanding the range of internal and external quality assurance mechanisms and agencies, the universities decided to establish an Academic Audit Unit (AAU), with the following terms of reference:

- to consider and review the universities' mechanisms for monitoring and enhancing the academic quality and standards which are necessary for achieving their stated aims and objectives
- to comment on the extent to which procedures in place in individual universities are applied effectively
- to comment on the extent to which procedures in place in individual universities reflect good practice in maintaining quality
- to identify and commend to universities good practice with regard to the maintenance and enhancement of academic standards at national level.

In fulfilling these terms of reference, the AAU focuses on mechanisms for:

- quality assurance in the design, monitoring and evaluation of courses and programmes of study for degrees and other qualifications
- quality assurance in teaching, learning and assessment
- quality assurance in relation to the appointment and performance of academic staff
- taking account of the views in respect of academic matters of students, of external examiners, of professional bodies, and of employers
- quality assurance in research, especially in the context of its relationship with university teaching.

The AAU is funded jointly by the universities but is otherwise independent of both the universities individually and the NZVCC itself. Its accountability is to the public, and its audit reports are public documents, with concomitant pressure on the universities to take very seriously any flaws that are identified in their mechanisms. There were several reasons that led the universities to establish yet another external quality body. One is that the government, through the Minister of Education, has expressed the view that the quality of academic performance of the universities is not sufficiently transparent to external constituencies. A second reason is the universities' recognition that the perceived quality of their programmes and qualifications is an important element of competitive advantage. Third, the universities are concerned to protect legitimate academic autonomy in their operations. And fourth, CUAP is a sub-committee of the NZVCC, not independent therefrom. It was deemed appropriate to have an independent external body commenting on the universities' quality mechanisms, both because this is becoming accepted practice world-wide, and because this occurs for other degree-granting institutions in New Zealand (through the NZQA).

The AAU has developed procedures for investigating the existence and effectiveness of various aspects of each university's quality assurance processes. The procedures stress the need for the university to carry out a self-audit first, and provide the AAU with a report on its quality assurance processes that incorporates the conclusions of this self-audit. The AAU's visiting panels include academics from New Zealand and overseas, and members of the business community. The audits are comprehensive, and universities are introducing or enhancing quality assurance processes where they are detecting gaps or shortcomings. It is noteworthy that the NZQA covers similar areas in determining the potential of a non-university institution for successfully offering degree programmes. Although the approaches used by the AAU and the NZQA are not identical, the overlap and similarity suggest that the audit function may be extended without too much difficulty (see below).

The polytechnics

The 25 polytechnics act collectively through the Association of Polytechnics in New Zealand (APNZ), which established the New Zealand Polytechnic Programmes Committee to act, under delegated authority from the NZQA, as the quality assurance body for the polytechnic system. It now has limited authority to approve unit standards at sub-degree level. Although the term 'degree' is defined in legislation, it is legitimate to ask whether polytechnic degrees should be different in character to university degrees and if so, in what way and how would the difference be achieved?

Over recent decades, the delivery of vocational education and training has shifted from the (compulsory) secondary education sector to the continuing education sector. Training formerly provided by technical high schools is now provided by polytechnics. Polytechnics provide a diverse range of vocational education resources and cover a large and increasing number of subjects at various levels of specialisation. There is an increasing recognition of the need to provide articulation and cross-crediting arrangements among different providers of tertiary education and training. As an illustration, a number of New Zealand provincial polytechnics are now recognised by universities as providers of their first year courses.

Colleges of education

There are four colleges of education, offering courses in teacher training, and all work closely with their nearest university. The New Zealand Council for Teacher Education (NZCTE) may receive delegated powers from the NZQA in respect of the colleges of education. It is also looking at an AAU audit model for institutional-level review.

Wananga

Recent legislative changes have also enabled the establishment and funding of *wananga*, that is, institutions of higher education in which instruction is in *Te Reo Maori* (Maori language) in accordance with *tikanga Maori* (Maori custom). Maori, the indigenous people of New Zealand, comprise 13 per cent of the New Zealand population. *Wananga* are able to provide tertiary education and training, whilst assisting the application of knowledge regarding *ahuatanga Maori* (Maori tradition) in accordance with *tikanga Maori*. *Wananga* qualify for funding on the same basis as other state HEIs.

Private training establishments

There are several thousand private institutions, mainly small, of which several hundred are registered with the NZQA. Recent legislative changes have also enabled them to become eligible for state funding. This introduces a new element of diversity and competition for state tertiary institutions.

Industry training organisations

Pursuing market-driven policies, the government enacted legislation authorising industries to set up Industry Training Organisations (ITOs) (e.g. printing, motor mechanics, engineering, etc.). The NZQA is recognising ITOs as National Standards Bodies. The concept is that an ITO will work out the educational needs of that industry, represent it in unit standards and qualifications, and submit these to the NZQA for registration on the NQF. A 'provider', typically a polytechnic or private training establishment, will then seek approval from the NZQA to offer such unit standards or qualifications (see Figure 4.1).

The government gives the funds to pay for such courses to the ITO, which then invites bids from approved providers, and contracts one or more of the bidders to mount the course for a specified number of students. This funding arrangement is intended to ensure that polytechnics are responsive to the training requirements of industry. Conversely, it usually means that some providers that have spent time and money preparing to give a course are not given a contract. Also, late allocation of funds by government to ITOs makes it difficult for providers to plan ahead. The government only announces its allocation of funds to the ITO pool late in the calendar (equivalent to academic) year, and by the time ITOs have decided on their preferred supplier of training it is well into the next year. Funds are therefore only available to providers after the training has started, and well after the course planning has occurred. It is clearly impossible to employ new specialist staff with an appropriate lead time. In practice, there is increasing collaboration between institutions and ITOs at the development stage.

Conclusion

The social changes in New Zealand in the last decade have altered the language of discourse and the basic assumptions in all spheres, including education. Many people have enthusiastically embraced the language of the market place: providers, products, customers, outputs, etc. Many people reject it entirely. Both reactions are inappropriate. Education is not a commercial production line, but often a rephrasing brings out alternative truths. Just as the wave and particle theories in physics are incompatible but both true, we in education would do well to embrace the truths and insights that come, even if from unlikely directions, while rejecting those aspects that are inappropriate.

     This is the challenge for New Zealand and also within quality assurance agencies, and within institutions. It is clear that the New Zealand education system is changing. There are definite decisions and directions, but there are also issues that are still subject to discussion and negotiation, and there are some basic differences of principle and philosophy that will not easily be reconciled. The task of the AAU is to fit into the framework of quality-related organisations and procedures, assisting the universities to maintain and enhance their academic quality. It will be some years before the whole picture of quality assurance in New Zealand higher education settles down into a firm pattern.

References

Barker, A. (1993) *Quality Assessment and Quality Improvement Within Higher Education: The New Zealand Perspective.* Paper presented to the INQAAHE Conference, Montreal, May.

Blackmore, T.J. (1995) *Submission to the OECD Thematic Review of New Zealand Tertiary Education Policies.* New Zealand Vice-Chancellors' Committee.

La Rocque, N. (1995) *Developments in the Higher Education Sector in New Zealand.* New Zealand Treasury.

Malcolm, W. (1993) *The Development of an Academic Audit Unit in New Zealand.* Paper presented at the INQAAHE Conference, Montreal, May.

New Zealand Government (1990) *Education Amendment Act.*

New Zealand Qualifications Authority (1993a) *Quality Management Systems for the NQF.* NZQA.

New Zealand Qualifications Authority (1993b) *Guidelines, Criteria and Regulations for the Registration of Units and Qualifications for National Certificates and National Diplomas.* NZQA.

New Zealand Qualifications Authority (1996) *Tertiary Action Group Report to the Board of the NZQA on the Implementation of a Harmonised Qualifications Framework.* NZQA.

New Zealand Vice Chancellors' Committee (1996) *Committee on University Academic Programmes: Functions and Procedures.* NZVCC.

Preddy, G. (1993) *The Transition from Elite to Mass Higher Education.* Sydney: DEET/OECD.

Woodhouse, D. (1994) The Academic Audit Unit in context. 'QA', August, 2–6.

Chapter 5

Evaluation à la Française
The CNE[1]

Marie-Odile Ottenwaelter

Background

Statutes and organisation

The Comité National d'Évaluation des établissements publics à caractère scientifique, culturel et professionnel (CNE) was created by the higher education legislation of 26 January 1984 – legislation which granted universities administrative, pedagogical, research and financial autonomy. Based on legislation of 10 July 1989, the CNE enjoys full administrative autonomy: it reports directly to the President of the Republic and, thus, is not under the authority of the Minister in charge of higher education.

The CNE consists of 17 members appointed by the President of the Republic for four years; this membership is non-renewable. Eleven members represent the academic and research community (chosen from lists of 11 names presented respectively by the department chairmen of the National Council of Universities [*présidents de sections du Conseil National des Universités*], the department chairmen of the National Council for Research [*présidents de sections du Comité National de la Recherche Scientifique*], and the French Academies [*Institut de France*]); four members from the Economic and Social Council (*Conseil Économique et Social*) which is the third parliamentary chamber; a member from the State Council (*Conseil d'État*); and a member from the State Audit Office (*Cour des Comp-*

---

1   This chapter was translated into English by Andrée Sursock of the CNE.

tes). The CNE president is selected from among the members of the *Comité*. Half of the *Comité* membership is renewed every two years. The CNE general secretariat consists of a permanent staff of 24 members. The CNE is financed by the state and has its own budget.

Missions and activities

The CNE's mission is to evaluate research, cultural and vocational public institutions (*établissements publics à caractère scientifique, culturel et professionnel*) comprising the universities, the schools and the *grands établissements* that are under the authority of the Minister in charge of higher education. The CNE may also evaluate institutions of higher education that are under other ministries' authority. The CNE evaluates institutions in the areas corresponding to the public service missions of higher education. These missions are education and continuing education, research, and development (i.e. the integration of each institution in the regional, national and international spheres). It also examines the governance of institutions, their policies and management practices. The CNE is not charged with the evaluation of individuals, nor does it have responsibilities in accrediting degrees or apportioning state funds. It has no power to regulate or manage institutions. It is up to the Minister and his administration, as well as the institutions themselves, to implement (or not) the CNE's recommendations.

Based on the decree of 21 February 1985, the CNE organises its activities independently: it plans its own programme and determines the methodology of its evaluations. The CNE conducts about 20 evaluation programmes every year. It is involved in three types of activities. First, it carries out institutional evaluations, that is, evaluations of universities and *écoles*. In 1996, it will have completed the evaluation of all French universities and that of about 20 schools (it has published over 100 reports). The CNE has started the evaluation of universities that had already been evaluated (second-round evaluations) to assess the implementation of its initial recommendations and to measure change; it plans to conduct such evaluations on a five-year cycle. Second, the CNE undertakes cross-cutting and comparative evaluations which assess either a specific discipline (geography, sciences or information, dentistry, and chemistry) or a degree (*magistères*). And third, based on knowledge acquired through the institutional and disciplinary evaluations, the CNE studies the missions of universities. In both its annual report to the President of the Republic and its thematic studies, the CNE examines general higher education policy issues.

Principles and method

The main elements of the French model of evaluation are as follows. An evaluation rests on a quantitative and qualitative approach, with the statistical data used as a basis for analysis and for homogeneous data-gathering nation-wide. The CNE thinks, however, that the evaluation of higher education has to be primarily qualitative; this is why it does not believe in the use of performance indicators but takes into account the context, the specific situation, the evolution, and the specific objectives of each institution being evaluated. An evaluation always includes both an internal and an external phase. Through a questionnaire, the institution being evaluated prepares its own internal evaluation and analyses its strengths, weaknesses and future prospects. An external phase comprises a peer review that includes a site visit and results in confidential reports. On the basis of the internal evaluation report and the experts' reports, the CNE writes an evaluation report which is published.

The evaluation reports analyse how institutions define their project and fulfil their mission. Thus, these reports serve to inform public opinion first and foremost, the users and partners of the institutions, in particular the state, and other funding agents. In addition, thanks to their recommendations, the reports constitute strategic tools at the disposal of institutions, specifically presidents and their teams, to allow them to implement policies and improve the quality of teaching, research and management.

The evaluations are based on a dialogue. Thus, the criteria and indicators currently in use were established in 1986 and redefined in 1994 in a dialogue between the CNE and the Conference of University Presidents. Each evaluation involves numerous exchanges between the institutions and the CNE: joint preparation of the methodology and the questionnaire used for the self-assessment, site visits of CNE and staff members, and site visits by the experts. The draft report itself is submitted for comment to the heads of institutions who are also responsible for the accuracy of the facts presented in the report. The president of the institution being evaluated has the last word since his/her response is published at the end of the evaluation report.

Recent developments

At the conclusion of its first ten years of activities and its first *tour de France* of universities, the CNE started to return to the universities that had already been evaluated, to pursue its institutional evaluations. It also started a new evaluation programme: that of the IUFMs (Teachers' Training Schools). Finally, it will develop further its cross-cutting and comparative evaluations.

The second-round evaluation of universities

Before it even ended its evaluation of all French universities, the CNE had started to return to institutions for a second-round evaluation. On the basis of a few pilots, it developed a new methodology, applied for the first time in 1994 for the second-round evaluation of the University of Strasbourg I. As at August 1996, five second-round evaluations have been completed. The elaboration of this methodology took into account a number of factors linked to the general environment. First, important changes have taken place in the past ten years in the French higher education landscape, especially in relation to the significant increase in student numbers, and in human and material resources. Second, changes in the relationship between the ministry and the institutions, that took place with the introduction of the contractual policy, require universities to prepare a four-year strategic plan which the CNE is legally required to evaluate. Third, new partnerships between universities and both local authorities and firms with regard to research and teaching activities have developed; and finally, lessons have been drawn from the different evaluation procedures in Europe despite the existing differences among higher education systems.

Taking into account these significant changes in the higher education environment, the CNE developed its second-round evaluation methodology on the basis of the following principles: the selection of the institutions is done by the *Comité*; the evaluation takes into account the *politique de site*, that is, the institutional policies regarding the place of the institution in its regional environment (see below); the evaluation implies the active participation of an institution (see below); it is selective (see below); it takes into account the dynamic dimension of an institution; it emphasises quality issues; the principle of peer review is maintained; and the evaluation report is public (Comité National d'Évaluation 1995a).

The main innovations

The main innovations include the *politique de site*, the increased importance of an internal evaluation stage, and the selectivity of evaluations. Each of these deserves further elaboration.

The politique de site

Because of both the development of closer relationships with the local authorities and the firms, and the co-existence of several institutions (sometimes with the same disciplines represented) within a single town or region, it has become necessary to analyse the coherence of policies developed by institutions or local authorities with regard to the regional site. A first programme is underway in Lyon. In the first phase, the CNE started the evaluation of eight institutions established in Lyon: three universities (which have already been evaluated in the first ten years), four schools and the Teachers' Training School. In a second phase, starting in autumn 1996, it will conduct a cross-cutting evaluation to examine the relationships among the different entities: not only the eight institutions already mentioned, but all other institutions in the city, including private ones. These evaluations will lead to two types of reports: a specific report for each institution, and a site report. Two new programmes will be launched in the next few months: Aix-Marseille and the greater periphery of the Paris region.

The increased importance of an internal evaluation phase

From the start of the CNE activities, the universities presented a quantitative and qualitative document that served as the basis for the evaluation. But, on the one hand, many encountered difficulties in gathering all the required data and, on the other hand, the documents were neither synthetic nor analytical, but simply descriptive of the institution. The CNE and its experts were in charge of the analysis and synthesis of these documents. Thus, the first-round evaluation reports, although essentially descriptive, provided an exhaustive panorama of French universities.

The changes that have occurred in higher education, however, enabled the adoption of a new method: institutions enjoying greater autonomy and responsibility must be able to know themselves better, to gather the necessary data and analyse them. This is why, in the internal evaluation phase, they are asked to produce, under the president's accountability, an internal evaluation report that includes a discussion of all university units and activities. The CNE provides universities with documents, questionnaires, analytical tables, and staff support to facilitate this work. The main obstacles encountered by institutions in this internal phase are to learn to describe themselves in a coherent and exhaustive manner and, even more, to assess their strengths and weaknesses, and to judge strategically their organisation, activities and development plan.

A selective evaluation

Since the aim is to evaluate all institutions on a shorter, five-year cycle, it is essential to lighten the procedure: this is why the external evaluation is now selective. The internal evaluation report, which as we have seen is exhaustive, allows the CNE to bypass the heavy task of describing all aspects of an institution at the same time as it highlights the main issues facing an institution. The selection of issues that constitutes the focus of an evaluation is done by the CNE on the basis of the following elements: the initial evaluation report and its recommendations; the second-round internal evaluation report which must highlight the issues faced by the institution and how it has resolved or plans to resolve them; the requests of the university president that the CNE focuses on a specific sector; and the focus on a specific general interest issue, with the long-term plan of a comparative evaluation. In practice, the choice of issues is not easy. It was decided to focus systematically on two topics: the implementation of the CNE recommendations and any initiative taken by the university since the initial evaluation. A balance must be reached in the analysis of strengths and weaknesses in order for an evaluation to be constructive and not to slide into an inspection.

The evaluation of the Teachers' Training Schools

If the creation of the new Teachers' Training Schools (IUFM) in 1990 did not solve all the problems facing this sector, the initiative nevertheless represented a significant change, surrounded by a heated debate. The 29 IUFMs are public higher education institutions attached to one or several universities. The Conference of IUFM Directors requested their evaluation in 1994. The CNE started in 1995, estimating that the schools had matured sufficiently to be evaluated. The creation of IUFMs led to a flurry of reports. The CNE procedure, however, was original in that it decided first to conduct institutional evaluations on which to base its judgement of the 'IUFM institution' as such, instead of proceeding in a more general way and risking falling prey to ideological presuppositions. The CNE developed a specific methodology, in a dialogue with the Conference of IUFM Directors, and launched three experimental evaluations (Lyon, Grenoble, Caen), whose evaluation reports will be published in autumn 1996.

On the basis of this experimental programme, the CNE will be able to perfect its methodology, make decisions regarding future institutional and comparative evaluations, and prepare a general study focusing on national policy issues regarding teachers' training: whether they concern research (science of education, didactics), recruitment of IUFM teachers, relationships with universities, internships and practical training, relationships with public and private schools, or the variety of teachers' recruitment policies.

The evaluation of disciplines

Several reasons justify the CNE plan to develop discipline-based evaluations. First, institutional evaluations have highlighted many discipline-based problems shared by universities which require a national analysis. Second, a comparative procedure is possible, which is not the case for institutional evaluation because of the heterogeneity of institutions (size, history, geographical location, disciplines represented, research activities, resources, etc.). And third, an international perspective, particularly a European one, is more easily done at the discipline level. This approach is in fact essential if the goal is to develop degree equivalencies in Europe, without necessarily ending with degree standardisation.

In practice, existing obstacles require certain choices. First, the selection of a disciplinary area is sensitive. The disciplinary field must be well defined epistemologically and sufficiently homogeneous to allow the use of a single set of indicators. It was the case for dentistry whose institutional structure in France is the same nation-wide and whose curriculum is uncomplicated – train oral surgeons and grant them a single national degree. For this evaluation, it was possible to develop a grid of questions and also to apply, for each of the 16 faculties, a five-point rating scale under five headings. Second, the presence of a single discipline or subdiscipline in a great number of universities does not allow the experts to visit all the sites, so the external evaluation must strike a balance between the analysis of documents and site visits. Third, the CNE decided in July 1996 to launch the evaluation of pharmacy, general medicine, and later the sciences of education (whose importance became evident during the IUFM evaluations). In order to develop a coherent programme the CNE envisages a study conducted both at the epistemological level and in terms of the global structure of degrees and their articulation, while taking into account the experience in other countries. Finally, the CNE plans to experiment with a comparative evaluation with other interested European countries. It offered a proposal for such a study as a follow up to the *European Pilot Project for Evaluating Quality in Higher Education* (Comité National d'Évaluation 1995b).

The publication of reports

As a matter of principle, every CNE evaluation report is published. Currently, the CNE prints 1000 copies of each report and mails 700 of those immediately. New technological developments, however, and financial concerns (both for printing and mailing), have led the CNE to look into other ways of publicising the reports. It is now possible to consult them on the Internet (http://www-cne.mesr.fr/) where all 1995 reports (and particularly the reports on the 'new universities') are to be found. In the short term, this mode of communication will obviously have important repercussions on the working relationship of the CNE with the institutions evaluated, as well as with other evaluation agencies.

References

Comité National d'Évaluation (1995a) *Evolution des Universités, Dynamique de l'Évaluation: Rapport au Président de la République 1985–95.* Paris: La Documentation Française.

Comité National d'Évaluation (1995b) *Projet Pilote Européen Pour l'Évaluation de la Qualité dans l'Enseignement Supérieur: Rapport National – France.* Translated into English and German. Paris: la Documentation Française.

Chapter 6

The Balance Between Accountability and Improvement
The Danish Experience

Christian Thune

Introduction

The last few years have witnessed a remarkable European trend towards accountability and improvement of higher education. Government policies of decentralisation, value for money, and internationalisation of higher education have all contributed to this development. Government initiatives have established national agencies, for example in France (1987), the Netherlands (1988), the UK (1992) and Denmark (1992), charged with the task of systematically assessing their respective higher education sectors. An increasing number of initiatives have also been taken by the higher education institutions (HEIs) themselves in the face of the move from elite to mass higher education. An understandable and fundamental perception of HEIs is that government initiatives, and government ownership of such developments, do not foster and fulfil the universities' expectations and goals of quality improvement.

Much of the recent discussion on quality matters seems, in relation to universities and university-based research, to take its starting point from the premise of a fundamental linkage between the central initiatives of governments and evaluation systems that are: government owned; fundamentally external and bureaucratic in their nature and procedures *vis-à-vis* the sensitivity of universities; assessing quality against standards defined by peers; and focused on accountability which is often perceived in terms of efficiency or productivity. The contrary belief is that if initiative and ownership are left to HEIs themselves procedures will be internal, non-bureaucratic and acceptable to universities; a 'fitness for purpose' approach will ensure that quality is established as a result of institutional practice being close to, or identical with, stated aims and goals; and the focus will be on quality assurance and improvement rather than accountability.

Much of this argument has a distinctly UK bias: the basis being that the UK funding councils are owned by government with a focus on accountability, whereas the UK Higher Education Quality Council is owned by the universities with a focus on quality assurance and improvement. The Dutch system also has a government-owned as well as a university-owned level, but the systematic evaluations organised by the VSNU (the Dutch Rectors' Conference) have a focus on both accountability and improvement. And in Denmark the government owns the evaluation system, but the main focus is on quality assurance and improvement. In other words the character of the process is a different issue from, and independent of, the matter of control.[1]

However, there is a principal dilemma which relates to purpose: there is a dilemma between an essential quality improvement-related purpose and a purpose which is focused on external accountability. There is a conflict in terms of the differences in method used by each, which follows from differences in the purpose of the quality system that has been set up. But there need not be such a simple and direct relationship between, on the one hand, who initiates and owns the evaluation system and, on the other hand, the balance between quality assurance and improvement, and accountability.[2] Of course this statement begs the obvious question: what in an operational sense are the criteria for identifying the goals and objectives of quality assurance and improvement, and those of accountability, respectively? Both concepts are ambiguous in themselves or are often used ambiguously, but for the purposes of this chapter the following may offer more clarification:

---

1   I am indebted here to Ronald Barnett's very interesting analysis of the 'messiness, overlappings, and lack of clarity' of the quality language discussion (Barnett 1994).
2   This argument evidently also covers the UK scene. Cf. the points made by Martin Trow and Paul Clark respectively, in (1994).

The *criteria for improvement* are those procedures that are conducive to strengthening the conditions, motivation, and scope and level of information of HEIs in this direction. In other words, they are procedures that engage institutions in a self-learning process. Procedures should aim at promoting future performances (formative evaluation) rather than judgements on past performances (summative evaluation). Procedures should lead to ends that are specifically in the interest of HEIs, and towards the specification of quality according to goals and criteria that are internal or may be made internal by institutions.

The *criteria for accountability* are procedures that lead to the assessment of quality of teaching and learning in terms of criteria set down by external authorities and institutions, and with the goal of strengthening external insight and even control – opening the door for eventual external corrective action.

But *empirical realities do not necessarily conform to theoretical positions and ideal types* (Barnett 1994). It is the argument in the rest of this chapter that the implications and consequences of the self-chosen strategy of the Danish Centre for Quality Assurance and Evaluation of Higher Education have in fact been to combine quality assurance and improvement with that of accountability. The Danish approach has been to merge or synthesise the two in a dual approach in terms of procedures, methods and goals, but with an emphasis on the improvement dimension. The following sections will present the Danish context, first, in terms of the 1992 reform of higher education which provided the formal basis for the balanced strategy argued above to the extent that it changed the power relationships between the government and HEIs towards a more decentralised system, ensuring considerable autonomy of institutions; and second, in terms of the mandate and procedures of the Danish Centre for Quality Assurance and Evaluation of Higher Education.

The 1992 reform of higher education

In the spring of 1992 the Danish conservative-liberal minority government and Parliament arrived at a number of compromises on higher education which, seen as one entity, constituted a reform of the entire higher education system (Danish Ministry of Education and Research 1992). The stated objectives of the reform, or rather package deal, were: to ensure a higher degree of institutional autonomy combined with a tightening of each institution's management structure; to secure an undisturbed working environment through political compromises reaching several years into the future; to find a better balance between supply of, and demand for, study places; and to improve quality of the programmes, so that they came up to the highest international standards.

Accordingly the principles of the reform stressed institutional freedom and autonomy. The intention was to formulate the main objectives for, and framework of, the higher education sector and to give HEIs the autonomy to develop within this framework. Consequently the key words of the reform set out by the government were deregulation and decentralisation, combined with mechanisms to ensure quality. The cornerstones of the reform were:

- an agreement on budgets for higher education from 1993 to 1996

- an improved PhD programme

- better balance between supply and demand for study places and freer intake at most programmes

- a new uniform study structure for higher education with a three year BA programme, a two year masters programme, and a three year PhD programme

- a new University Act which reorganised the political and management structure of HEIs. Key elements in this new – and to HEIs highly controversial – Act were: massive authority transferral from the Ministry of Education to HEIs; preservation of the institutional democracy, but a reduction in the number of governing bodies and their members; significantly strengthened mandate and authority of rectors and deans; separation of the management of education from research; and external representation in the senate and faculty councils.

- Educational quality. An important message in the reform was that the changes caused by the reform and the pressure from a growing student population must not have a negative effect on the quality of programmes. Accordingly a number of special provisions contributed to

ensuring continued educational quality: stiffer admission
requirements to the most demanding programmes;
introduction of first-year tests in programmes where they
do not exist already; and strengthening central quality
assurance through the establishment of an evaluation
centre and through reorganisation of the system of
external examiners.

Institutions were sceptical about the reform package from the
outset. The criticism focused, in particular, on the new uniform
structure of studies, and on the new University Act. The serious-
ness of the intended process of decentralisation was also questioned as was, initially, the new centrally-based mechanisms for
accountability of quality. However, it could be said that, first, the
government needed evaluations as a means of steering the higher
education sector towards greater modernisation and decentralisation. The general development and trends of higher education
would be monitored through evaluations, which would simultaneously control the level of quality in individual programmes.
Second, HEIs had received considerable real autonomy as a consequence of the new University Act. Accordingly the presidents,
deans, and governing boards were now facing independent,
broad, and often difficult decision-making. Systematic evaluations
would provide the institutions with an insight into the quality of
their own study programmes. Good evaluations, which reflected
the relationship between institutional goals and realities, could
therefore form the basis for planning and prioritising tasks.

The Danish Centre for Quality Assurance and Evaluation of Higher Education

Accordingly the Danish Centre for Quality Assurance and Evaluation of Higher Education was established by the Ministry of
Education in 1992 and became operational on 1 July 1992 (Thune
1994a). The Centre is funded by the Ministry and in 1995 its total
annual grant amounted to 9.5 million DDK. The Centre is in
principle independent of the Ministry of Education, and of the
universities and other institutions of higher education. The Centre
is governed by a board composed of the five chairmen of the
National Education Councils, who had been key actors in the
discussions leading up to the decision to launch the Centre (Chair-

manship of the National Advisory Boards on Higher Education 1992). The Centre is staffed by a director, eight academics in charge of projects, three office secretaries, and a dozen experts and assistants employed in the short term in connection with various evaluation projects. *The mandate* of the Centre is: to initiate evaluation processes of higher education in Denmark; to develop appropriate methods of assessing programmes; to inspire and guide the institutions of higher education in aspects concerning evaluation and quality; and to compile national and international experience on evaluation of the educational system and quality development.

A substantial part of the Centre's work consists of regular and systematic evaluations of programmes on a rotating basis in which all programmes will be evaluated within a period of seven years. In addition, the Centre evaluates new programmes after their establishment period, and programmes for which the Ministry of Education, consulting bodies, or an HEI find that there is a need for an evaluation of the quality of the programme. The Centre must ensure that reliable methods are employed in connection with the execution of the various evaluations.

Method of evaluation

The Centre will initiate evaluations by arrangement with the initiator of the assignment, who could be one of the Danish National Education Councils, one or several HEIs, or the Ministry of Education. Generally an evaluation will comprise five phases spanning a period of 12 months:

Phase 1 – Planning

Phase 2 – Self-assessment

Phase 3 – User surveys

Phase 4 – Visit of experts

Phase 5 – Reporting

The evaluation model is shown in Figure 6.1.

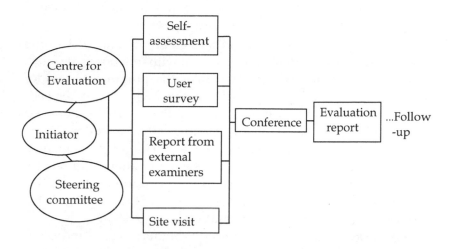

Figure 6.1 Evaluation model

The planning phase sees the establishment of the *steering committee* that will be charged with the professional responsibility of the evaluation. The steering committee covers, in principle, the functions of what in other contexts are called peer group, expert panel or visiting team. It is important to note that the steering committee follows the whole process of evaluation. Further, the composition of the four to five member committees typically reflects not only professional or academic expertise, but also comprises one or two employer representatives. The planning phase also includes a number of information and planning meetings with the institutions involved.

In *the self-assessment phase* the pivotal element of any evaluation is launched, that is, the self-assessment process. The HEI prepares a self-assessment report which should identify and discuss the central aspects of the evaluation and should contain an assessment of the strengths and weaknesses of the programme in relation to the objectives. Furthermore, the report should set out proposals of initiatives that may ensure the quality of the programme. The long-term objective of the self-assessment process is to encourage continued internal quality development of the programme.

In *the user survey phase* an inquiry is carried out among the users of the programme: students, graduates and employers. The observations of the external examiners will also be included in this phase.

In *the visiting phase* a panel consisting of representatives of the steering committee, often supplemented with independent (international or Nordic) experts, will visit the programmes under review. During the day-long visit, the panel will discuss the self-assessment report, the user surveys and the external examiners' report with senior management, teaching staff and students.

The *reporting* will be carried out in an evaluation report in which the steering committee will sum up the observations and recommendations for quality assurance of the programme. The evaluation report will be delivered to the initiator of the assignment for further processing and implementation.

The scope and level of activities within this model is indicated in the figures on evaluations completed within the first three and a half years of activities as shown in Table 6.1.

Table 6.1 Scope and level of activities

		Total
Discipline areas		22
Programmes/ Self-assessment reports		232
Initiator	Educational Councils	18
	Ministry	4
	H E Institutions	4
User surveys	Students	6
	Graduates	17
	Employers	17
Other surveys		4
External examiners' report	Yes	17
	No	5

Source: Evalueringscenteret

The feedback to the Centre from HEIs indicates, to a growing extent, that the basic methodology has in fact stood the test of trial in practice. Compared with the concern and sensitivity normally associated with external evaluations, the Centre has received very few decidedly negative reactions. On the contrary, many institutions accept the challenge and consequently express satisfaction with the process and the results of evaluation. Accordingly, the experience of the first two or three founding years has demonstrated that the Centre has established itself with a model of evaluation which those evaluated, that is the institutions, can accept, and which is able to produce the expected results. Several elements in the model contribute to this result. In general the Centre has succeeded in establishing a good and operational division of labour between the steering committees, the Centre itself, and HEIs. Other important factors include: a satisfactory running contact and dialogue between the Centre and the study programmes under evaluation; a relevant balance between quality assurance and accountability; a comprehensive, solid documentation; and a processual starting point without previously defined criteria of success, indicators of quality, or standards of excellence. In the following section the elements that contribute towards the priority of an improvement focus will be outlined and discussed.

The elements of improvement and quality assurance

Using a standard methodology

It is the basic mandate of the Centre to evaluate all study programmes in higher education and, from the outset, it has been a high priority to ensure that these systematic evaluations are based on a consistent, transparent and well known methodology. Given the difficult task of keeping to the six-year time-schedule for the first round of evaluations, there is a temptation to differentiate evaluations in terms of the basic effort and resources employed. The Centre, however, has decided against this, because it would be difficult to justify such action to the institutions. In particular, the Centre needs to ensure that there is no basis for accusing it of 'pre-evaluating' the study programmes in order to decide the level of methodological effort. Even more important in this context is that HEIs are given the real opportunity to prepare themselves for the evaluations within local mechanisms that are at one and the same time compatible with the basic methodology of the Centre and conducive to further improvement on local terms.

Careful documentation

In the development of the general methodology, the Centre has had four general aims concerning the quality of the documentation collected from the various study programmes. First, satisfactory documentation is required to enable recommendations and conclusions to be reached by the steering committee. Second, the study programmes must be able to accept the basic evidence on which the conclusions and recommendations of the experts rest. Third, the evaluation process, including the documentation, must aspire to further and continuing internal quality assurance and improvement in the study programmes; and finally, the initiator of the assignment must have a relevant basis for implementation of the evaluation. In order to achieve these aims there must be a relevant balance between the components of the evaluation. The final documentation must be comprehensive and consistent – including those cases where, for example, the self-assessment has neither been informative nor analytical, or in those cases where the site visit is less successful.

HEIs participate in the planning of the evaluation

The Centre gives a high priority to initial meetings with representatives of the study programmes under evaluation, not least with a view to identifying relevant areas for potential improvement.

Stress on self-assessment

The more the self-assessment is given priority in the process, the more the self-assessment will function as a means of training and preparing the institution or the study programme to take responsibility for its own quality development – and the less the self-assessment will be seen as merely producing information for the expert committee. Ideally, the self-assessment should reflect a subtle balance between qualitative and quantitative data. But there is no doubt that particularly the quantitative part, which borders on performance indicators, causes considerable work and some apprehension. Many Danish universities are not yet geared-up to compile and deliver that kind of precise data. But the Centre does try to avoid giving the impression that a technicist approach is being adopted through the unreflected use of performance indicators.

The self-assessment is the standard against which the institution can measure itself. It provides a framework for building up a definition of quality; it helps the institution decide how far it is achieving its strategic mission and goals; and it allows it to build an action plan for development. In the qualitative context, the self-assessment should be used to put more stress on inviting the study programmes to analyse their mission, values, goals, and strengths and weaknesses, respectively. Therefore, the second and perhaps even more important purpose of the self-assessment is to provide the institution and the study programme with a commitment, and a valid procedure and method to continue a process of quality assurance and improvement. It is very important to stress that the long-term perspective of the effort vested in the self-assessments is less on delivering the material for a control process, but much more on contributing to local quality improvement.

The experts on the steering committee have as a general rule their professional background – and loyalty – within the discipline area under evaluation

The Centre considers its experiences with, up until now, more than 20 steering committees as being very positive. Their continued professionalism combined with a serious and committed approach has ensured that there have been no hidden or 'political' agendas involved in the proceedings. Furthermore, the potential and implicit 'examining role' is generally more than balanced by the elements of collegialism and mutual trust among representatives – and even in some cases 'partisans' – from the same discipline area.

A heavy focus on enlisting users or consumers in the procedures

This reflects a general and long-standing Danish tradition for including users in the planning of higher education. The attitudes of all three groups – the students, the recent graduates and the employers – are surveyed intensively as part of the procedure of the individual evaluation. Furthermore representatives of employers are prominent on the steering committees. The focus is not to deploy evaluation as a means of steering HEIs more in the direction of the labour market. The dialogue between consumers and institutions should be balanced in such a way that the integrity and independence of the institutions are not in question. The role of the consumer is to provide information and advice, not to take over the institutions, to dictate the content of the educational provision, or to control the production. This balance is necessary because the consumers do not have the knowledge and scientific basis on which higher education must be built. If the consumers took on this role, there would be an obvious risk of higher education becoming fit for the society of yesterday and not for the society of tomorrow.

The evaluation reports contain recommendations targeted at the HEI as well as at the Ministry of Education

In fact the majority of recommendations ask for implementation by the HEI. However, an interesting dimension is that those evaluated, as a rule, criticise reports that are formulated in too general terms. But neither is it appreciated by those in focus when the critical impact of a report is very specific.

Emphasis on the recommendations

The Centre instructs the steering committees to focus on recommendations that are operational, constructive and realistic within the given conditions for the discipline area in question. Furthermore, there should be a clear priority of recommendations, and preferably it should be evident which recommendations are essential in the short-term as well as in the longer-term. Finally it should be clear who must carry the responsibility for follow-up or implementation.

The report is presented to the HEIs involved before publication

This final conference brings together, on the one hand, the Centre and the steering committee and, on the other hand, deans and course leaders from the study programmes evaluated. The latter have the opportunity for an open discussion with the former of the premises for the conclusions and recommendations of the report – which eventually may be redrafted in the light of points raised during the conference. The conferences as a rule produce very fruitful discussions and have a distinct potential as safety valves for the proceedings.

The follow-up procedure places the prime responsibility within the HEI

Once an evaluation is finished and a report is available in some form or other, the crucial phase begins of implementing the conclusions and recommendations. The follow-up of the evaluations is the prime responsibility of HEIs. As the aim of the evaluation process is the launching of a continuous process of quality assurance and improvement within the study programmes, it is crucial that the institutions themselves are committed to this follow-up. With the first evaluations finalised in 1993, it is still too early to say what kind of evaluation procedures are developing in the institutions. It is the firm belief of the Centre, however, that the institutions' incentive to initiate follow-up procedures is closely tied to the success of the self-assessment process and the openness of the self-assessment, on the one hand, and the operationality of the recommendations in the evaluation report, on the other.

Fitness for purpose and no ranking

There seems to be a general consensus among HEIs and the Ministry of Education that institutions should not be ranked. Institutions have different aims and objectives. Considering the diversity of institutions which exist within national higher education systems, it is important that quality assessment should assess the extent to which institutions actually achieve the aims and objectives which they set for themselves. This assessment of the relationship between aims and objectives and actual achievement focuses on the core of the quality issue.

No linkage to funding

In several countries a much commented on, and controversial, issue is any linkage between evaluation and government funding. The issue is whether a government's allocation of funding to universities should wholly, or in part, be based on the results of systematic evaluations. For the moment this is only the case in the UK. In Denmark the fact that funding and evaluation have not been linked explicitly has been a marked positive factor. At the same time positive evaluations should have the effect of attracting more qualified applicants, thus strengthening the possibilities of the HEI in question gaining from the taximeter-based funding system.

The elements of accountability

It could be argued that the elements of improvement listed above all contain elements of accountability as well. There is an element here of describing the 'glass of water as half full or half empty'. The same observation could cover the following list of elements of accountability and so confirm the reality of dualism or synthesis in the Danish approach to accountability and improvement.

In principle the recommendations of the experts must be within the context of the 1992 Parliament decision on higher education, especially in relation to financing, structure and duration of study programmes

The implication is that the institution should not entertain over-optimistic notions as to the possibility of reports recommending positive changes in funding and length of study programmes.

All reports are public and accordingly the criticism is also public

In some countries where evaluation procedures have been established the issue of openness has been controversial. The standard argument in favour of confidential proceedings has concerned the self-assessment. The argument runs that confidentiality should encourage the authors of the self-assessment to be more honest and critical. In Denmark openness is viewed as a cardinal point with regard to the overall target of making evaluations the platform for qualified knowledge of the merits of various study programmes. All reports are, therefore, published or available.

HEIs are not able to influence

- the structure of the documentation in terms of user surveys
- the appointment of the experts (members of the steering committees).

The role of the Ministry of Education in the follow-up process

The Ministry has recently approved a procedure according to which institutions hosting the programmes that have been evaluated must, within three months after the publication of the evaluation report, present individual action plans for the follow-up of the recommendations. After two and a half years the Ministry will, through the relevant Advisory Board Council of Higher Education, discuss with the institutions the extent to which the action plans have been implemented; however nothing has been stated yet as to the consequences if implementation is found wanting.

The Centre is funded through the Ministry of Education

The Centre is formally independent, but funded by the Ministry. Important in this respect, however, is the point that the Ministry has never interfered in the setting up of the Centre's procedures and methodology. The relationship has been harmonious, but, significantly, is of an arm's length nature.

External examiners

One essential dimension in the context of the need for accountability is the system of external examining (Thune 1994b). External examiners (*censorer* in Danish) are characteristic of the Danish educational system at all levels, from the upper classes of the primary schools and onwards to the graduate level of higher education. This system of permanent, salaried external examiners was initiated in 1871 at the University of Copenhagen. Traditionally, external examiners have joined internal examiners (teachers, professors etc.) in the grading of the individual examinations. In other words, at the typical Danish examination, the student faces a teacher from the institution in question and an external examiner.

The main tasks of the external examiners are to guarantee that the aims and demands of examinations are in accordance with the curricula; examination procedures are in accordance with the appropriate rules; and students receive an equal and just treatment, and their efforts a relevant and trustworthy appraisal. In 1992 the system of external examiners in higher education was reorganised in order to secure and strengthen: the independence of the external examiners *vis-à-vis* HEIs; the dialogue between external examiners and departments; the representation of the external examiners in relation to the employers of the graduates; and ways and means of using the system of external examiners to enhance the quality of the study programmes.

In the latter respect, the chairmen of the bodies of external examiners, within the various discipline areas, must now on an annual basis deliver a report of the findings of external examiners to the various departments. These annual reports should be based on the individual reports of those external examiners who have been involved in the examinations during the year in question. Reception among HEIs was initially somewhat less than enthusiastic. The general hesitancy of Danish institutions towards outside suggestions of change manifested itself in, and in particular was activated by, misgivings about a more bureaucratic system, and about appointing external examiners representing the employers of candidates. However, from the perspective of the need for accountability, it should be obvious that the reorganisation of the system has a potentially crucial role in ensuring that the level of quality in study programmes meets the relevant standards of quality.

Concluding remarks

There are evident advantages of external, systematic dimensions to quality assurance. Some of the key aspects would be: impartiality; credibility; authority; comprehensiveness; consistency; and transparency. The recipe for success would be the extent to which a linkage can be made to the aspects characteristic of internal, institution-based quality improvement, that is, trust, commitment and understanding. There is little doubt that a series of well-executed evaluations do not in themselves bring any merit to the concept of systematic evaluations. The proof of success will be the impact and follow-up in the longer perspective of the foundation for quality improvement launched by a successful evaluation. The ambition and intention of the Danish Evaluation Centre have been to set up procedures and methods that could motivate HEIs towards this end.

After a period of initial scepticism, the feedback from institutions is increasingly affirmative. At the conferences during the final phase of the evaluation, the institutional representatives speak their minds very freely in terms of their experiences of the strengths and weaknesses of the process. Not least the experience of the self-assessment phase is generally considered in quite positive terms. As it has recently been said at a conference by one university representative, 'if the Evaluation Centre had not been established the HE institutions would have had to invent it themselves, because they now realise the need for, and their interest in, a professional, external evaluation agency'.

References

Trow, M. (1994) *Managerialism and the Academic Profession: Quality and Control.* Higher Education Report No 2. London: Quality Support Centre.

Barnett, R. (1994) 'Power, enlightenment and quality evaluation.' *European Journal of Education 29,* 2.

Chairmanship of the National Advisory Boards on Higher Education (1992) *Quality Assessment of Higher Education in Denmark.* Copenhagen: Ministry of Education.

Clark, P. (1994) In *Managerialism and the Academic Profession: Quality and Control.* Higher Education Report No 2. London: Quality Support Centre.

Danish Ministry of Education and Research (1992) *Education Reform – a Danish Open Market in Higher Education.* Copenhagen: Ministry of Education and Research.

Thune, C. (1994a) 'Setting up the Danish Centre.' In A. Craft (ed) *International Developments in Assuring Quality in Higher Education.* London: The Falmer Press.

Thune, C. (1994b) The Danish experience of external examining. In Higher Education Quality Council, *External Examining in Focus.* London: HEQC.

Trow, M. (1994) In *Managerialism and the Academic Profession: Quality and Control.* Higher Education Report No 2. London: Quality Support Centre.

Chapter 7

Quality Assurance and Diversity
The Case of England

Ruth Williams

Introduction

The aim of this chapter is to explore the development and outcomes of the external quality assurance arrangements in the
United Kingdom. The context against which this will be done is
the move from elite to mass higher education and the creation of
a unified but diverse sector – diverse in the sense that it is characterised by differences in the nature, purpose and scale of higher
education institutions, an increased and more heterogeneous student body, changing curricular structures and content, and new
methods of teaching, learning and assessment. The move to mass
higher education, which has taken place over the last three decades, has created a higher education system which Brennan describes as 'a system no longer characterised by exclusiveness of
entry,…a system with a plurality of purposes and clients and
which is often only imperfectly understood, even by those working in it' (Brennan *et al*. 1996, p.11).

   The focus of this discussion is on those arrangements for quality
assurance which affect the teaching function of higher education
institutions in England, although many of the points raised will
also apply to institutions in Northern Ireland, Scotland and Wales.
The chapter begins with a brief look at the history of the new
unified higher education system and the reasons why the current
externally-set arrangements for accountability and quality assurance were established. It then looks at the arrangements themselves – quality assessment as conducted by the Higher Education

Funding Council for England and quality audit by the Higher
Education Quality Council – and the outcomes and issues emerging from these two processes. The chapter explores some of the
reasons why the current external arrangements have proved un-
popular and the reasons for the increased focus on academic
standards. The chapter concludes with a look at the future quality
assurance arrangements in the UK.

Historical background

The Further and Higher Education Act of 1992 (Department of
Education 1992) marked a major reshaping of UK higher education, ending the binary line which had operated since the late 1960s
and placing all of higher education in a single regulatory framework. Three major changes were made:

- It established the funding councils for England, Scotland
  and Wales and gave them responsibility for securing that
  provision was made for assessing the quality of education
  in the institutions they funded.

- It abolished the Council for National Academic Awards
  (CNAA) as the degree awarding body of the polytechnics
  and colleges of higher education.

- It ended the binary policy by allowing polytechnics to use
  the title 'university' and allowing them their own degree
  awarding powers.

In addition to these developments, the Committee of Vice-Chancellors and Principals (CVCP) established the Higher Education
Quality Council (HEQC) which extended the remit of the CVCP's
existing Academic Audit Unit to cover all universities and colleges
in the new sector that subscribed to the new body. Two new forms
of external quality assurance and accountability arrangements
were established therefore – one state controlled through the funding councils to assess the quality of educational provision at subject
level, and one owned by the academic community through self-
regulation to scrutinise the effectiveness of institution-wide quality assurance procedures.

Reasons behind the establishment of these arrangements lie in
the political climate that had developed from the late 1970s which
was to demand greater public accountability from public sector

organisations for the central funding they received. Kogan (1986, quoted in Wright 1989) makes the point that this demand for public accountability lay in 'a weakening consensus (in Britain as else-where) that public institutions are beneficent and led by profes-sionals who can be trusted to provide society with what it needs' (p.151). Moreover, the White Paper preceding the 1992 Act out-lined the government's requirements for public accountability which it linked to its free market policy thus:

> ...there is a need for proper accountability for the substantial public funds invested in higher education. As part of this, students and employers need improved information about quality if the full benefit of increased competition is to be obtained. As demand for higher education expands further, and as competition among institutions increases...the gov-ernment considers that new arrangements for quality in higher education will be required (Department of Education and Science 1991, p.24).

The former polytechnics had always been used to external scrutiny – through the CNAA, Her Majesty's Inspectorate (HMI) for the former Polytechnics and Colleges Funding Council, and profes-sional and statutory bodies where it was required. The universities, however, had not been subjected to any such requirements (except in teacher training provision and by professional or statutory bodies where it was required) until the CVCP set up its Academic Audit Unit in 1990, albeit on a voluntary basis. The requirements of the new unified sector were to change this imbalance with a new set of arrangements.

Why did two arrangements develop separately and in parallel? As mentioned above, the government had developed a mistrust of self-regulation by public organisations because it believed that self-regulation did not provide genuine accountability for public funds. Although the setting up of the Academic Audit Unit by the CVCP was possibly seen within the academic community as a move which might 'see off' any state intervention in the future, the government was not convinced that such collegial forms of aca-demic quality control by themselves would ensure public account-ability. Quality assessment by the funding councils was thus established (along with the establishment of HEQC which the government's legislation (DES 1991) recognised and encouraged because it was seen as an additional layer of public accountability).

Such government action, which established quality assessment, has been labelled by Trow (1994) as 'hard managerialism' which he says is 'a substitute for a relationship of trust between the government and university, trust in the ability of the institutions of higher education to broadly govern themselves' (p.11). It was action imposed from outside the academic community to 'reshape and redirect the activities of that community through funding formulas and other mechanisms of accountability' (p.14). If Trow's observations are correct then there are possible implications for diversity and these will be explored further below. What then has been the impact of quality assessment, has it reshaped and redirected higher education as Trow asserts, and what are the issues to emerge from quality audit?

Quality assessment

The purpose of quality assessment as outlined by the 1992 Act is to ensure that quality is satisfactory or better, to encourage improvement, and to inform funding and reward excellence (HEFCE 1993). The aim is to examine the quality of the students' learning experience and achievement against the subject-provider's aims and objectives through a process of self-assessment and external peer review within the context of the subject-provider's aims and objectives. The fact that quality assessment is based on the subject-provider's aims and objectives is an attempt by the Funding Council to acknowledge and encourage diversity, although the extent to which this has proved to be the case is explored below.

The process of quality assessment involves the submission of a self-assessment by the department providing the subject to the funding council, a visit to the department by external assessors (mainly academic staff employed in other institutions) contracted and trained by the funding council, and judgements made on the quality of education through the observation of teaching and learning, scrutiny of students' work and discussions with staff and students. Initially the method developed by HEFCE involved selective visits to subject-providers on the basis of the self-assessments submitted, and this resulted in the award of an excellent, satisfactory or unsatisfactory grade. Where no visits took place, subject-providers were awarded 'satisfactory' grades. Criticisms about the selectivity of visits, the insensitivity of external assessors to institutional and subject aims and objectives, and the use of a three-point scale which effectively ranked institutions, persuaded the Funding Council to revise its method.

The revised method is based on an assessment process geared around the production of a graded profile of a subject area, constructed against six aspects of provision (i.e. the curriculum; teaching, learning and assessment; students' progress and achievements; the support and guidance provided; learning resources; and quality assurance arrangements), and all providers are visited in a particular subject area. The aspects of provision provide the structure of the self-assessment, the focus of the visit, and the outline of the published report. The graded profile results in an overall summative judgement which states whether quality has been approved, or not. A report of each visit is published describing the assessors' principal findings, the graded profile, and the overall judgement (HEFCE 1994).

HEFCE has published the outcomes of the *initial* method which was carried out between 1992 and 1995 (HEFCE 1995). Selective visits were made to subject-providers on the basis of the self-assessment report where the Funding Council believed that a *prima facie* case had been established for excellent provision, where it felt quality was at risk, and on a sample basis of those institutions claiming satisfactory provision. The report demonstrates that of the self-assessments received from former University Funding Council (UFC) institutions 88 per cent (373) made claims for excellence compared with 43 per cent (213) received from former Polytechnics and Colleges Funding Council (PCFC) institutions. Of the UFC institutions 75 per cent (281) made a *prima facie* case, and of the PCFC institutions 50 per cent (106) did so. In relation to the outcomes of the assessment visits, the information which has emerged is outlined in Table 7.1.

The overall outcome of the quality assessment exercise (which includes those institutions visited and those institutions awarded satisfactory without an assessment visit) was that 26 per cent of providers were excellent, 73 per cent were satisfactory and 1 per cent were unsatisfactory. These figures are described in greater detail in Table 7.2.

Table 7.1 Outcomes of quality assessment visits, 1992–95

	UFC	PCFC	FE	Total
Excellent	61% (193)	25% (55)	7% (1)	45% (249)
Satisfactory	39% (124)	71% (156)	80% (12)	53% (292)
Unsatisfactory	(1)	4% (9)	13% (2)	2% (12)
Total	**100% (318)**	**100% (220)**	**100% (15)**	**100% (553)**

Source: HEFCE (1995)

Table 7.2 Outcomes of the overall quality assessment exercise, 1992–95

	UFC	PCFC	FE	Total
Excellent	46% (193)	11% (55)	2% (1)	26% (249)
Satisfactory	54% (226)	87% (434)	94% (51)	73% (711)
Unsatisfactory	(1)	2% (9)	4% (2)	1% (12)
Total	**100% (420)**	**100% (498)**	**100% (54)**	**100% (972)**

Source: HEFCE (1995)

This information plainly shows the differences in grades awarded between the former UFC and PCFC institutions. More UFC institutions claimed excellence and more were awarded excellence than PCFC institutions. This raises questions about the acceptability and understanding of diversity in British higher education. It raises issues about the external assessors who make decisions based on their reading and understanding of the self-assessment reports, and their visits to the institutions. It raises issues about external assessors' knowledge and ability (and willingness) to understand and ultimately accept the different contexts within which a subject might be provided. It raises issues about the legitimacy of the peer review method in a system where teaching and learning provision is diverse.

It also raises issues about quality and the links between high quality teaching and well-funded research, on the one hand, and, on the other, the differences between the relatively richer and poorer institutions. In terms of the link between teaching and research, preliminary work conducted by HEFCE suggests that there is 'some validity' in the relationship between well-funded research departments and high quality teaching, although the work has also demonstrated that 'the highest achievement in teaching and learning can be secured without the highest achievement in research' (HEFCE 1995). However, if there is a close correlation, and if there is a move towards greater selectivity of research funding in the near future, which the Council has indicated should be no less than at present (HEFCE 1996), then the differences will remain apparent, but in sharper relief.

The Funding Council has indicated that the suggestion that richer institutions are more successful in obtaining excellent grades than those not so well-off, in relation to the funds received from the Council and other private income, can only be 'tentative and speculative' (HEFCE 1995). It makes this observation because any examination of a relationship is impossible given that the method by which it distributes funds to institutions is not at the level of the unit of assessment (i.e. the subject). However, the Funding Council's examination of the relationship between grades awarded and 'total income per student' has demonstrated that excellent provision is concentrated in the richer institutions, though without proper research it is difficult to draw firm conclusions. What evidence is available, then, shows that it is the rich research-oriented institutions that obtain the rewards from the quality assessment of teaching and learning. Continuing operation of the current quality assessment method, in a time of diminishing resources, may further compound these distinctions between institutions with possible implications for the continuing diversity of UK higher education.

Quality audit

In contrast to quality assessment whose focus is at the subject level, quality audit, undertaken by HEQC, is concerned with institutional systems and procedures which assure quality and standards. However, like quality assessment, quality audit is carried out within the context of institutions' stated aims and objectives. Its purpose is to ensure public accountability for the maintenance and improvement of academic quality and standards by finding out how higher education institutions discharge their obligation to provide high quality education and (more recently) how they satisfy themselves about the academic standards they seek to uphold (HEQC 1995a).

The process involves scrutiny of documentation supplied by the institution and a visit by a team of auditors. Visits focus on a number of aspects concerned with institutional procedures (such as the design, approval and review of programmes, teaching and learning and the student experience, and student assessment and the classification of awards) through inquisitorial 'question and answer' sessions with staff and students. The outcome of a quality audit is a published report. It describes the institutional systems and procedures, and the auditors' perceptions of their effectiveness, with comments on areas of good practice and suggestions about areas for improvement. The more recent focus of audit, on how institutions determine and maintain their academic standards, arose in response to government concerns about the quality and standard of UK degrees as a result of the rapid expansion in student numbers. Government action was to ask HEQC 'to place more emphasis on broad comparability in the standards of degrees offered by different institutions' (Patten 1994) to maintain the academic reputation of UK higher education. How this work has taken shape and the issues emerging is explored later in this chapter.

Like HEFCE, HEQC has published reports describing the issues emerging from quality audit. The first report (HEQC 1994) was based on the first round of audit which mainly comprised the pre-1992 universities. The report highlighted the diversity of institutional mission and tradition in the UK which was similarly reflected in the institutional approaches to quality assurance. Whilst the former polytechnics appeared to be moving to quality assurance procedures characterised by a 'lighter, but no less effective touch', the pre-1992 universities were moving away from an 'informal, implicit' culture of quality assurance to one characterised by more formal and codified procedures. The report also noted the continuing dominance of the research culture in the pre-1992 universities which was given greater status and reward than the teaching function, and raised serious questions about the effectiveness of the external examiner system.

The second report (HEQC 1996a), based on the subsequent round of audits, which comprised a more diverse set of institutions, noted amongst other things that formal systems of quality assurance are now the norm within the higher education sector – the case for the norm most probably lying in the very existence of the external quality assurance arrangements and their impact. However, it also noted that institutions are becoming aware of the significant resource required to run effective quality assurance procedures – an important consideration when funding to higher education is being cut. The report also notes the tension between research and teaching which has been made sharper given the competitive funding method and the pressures on institutions and academics to produce research output. The ways in which institutions determine and maintain academic standards have also been raised as a concern; audit has found an overwhelming reliance on the external examiner system which, the report states, clearly demonstrates a lack of articulation into the meaning of academic standards at the institutional level. The current trend to modularise the curriculum has raised issues, especially those relating to academic standards, which in the past were implicit; issues which have now become more transparent and questioning about the consistency of approach of academic practices and traditions across subjects, for example, in the definition and the operation of the degree classification system.

Some problems

Whilst quality assessment and quality audit have attempted to be sensitive to the diverse nature of higher education by focusing on institutional and subject-provider aims and objectives, there have been criticisms nevertheless. These must be understood within the overall context of the UK's framework for quality assurance. This framework additionally includes those quality assurance procedures operated by individual institutions themselves, as well as the accreditation processes operated by professional and statutory bodies, where they apply, and the requirements of other bodies such as the Teacher Training Agency. In this overall context, therefore, the combined processes can appear episodic to those on the receiving end; no sooner is one process completed than another one appears and with limited relationships between them. The combination of processes also produces overlap and duplication, and causes distraction from normal day to day institutional activity. At a time when the resourcing of higher education forces institutional purse strings to be tightened, the cumulative effect is to rationalise resources and the effort expended on quality assurance. Thus, one of the dangers of over-elaborate bureaucratic systems of external quality assurance is that they can lead to a 'compliance culture' to the detriment of any quality improvement dimension that might be gained from the process. They can also lead to internal institutional processes becoming determined by external requirements, but at the expense of what is good for the institution. Thus, innovation may suffer for fear that it will not be understood.

External arrangements, such as those described above, which are premised on the concept of peer review, need to instil confidence, legitimacy and credibility in the peers if actions are to be taken on the outcomes. Therefore peers, in the classical sense, should be recognisable and relevant; they should be expert and possess specialist knowledge; they should be competent; they should carry status, authority and legitimacy; and they should be objective. As Brennan, El-Khawas and Shah (1994, p.22) point out:

> Peer judgements possess a *moral authority* based on the shared membership, knowledge and values of the peer community. These are most clearly seen in subject-based groupings of peers which claim exclusive possession of specialist knowledge and competence. Members share a common educational background and professional situation which are the basis of shared interests and loyalties between reviewers and reviewed. It may be hypothesised that these characteristics will be associated with a high degree of legitimacy of peer judgements within the peer community itself.

In research, for example, most academics are able to identify their peers because it 'has high status and is public in its nature, in its legitimation and in its production' (Barnett 1996, p.152). Teaching on the other hand is a relatively private and low status activity, so the identification of peers in teaching is not as transparent as in research. Identification and 'match' of peer is made even harder in a diverse higher education sector where practice varies, for example, in terms of curricular content and structure, and teaching and learning methods. Moreover, one might challenge the use of the term 'peer' in the classic sense as described above; both HEFCE and HEQC train their assessors and auditors which, a purist might argue, transforms the peer into the inspector whilst the peer title is retained in order to give legitimacy to the process and outcome.

Academic standards

Alongside the debate about the effectiveness of the current external quality assurance arrangements is the debate about academic standards which Brennan notes:

> ...cannot be divorced from the broader debates about the roles and responsibilities in quality assurance of institutions, HEQC and the funding councils and, more generally, about the respective responsibilities of the state and of higher education in steering the future direction of higher education. It is a debate about coming to terms with mass higher education...(1996, p.11).

The debate about academic standards was taken up by HEQC as a result of the concern expressed by the government. However, the debate and the issues which have emerged therefrom have not instilled confidence that the quest for broad comparability of academic standards will be achieved, or achieved easily. The basis for this lack of confidence lies in the problems surrounding the concept and understanding of academic standards, and the diverse nature of higher education. The HEQC-led debate has centred on developing threshold academic standards and it has taken place through quality audit which looks at how institutions articulate and assure their academic standards, and through the Council's Graduate Standards Programme. However, audit has shown that in the articulation and assurance of academic standards, there is an over-reliance by institutions on the external examiner system. This over-reliance stems from the fact that it has always been explicitly stated (by both the CVCP and the former CNAA) that one of the dual purposes of the external examiner system is to ensure that degrees awarded in similar subjects are comparable in standard across higher education. However, a recent study for HEQC (Silver, Stennett and Williams 1995) on the effectiveness of the system has shown that this purpose is no longer possible in today's system of a mass and diversified higher education, a conclusion which has been confirmed through further work by HEQC (HEQC 1996b).

Because of factors such as the nature, purpose and scale of institutions, an increased and more diversified student body, changing curricular structures and content, and new methods of teaching, learning and assessment, it is no longer possible to claim that there is a national academic standard which external examiners help to maintain and compare across the sector (and it probably never was). Academic standards, therefore, must vary in today's higher education system. That variation will occur between programmes of study within subjects because of differences in educational purpose and subject breadth, between similar programmes of study across institutions because of diversity of mission, and between subjects *per se* because of custom, practice and tradition. What the study suggested is that external examiners would need to 'operate at the intersection of national academic policies, the academic standards of their subject area, albeit loosely defined, and the academic standards as defined by the receiving institution and the programme of study' (Silver and Williams 1996, p.45).

However, work undertaken by HEQC (HEQC 1995b) has concluded that the process of articulation and definition of standards by institutions is itself problematic. This work, alongside the quality audit process, has been premised on the notion that institutions are responsible for defining academic standards. However, the work has highlighted the vagueness of the term academic standards – first, it means different things to different people and second, standards will vary depending on what is being looked at, and both are influenced by the diverse nature of higher education. For example, academic standards can focus on the different 'stages' of the educational process and the relationships between those stages such as inputs, processes and outputs. Educational input standards can be defined in terms of students' entry characteristics through their qualifications and experiences influenced by institutional admissions policies, and through the quality of the teaching staff. Educational process standards might relate to the student's learning experience and progress influenced by the content and organisation of the curriculum, the teaching, learning and assessment strategies, the learning resources and support available, and the quality assurance mechanisms. Educational output standards will be defined by the inputs and processes, and determined by the knowledge, skills and/or understanding acquired by students.

It is a complex picture which is complicated further by the diverse nature of institutional purposes and missions at one level and subject tradition and practice at another, which leads to a lack of consensus about the definition and understanding of standards across the higher education sector. The attempt to define threshold standards has created more questions than it has answered. Should academic standards be defined in terms of subject discipline or should they be non-discipline specific? What will they define: inputs, processes and outputs, knowledge, skills and under-standing, or a combination of all of these? If standards do become defined (which seems unlikely given the lack of consensus), will there be an attempt to compare these standards across the higher education system? How will this be done given the current defi-ciencies in the external examiner system? What picture will emerge and how will it be interpreted by external bodies, students and employers? Will further rankings of institutions emerge based on the perceptions of those academic standards? There are dangers in any attempt to define threshold academic standards and none more so than the dangers of constraining innovation and institu-tional autonomy and diversity in favour of uniformity and 'accep-tance'.

The future

What then is the future of the external quality assurance arrange-ments and the issues raised by the diverse nature of higher educa-tion? Because of the criticisms levelled against the separate systems of quality audit and quality assessment reported above, the Secre-tary of State made a decision at the end of 1994 to review the arrangements, and to bring them together under a single agency. Conditions were applied which include, amongst other things, the need to assure that academic standards are maintained and broadly comparable, assure the quality of teaching and learning, respect academic autonomy, diversity and freedom, but provide value for money and accountability, and avoid unreasonable bur-dens on institutions. A further condition ensures that the funding councils will continue to exercise their statutory rights in respect of quality assessment to ensure public accountability, underlining the government's continued mistrust of self-regulation.

The proposals put forward for the single agency have produced an integrated process of quality assurance focused on the subject level. They suggest that the new agency should be an independent body, with representatives from institutions, the funding councils, and the wider community with an interest in higher education. The integrated process should replace the functions currently carried out by HEQC and take over quality assessment from the funding councils. The integrated process aims to eliminate overlap and duplication, and to provide flexibility in relation to institutional academic structures. It aims to promote negotiation between institutions and the new agency regarding the number, scope and timing of subject level reviews. It aims to harmonise internal and external review arrangements, and to involve institutions in the selection of reviewers. At present the proposals are embryonic and, of more importance, are subject to the support of the academic community. However, it is likely that they will be accepted for two reasons. First, they make real attempts to be aware of, and sensitive to, institutional differences, and second, they appear to remedy some, if not all, of the problems which have emerged from the current external quality assurance arrangements.

References

Barnett, R. (1996) 'The evaluation of the higher education system in the United Kingdom.' In R. Cowen (ed) *The Evaluation of Higher Education Systems*. London: Kogan Page.

Brennan, J., El-Khawas, E. and Shah, T. (1994) *Peer Review and the Assessment of Higher Education Quality: An International Perspective* (Higher Education Report No 3). London: Quality Support Centre.

Brennan, J., Frazer, M., Middlehurst, R., Silver, S. and Williams, R. (1996) *Changing Conceptions of Academic Standards* (Higher Education Report No 4). London: Quality Support Centre.

Department of Education and Science (1991) White Paper (Cm.1541) *Higher Education: A New Framework*. London: HMSO.

Department of Education and Science (1992) *Further and Higher Education Act*. London: HMSO.

Higher Education Funding Council for England (1993) *Assessment of the Quality of Education* (Circular 3/93). Bristol: HEFCE.

Higher Education Funding Council for England (1994) *The Quality Assessment Method from April 1995*. Bristol: HEFCE.

Higher Education Funding Council for England (1995) *Report on Quality Assessment 1992–1995*. Bristol: HEFCE.

Higher Education Funding Council for England (1996) *Funding Method for Research* (Consultation 2/96). Bristol: HEFCE.

Higher Education Quality Council (1994) *Learning From Audit*. London: HEQC.

Higher Education Quality Council (1995a) *Notes for the Guidance of Auditors*. Birmingham: HEQC.

Higher Education Quality Council (1995b) *Graduate Standards Programme Interim Report*. London: HEQC.

Higher Education Quality Council (1996a) *Learning From Audit 2*. London: HEQC.

Higher Education Quality Council (1996b) *Strengthening External Examining*. London: HEQC.

Kogan, M. (1986) *Educational Accountability: An Analytical Overview*. London: Hutchinson.

Patten, J. (1994) Speech by the Secretary of State for Education to the Higher Education Funding Council for England conference, 12 April.

Silver, H., Stennett, A. and Williams, R. (1995) *The External Examiner System: Possible Futures*. London: Quality Support Centre.

Silver, H. and Williams, R. (1996) 'Academic standards and the external examiner system.' In J. Brennan *et al. Changing Conceptions of Academic Standards* (Higher Education Report No 4). London: Quality Support Centre.

Trow, M. (1994) *Managerialism and the Academic Profession: Quality and Control* (Higher Education Report 2). London: Quality Support Centre.

Wright, P.W.G. (1989) 'Who defines quality in higher education? Reflections on the role of professional power in determining conceptions of quality in English higher education.' *Higher Education 18*, 149–165.

PART TWO

A UK Debate about Standards

The previous chapter on developments in Britain deals with three main issues: quality assurance, the roles of the Higher Education Funding Council for England (HEFCE) and the Higher Education Quality Council (HEQC), and academic standards. As the theme of academic standards has been a matter of intense debate in Britain in the past few years, it is explored in greater depth in the following chapters. The main issue under debate, arising from a question posed in a speech given in 1994 by Mr John Patten, a former education minister, is whether some form of comparability of standards across higher education institutions can be achieved. The authors of the next four chapters attempt to answer the question, each from the perspective of his/her own role in higher education in Britain, and from her/his value position. Consequently, they provide widely divergent responses which converge around a few core issues which will be highlighted below.

Roger Brown's is the most wide-ranging chapter, written from the standpoint of his role as chief executive of HEQC. He writes about the role of his organisation in maintaining standards across institutions through audit visits to institutions and the subsequent reports, but in particular mentions the work of the Graduate Standards Programme. In doing this, he outlines some of the key dimensions being raised at present:

- the specification of academic standards; their definition, the need to be explicit about what they are; and making them transparent to all affected by them
- control and maintenance by developing norms, by quality assurance procedures, monitoring and review
- judgement of what counts as a standard
- the role of external examiners in maintaining academic standards

119

- comparability across institutions; whether there can be a measure of uniformity and if so, across which dimensions.

This overarching perspective places the other three chapters into context, and provides readers with a means by which they can link the four contributions.

David Watson's chapter is written from two perspectives: he was, at the time, the chairman of the Quality Assessment Committee of the HEFCE, but at the same time is the director of a university. In the first part of his chapter, he discusses the maintenance of academic standards, and how institutions have accepted collective responsibility for their maintenance through an academic culture of institutional reciprocity. He views the major issue impacting on maintenance as the greater diversification of institutions, academic subjects, and the student body. One way of reconciling differences and dealing with diversity is by collective action and making a buffer organisation responsible. This entails the marriage of subject assessment and institutional audit requiring, on the one hand, the responsible body to determine how standards are set and on the other, how it measures the achievement of standards against these criteria. He picks up Brown's view on external examining which he labels as 'the worst-best system' for maintaining standards, and mentions the external examiner's important role. He outlines how his institution has developed a procedure for obtaining more precise information from external examiners which makes their reports more useful in making decisions on academic standards.

The third contribution is from another vice-chancellor of an English university who writes here largely from her own experiences as an academic. Janet Finch takes up Brown's notion of judgements, and expands on it by exemplifying the different roles that she as a peer has played in safeguarding academic standards. She uses, in particular, Max Weber's notions of control and legitimacy to explain how important it is for buffer organisations – which have the power to do so – not to make judgements on academic matters but to rely on the judgements made by members of the academic community. As the buffer organisations do not have the expertise in the subject disciplines, their decisions will lack the legitimacy necessary for their acceptance. She states that the exercise of academic peers' judgements is based on a clear collective view in a particular discipline of what the standard is.

She emphasises that this view is shared among established and experienced academics. This provides for social order within disciplines, so that there is a clear understanding among peers that a particular piece of student work counts as good or less good. By making judgements, academics are continually defining and re-enforcing academic standards.

The final chapter in this section is by Tony Becher, the well-known writer on higher education and author of the book *Academic Tribes and Territories*. He reiterates the point made by all the contributors that sound academic judgements are the key to high academic standards. The added dimensions he brings to the exercise are those of comparability and context. He draws on the results of subject assessments and examination results to show that there is not necessarily comparability of judgements across disciplines, but that does not necessarily invalidate the judgements made. This is where the issue of comparability comes into play: the different contexts in which the disciplines play out their conceptions of academic standards bring to bear different notions of what counts as excellent or less good work. He lays great emphasis on the exercise of connoisseurship in judgements. This is a feature of academic life which is not susceptible to audit and assessment, for he agrees with Finch that it comes from knowledge of the field and experience in making judgements.

All the chapters point in one direction: the futility of trying to develop threshold standards which will apply uniformly across all institutions. From their particularistic viewpoints, the chapters disaggregate the notion of academic standards and lay bare many of the assumptions made on what they are and how they are achieved, enhanced and maintained.

Chapter 8

Learning from the HEQC Experience

Roger Brown

Introduction

The basic message of this chapter is that if we do not pay sufficient attention to the definition of standards and to ways of protecting them, the academic community may be in danger of losing the control it has traditionally enjoyed over the standards of attainment associated with the award of the degree or diploma. The argument is prefaced by the definition of the Higher Education Quality Council (HEQC) of academic standards: explicit standards of academic attainment which are used to describe and measure academic requirements and achievements of individual students or groups of students.

The chapter will expand on this definition by detailing what has come out of HEQC's work so far, outlining what we see as the main issues which arise for the academic community, and suggesting how standards might be handled in a single system of external quality assurance.

The description will begin with a summary of HEQC's work so far. Virtually all of the work touches on standards in some way or other. The areas which will be highlighted are:

- academic quality audit
- external examiners
- the Graduate Standards Programme.

Academic quality audit

From its inception audit has been concerned with the ways in which institutions maintain their academic standards. However since October 1994, in the light of the speech by John Patten, former Secretary of State for Education and the sector's response, the Council's audit teams have treated this as a discrete area of scrutiny. Institutions have been asked questions designed to establish how they define and determine their standards, what comparators they use to ensure that their standards are broadly in line with those of other institutions, and how they ensure that their standards are in fact being maintained and improved.

Very few institutions have rejected HEQC's definition, although one claimed that its best minds had been applied to the definition but could not understand it, whereas another has challenged its fundamental validity. However, the responses to auditors' questions were remarkably uniform in that almost total reliance appeared to be being placed on the external examiner system as the guarantor of standards. It was widely believed to provide the necessary safeguards and security, despite the lack of clarity about precisely what it was that was being safeguarded. A preliminary conclusion which might be drawn from this, and which would also reflect one of the findings of the Council's Graduate Standards Programme, is that institutions have not yet fully engaged with the question of what explicit and comparable standards are within a much larger and more diverse higher education system, and indeed lack a conceptual and theoretical framework within which to discuss them.

One interesting finding from these audit visits is that a number of institutions were undoubtedly caught unawares by this line of questioning. More recent audit reports suggest that once the significance of the development was appreciated, institutions quickly began to ask themselves the demanding questions which they knew audit teams might pose. It nevertheless remains the case that, at least to judge from audit, few institutions appear to have a coherent, explicit and consistently applied notion of the academic standards appropriate to their awards.

External examiners

One of the most striking findings of audit has been the heavy reliance upon external examiners. The finding has emerged from the two major consultations on the role of external examiners in the more diversified system which has now been created, carried out by the Council's Quality Enhancement Group (QEG). The first study was commissioned essentially to map existing practice and the impact of change, whereas the second was asked to clarify ways in which external examining might be strengthened. As one would expect, the consultations confirm that whilst virtually all institutions use external examiners, there is a wide range of ways in which they use them such that the traditional model is seriously outdated. Nevertheless there is a very strong attachment to external examining, and not only in the context of protecting standards.

HEQC's conclusions will be announced and disseminated later when a detailed report will be published on the second consultation.

The revised purposes will be:

- to assist in the comparison of academic standards across higher education programmes and awards within the boundaries of comparability sought, defined and agreed by institutions

- to verify that standards are appropriate for the award or award elements for which the external examiner takes responsibility

- to ensure that the assessment process is fair and is fairly operated in the marking, grading and classification of student performance.

Institutions may of course wish to 'add' further purposes to satisfy their local needs.

The Graduate Standards Programme

The findings of audit and the consultations and work on external examiners have fed into another QEG-led project, the Graduate Standards Programme (the GSP). The Interim Report has been published and widely read and quoted (Middlehurst 1996). The underlying aim of the project is to see how some measure of comparability between institutional programmes and awards might be established and assured, assuming that this is agreed to be necessary or desirable.

As Middlehurst's article asserts, arriving at a standard involves five stages:

- specifying and articulating the characteristics and level(s) of performance required at both exit and entry to the programme
- designing an appropriate educational process
- providing teaching and learning support to enable expected performance levels to be achieved
- measuring and recording achievement against the specification
- monitoring and reviewing the process.

The comparability of the standards which result has then two aspects or *dimensions*: an application dimension and a process dimension.

The *application* dimension refers to the range of awards which are under discussion. The question is whether the issue under discussion is the degree of comparability of:

- all degrees
- all degrees of a particular type (vocational, theoretical/research oriented, generalist)
- all degrees in a particular subject or sub-discipline
- all degrees of a particular type in a particular subject etc?

The *process* dimension refers to ways in which comparability might be achieved through curriculum content; assessment mode; skills e.g. generic academic attributes or subject specific cognitive skills; and consistent processes, for example, agreement over the levels of awards, over grading and classification criteria, over marking practices and the use of data, over credit rating and quality assurance.

HEQC within the GSP is currently looking at two of the possible range elements (levels and titles of awards, types of programmes), as well as at two of the possible process dimensions (the notion of 'graduateness' and the potential of greater consistency in processes) to see whether these might offer a way forward. It will be reporting in the early autumn on the outcome of this and associated work, which covers both under- and postgraduate provision. It will then be able to see more clearly whether the determination of some sort of agreed sector-wide threshold standards might be possible. These will clearly raise a number of major issues.

Before turning to these issues, however, the following points may clarify any misapprehensions there may be about the purpose and scope of the Council's work on standards generally and the GSP in particular. The basic aim of this work is to assist in the clarification of the standards – the kinds and levels of knowledge, understanding, skills etc. – which institutions, departments and individual academics *currently* expect their students to achieve. It is not about making everything explicit since standards are ultimately a matter of judgement residing in the minds of those concerned with teaching, learning and assessment. It is not about creating a uniform, homogeneous system; on the contrary, the Council wishes not only to protect but to promote diversity as even a most cursory glance at any of the audit reports indicates. Nor is it about lowering standards: a threshold can be set and agreed at any level, high or low, depending upon the purpose for which it is intended. Nor, finally, is it about doing the government's business: HEQC is not expecting institutions, departments or individual academic staff to do anything which they are not doing, or should not do anyway as professionals in charge of the standards associated with their intellectual 'product'.

Issues

Whilst HEQC can, with the full engagement of individual institutions, lead the necessary technical and preparatory work, the Council cannot *determine* what the range of comparability – the basic meaning of threshold standards – should be. This is a matter for the sector. A particular source of encouragement is the statement by the Chairman of the Committee for Vice Chancellors and Principals (CVCP), Professor Gareth Roberts, following the CVCP conference in Belfast in 1995 that:

> UK universities are responsible for defining and assuring the standards of their own degrees and awards. This is a responsibility they have, formally, as individual institutions and which they share, collectively, as an academic and profes-

sional community. At a time of unprecedented change and major expansion of the sector, CVCP (with the support of SCOP)[1] has instigated this review to assist in articulating what those standards are and in assuring that they are met.

If we, as an academic and professional community, cannot define and protect some measure of comparability, then we are laying ourselves open to a number of dangers, of which three are perhaps most immediately apparent.

The first is that others will try to set standards where we have failed. The pressures for some degree of comparability, from both outside and inside the academic community, will not disappear. There is a clear risk that institutions will have comparability imposed on them in ways which could parallel the introduction of the national curriculum and of national testing and assessment in schools. The second is that the academic community will break up and standards will be established and protected by individual institutions or groups of institutions in response to what they see as being the requirements or needs of their particular bit of the 'market'. There are indeed beginning to be signs of this happening. The third is that academic awards will in effect be left on one side and a new category of 'general vocational' standards be introduced which enjoys wide support not least because of a greater assumed underpinning of comparability.

Quality assurance of standards

The final section of this chapter will be on how the protection of standards might be handled in a single system of external quality assurance. One of the fundamental points in the discussions about such a system is that the new arrangements should be concerned with both quality and standards. How might this be achieved?

It can be inferred from the arguments hitherto that if institutions are discharging fully and appropriately their responsibilities for the academic standards associated with their awards, they will have both formal and informal quality control mechanisms in place, in relation to each of the five stages of standards specification mentioned earlier, namely specification; design of process; provi-

---

1   SCOP – Standing Committee of Principals (of higher education institutions)

sion of teaching and learning; measurement of achievement; monitoring and review. In other words, the institution will already be asking itself:

- what standards are being set?
- are the standards appropriate to the award?
- are the programmes being designed to enable those standards to be met?
- are the programmes being delivered i.e. taught and assessed in ways which enable those standards to be met?
- are the standards actually being delivered?
- how do we know?
- how can we improve or change these standards?

A number of issues then arise as a result of this self-examination. What kind and level of externality does this process need in order to be effective? How is it best obtained? Who takes what action when these processes either do not exist or do not work as well as they might?

First, whether or not comparability is a formal aim. Very few institutions do not have some means of benchmarking their standards, however informal. In many professional and vocational areas, of course, such benchmarking is compulsory or virtually so. Whilst there may be questions about how it is secured, there is surely no contesting the basic principle that in determining the questions just set out, external academic reference points are needed.

Second, how are external reference points achieved? One of the main findings of the GSP has been that academic standards very often emerge towards the end of the teaching and learning process. Typically, in other words, they are 'fixed' as part of student assessment. Yet if standards are to be more explicit and more transparent, they need to be available at the beginning of the process in a form which is accessible, and arrived at in a systematic way taking account of external reference points. This will in itself be a great service to students, potential students and indeed everyone else involved. It will also be a service to institutions and the academic community because it will protect them against potentially arbitrary observations or judgements made by others at a later stage on much less secure or widely based grounds.

Third, what happens if internal quality processes do not work and, as a result, student attainment is consistently below the level set and/or those levels are inappropriate to the relevant award? There is agreement that it will not be possible for external *judgements* to be made about the appropriate levels of attainment for a particular award until there is collective agreement about what kinds and levels of attainment are acceptable to the academic and professional community as a whole and/or to relevant sub-sets. In the meantime the new integrated quality assurance process could seek information about the ways in which institutions identify and confirm the achievement of appropriate standards, and seek to improve them. Besides encouraging institutions to clarify and articulate the ways in which they establish their standards, this will provide information which will be helpful in determining the acceptable range of diversity. Provided the right questions are asked, and the right evidence sought, this should in itself be extremely helpful in taking us forward. It will of course require adequate coordination, but I see no difficulties of principle in achieving this since it would be one of the benefits of having a single system with enhancement as its principal aim.

Postscript

No summary will be provided of the above; however, to stimulate further debate the following questions which have arisen in the course of the GSP will be presented:

- Who will be responsible for defining threshold standards? How will they be assessed and reviewed? Is a modification or abandonment of the present classified degree avoidable?

- Who will take responsibility for a clear framework of awards, including levels, titles and interrelationships? How can collective agreement to adopt the framework be achieved? What account will be taken of international factors?

- How, precisely, will the judgements of academic peers be fed into the definition, articulation and monitoring of standards? What structures and processes are needed to

enable them to fulfil this role consistently and
systematically?

- What will be the role of externals i.e. persons external to
the academic process? How will they be prepared and to
whom should they report?

However the underlying question is whether and how the academic community can demonstrate its professionalism and thus retain control over its academic standards.

References

Middlehurst, R. (1996) 'Degree standards and quality assurance: a
discussion.' In J. Brennan, M. Frazer, R. Middlehurst, S. Silver and R.
Williams *Changing Conceptions of Academic Standards* (Higher
Education Report No 4). London: Quality Support Centre.

Chapter 9

Quality, Standards and Institutional Reciprocity

David Watson

Introduction

This paper should be called 'a view from the sector'. The three main propositions that will be advanced may not be universally shared or popular. But they are claimed to be in tune with historical commitments of the sector as a whole, despite the fact that the somewhat fevered atmosphere of recent discussion of the issues has obscured such commitments.

Institutional reciprocity

At the heart of the argument is the proposition that a key characteristic of the UK system of higher education has been the willingness of relatively autonomous institutions to accept collective responsibility for the standards, the strategy, and to a certain extent the image of the sector as a whole. There have been several historical manifestations of this as the system expanded out of the magic circle of Oxford, Cambridge, and some other early foundations: the role of 'validating' and 'awarding' universities; the external examiner system; the 'academic advisory' committees of the post-Robbins universities (Robbins 1963, para. 395); the Council for National Academic Awards (CNAA) and its predecessors; and, more recently, the participation of academic and professional peers in the processes of audit and assessment required by the Further and Higher Education Act of 1992 (Scott 1995).

The effect of these practices on UK higher education has been considerable, and in certain cases decisive. For example, the act of 'validating' new courses (and hence authorising 'entry' into higher education for emerging and developing professional areas) has relied on a broadly-based, expert, and above all external judgement about the appropriateness of the curriculum and the standards set. Similarly, despite the ultimately autonomous responsibility of institutions with degree-awarding powers (through charters and, significantly after 1992, through legislation), academic boards and senates have always relied upon external endorsement of the individual judgements made (to the extent of requiring external examiners to sign pass-lists). Finally, the scope of such activity has contributed to building and maintaining networks of academic peers, especially on a subject basis, and developing in new entrants to the profession an understanding of the wider culture to which they are inescapably contributors.

It is unfashionable in these days of competitive marketing and aggressive boosting of the so-called 'diversity' of the system to recall such features of the UK academic enterprise. However, it is salutary to note that none of these features has been explicitly repudiated or overthrown. Indeed, it could be argued that it is at least partly as a result of this approach that the UK system has enjoyed a number of favourable performance characteristics: relatively high completion/graduation rates; a strong international reputation; relative ease of absorption of major changes in overall strategy (for example, the ending of the binary line); and relatively high levels of consumer satisfaction. It is easy to forget that, compared with the experience of our peers within the customary OECD group for analysis, UK higher education has exhibited rather low levels of turbulence (Swain 1996, pp.2–3).

In sum these 'reciprocal' processes could be said to represent the 'collaborative gene' in the development of the system. That they should have survived the official encouragement of, and the institutional enthusiasm for, the 'competitive gene' throughout the past decade and a half in such good shape is perhaps remarkable. It is probably not an exaggeration to say that the survival of the collaborative gene is at stake in the current situation, although my feeling is that this is more a result of the funding situation than of any naturally centrifugal feature of the system. Quality and resources are, of course, inextricably mixed, although not in the simple linear relationship that some in the system (usually those with least resources) try to contend.

To elaborate this argument the implications of the information in two recent publications from the Higher Education Funding Council for England (HEFCE) will be compared: the *Report on Quality Assessment 1992–95*, and the more recent *Circular 28/95* on institutions' aggregated financial forecasts and strategic plans (HEFCE 1995a, 1995b). The former sets out the conclusions of approximately the first 1,000 assessments conducted by the HEFCE's Quality Assessment Division. The broad picture, in terms of academic health, is encouraging, with about the same small proportion of provision being found unsatisfactory (1%) as in Scotland, and a slightly smaller proportion excellent (23%, as opposed to 26%). The core characteristics of 'excellent' provision are unsurprising, given that this is an exercise driven by academic and professional peers. Indeed, a number of important questions are raised about the processes of peer review itself, without really challenging the generally-held opinion that this is probably the least worst system of academic regulation (Royal Society 1995). The broad conclusion has to be that, whatever the degeneration of the historical 'quality of life' (for students at least as much as staff within institutions), the sector has coped heroically with increased numbers and relentless pressure on the unit of resource per student.

The message from the financial forecasts is quite different, and sharpened by the thought that they were submitted before the higher education settlement in the November 1995 budget statement. The stark question is whether or not we have reached what John Beavan used to call the 'impending precipice'. The advocates of 'consolidation', and now retrenchment, would clearly have preferred a quality crisis to prove the merits of their case. This the sector has resolutely refused to deliver. Instead of which we may experience a financial crisis (which would be defined as a significant minority of institutions being unable to meet the terms of the financial memorandum) in advance of any possible quality crisis. Figures 9.1 and 9.2 are drawn from the Circular 28/95. They demonstrate that this conclusion is not irresponsible scare-mongering. The discipline of relentless efficiency gains has not simply sweated out a very few poorly managed institutions, but instead reduced the sector as a whole to margins which are wafer-thin.

Table 9.1: 1995 Financial forecasts

	1993/94 £000	1994/95 £000	1995/96 £000	1996/97 £000	1997/98 £000	1998/99 £000
Total income	7,591,000	8,005,146	8,373,288	8,604,632	8,858,375	9,106,410
Total expenditure	7,344,642	7,846,711	8,306,829	8,578,887	8,835,984	9,090,723
Surplus/(deficit) after depreciation of assets at valuation and tax	245,192	157,616	65,683	24,839	21,347	14,631
Historical cost surplus/ (deficit) after tax	285,015	204,038	110,925	68,544	64,578	57,670

Source: HEFC 1995

Table 9.1 shows a sharp drop in the retained and forecast surpluses of the sector as a whole (calculated in two ways). Table 9.2 shows the vulnerability of these surpluses to adverse shifts in the assumptions made. For example, it would only take an increase in pay of 1 per cent above that forecast or a 5 per cent shortfall in research contract income to pitch the sector as a whole into deficit in the next financial year.

Table 9.2 Sensitivity analyses

Analyses of sensitivity of financial forecasts to changes in key assumptions

	1995/96 £m	1996/97 £m	1997/98 £m	1998/99 £m
1 per cent increase in pay inflation	-32	-65	-101	-140
1 per cent increase in non-pay inflation	-21	-40	-60	-82
0.5 per cent increase in efficiency gain on Council funding	-11	-26	-41	-57
5 per cent shortfall in research contract income	-14	-25	-37	-51
1 per cent shortfall in UK and EU full-time student recruitment	-12	-21	-30	-39
3 per cent shortfall in part-time recruitment	-7	-12	-16	-23
2 per cent shortfall in recovery rates on research contracts	-7	-11	-15	-20
1 per cent increase in interest payable	-5	-10	-14	-19
1 per cent shortfall in overseas student recruitment	-4	-6	-10	-13

Source: HEFC 1995

It has been a frequent response in the past to suggest that institutions forecast conservatively, in order (a) to assist the case for public investment and (b) to keep their Boards and Councils happy with regular over-achievement. Two features suggest to me that those days are over. First, lenders are now privy to these financial forecasts, and a degree of relevant advocacy (sometimes apparently a little desperate) is beginning to creep in. Second, the other main lesson of Circular 28/95 (Figure 9.1) is that all of the institutions think that they can win in all of the markets all of the time.

HEFCE Circular 28/95

1993–99

Full-time and Sandwich (Full-Time Teaching Equivalent) (FTE) overseas students up 27 per cent (all institutions)

Part-time overseas students up 32 per cent (all institutions)

80 per cent of institutions increasing postgraduate provision

66 per cent of institutions increasing part-time provision

33 per cent of institutions increasing employer links in Continuing Vocational Education (CVE)

Home and European Union part-time numbers up 40 per cent (all institutions)

100 per cent replacement of Teacher Training Agency (TTA)-related reductions

Overall improvement in Research Assessment Exercise (RAE) ratings

---

Source: HEFCE (1995)

Figure 9.1 Aggregated strategic plan highlights

Proposition one: a financial crisis in UK higher education is likely to precede any quality crisis.

Quality and standards

Today's accepted wisdom declares that the most significant challenge to the system is to bring the processes of external regulation of quality and standards under control. The recently established Joint Planning Group of the representative bodies Committee of Vice-Chancellors and Principals (CVCP) and Standing Committee of Principals (of higher education institutions) (SCOP) and the Funding Councils is supposed to bring about a regime in which all of the current functions of audit, assessment and professional recognition are absorbed, the thorny issue of 'standards' is incorporated, and institutions feel that less is being demanded of them (Shephard 1995). Table 9.3 summarises the functions currently specified and the tasks required of the system to be devised by the

Joint Planning Group. It deliberately suppresses separate reference to those activities directed by both agencies Higher Education Quality Council (HEQC and HEFCE) at 'enhancement' or improvement. Despite the fact that these represent the major purposes of the whole exercise, for those centrally involved, and their clients, they are essentially 'elective', non-statutory activities.

Table 9.3 Joint Planning Group: before and after

	Before	*After*
Subject-based assessment	✔✔	✔
Limited cycle	✔	✔✔
Published reports	✔	✔
'Negotiated' timetable	✔	✔✔
Institutional overview (audit)	✔	✔
Assessor/auditor training	✔	✔✔
Agreed framework for standards	?	✔
Coordination with professional bodies	✔	✔
Advice on degree-awarding powers and university title	✔	✔
Access course recognition	✔	?

Key: ✔ required
         ✔✔ required with extra force
         ? uncertain or ambiguous
Source: Author

Expectations are high for the resolution of what might be called 'Mrs Shephard's fork' (doing more and appearing to do less). However, the frenzy of attention to this problem has missed an even more important challenge: to police the outer limits of diversity. This is where the issue of standards is pivotal.

Views on the standards question tend to polarise between those who think it simply can't be done, and those who would police it with the same rigour as the national curriculum within the compulsory school system. The enthusiasm of the latter confirms the misgivings of the former. Neither of these two extremes looks seriously at the possibility of tapping into and adapting the 'culture of reciprocity' which was described at the beginning of this paper. For example, it should be perfectly possible for a redesigned system of 'quality assurance' (*the JPG's term of art*) to examine (at both the subject and the institutional level) how the college or university *identifies and confirms the achievement of appropriate standards for the awards made*. This approach would mean, within the grain of other expressions of collective responsibility, that institutions could not simply assert their standards, but would have to calibrate them in some overt and satisfactory ways (including the external examiner system). It also has the merit of bringing together the evaluation of two processes: how the institution chooses (sets) standards, and how it measures the achievements of students against them. In this sense it is a quintessentially 'merged' inheritance of both 'assessment' (of subject-based achievement of objectives) and 'audit' (of institutional systems).

Finally, it leaves open to the sector the option (which hopefully it will take) of defining more precisely what it will accept as conditions for awards, and hence of accepting responsibility (as the former more integrated systems of 'validation' such as those of the CNAA emphatically did) for the boundaries or limits of diversity. The CNAA, for example, anticipated much of the current discussion of 'graduateness' or 'core qualities' in its principles underlying the validation and approval of degrees (set out in Figure 9.2).

At this stage it would be appropriate to acknowledge and challenge an objection to the analysis. Recapturing a collective sense of, and responsibility for, standards is not inimical to diversity. The whole history of external contributions to 'validation' as well as to examination should be testimony to this. At its best, external scrutiny compels a providing institution to be clear about its aims and its criteria for success. Designing and then operating a course, with such external scrutiny, establishes that the relevant academic and professional peer group is satisfied that both (aims and criteria) are above a threshold of acceptability. In this sense collaboration trumps competition and the system takes responsibility for the boundary of authorised diversity. There is no firm evidence, beyond the natural conservatism of peer review, that this has, in the end, precluded innovation. Indeed it could be said to have assisted it, by establishing immediate confidence in the curriculum for its potential clients. In circumstances where the reverse is true (competition trumps collaboration) the dangers are obvious: diversity can be used as an excuse for breaching the boundaries (including as a result of inadequate resources), and can potentially

Aims and Objectives of the Programme

Aims

The aims must include the CNAA's *general educational aims*:

the development of students' intellectual and imaginative powers;

their understanding and judgement;

their problem-solving skills;

their ability to communicate;

their ability to see relationships within what they have learned and to perceive their field of study in a broader perspective.

The programme must aim to stimulate an enquiring, analytical and creative approach, encouraging independent judgement and critical self-awareness.

Objectives

The statement of objectives must show how the programme will fulfil the aims.

The statement of *course-specific* objectives will specify the knowledge and skills appropriate to the field of study and identify the ways in which these will be developed and evaluated in the students.

The statement of *general objectives* will identify the ways in which the students' transferable skills will be developed and evaluated, in particular their ability to:

communicate clearly in speech, writing and other appropriate modes of expression;

argue rationally and draw independent conclusions based on a rigorous, analytical and critical approach to data, demonstration and argument;

apply what has been learned;

demonstrate an awareness of the programme of study in a wider context.

Source: CNAA 1991

Figure 9.2 CNAA general regulations for approved programmes of study

degrade into 'anything goes.' Thus to see a government that has specifically nourished the competitive gene at the expense of the collaborative, and its reliance on sector-wide patterns of self-regulation, suddenly express concern about possible failures collectively to guarantee standards is deeply ironic.

The conclusion that could be drawn is that the institutional campaign against external agencies of quality assurance has caused institutional heads in particular (there seems to have been greater understanding of these issues within subject communities) to take their eyes off the ball (Watson 1995).

Proposition two: confirming the 'limits of diversity' is more critical to the academic health and reputation of the system than bringing the agencies of public accountability under institutional control.

External examiners

In discussing comparability of standards for many the story begins and ends with the external examiner, arguably the most distinctive element in the UK system of academic self-regulation. As on quality in general, opinions are polarised about its value, significance and effectiveness. In the pre-audit days, for example, the CVCP attempted to boost it as an alternative to any more centralised pattern of scrutiny (CVCP 1984). More recently, it has become fashionable to announce its passing, under the weight of increased numbers, modularity, credit accumulation and transfer schemes (CATS) and a host of other features of a more flexible and accessible service (Silver *et al.* 1995). One very real danger is that from these concerns, and the resulting critique, will spring a self-fulfilling prophecy. This tendency can and should be resisted.

At the University of Brighton the Academic Board's Academic Standards Committee has been taking a long and hard look at the operation and effectiveness of the external examiner system. In doing so we have undoubtedly confirmed some of the misgivings about the operation of the system as collated by the HEQC, but also uncovered some more hopeful signs. The first point to recognise is the size and potential authority of this external group of academic and professional peers. In 1995/96 the university has engaged 274 external examiners for its taught courses, including

50 working within the Institute of Nursing and Midwifery (INAM). Of the 224 non-INAM appointees, 171 come from academic institutions and 53 from the relevant professional community. At least 60 per cent have senior or strategic responsibilities within their own organisations. In addition to examining or assessing experience 'at home' 21 per cent have held three or more external examining appointments in the last five years. Such experience is, of course, of limited use unless it can be appropriately focused on the task in hand. In common with other institutions the University of Brighton has attempted to sharpen its charge to external examiners, and to motivate them to address the comparative part of their brief more fully and effectively. Table 9.4 sets out the main questions that all examiners of taught courses are guided to address.

Table 9.4 External examiner's annual report

The areas to be covered by the report include:

(i)   the general standard of the work assessed an comparability with similar levels of work nationally

(ii) the overall performance of the students in relation to their peers in other institutions

(iii) the strengths and weaknesses of students

(iv) the quality of knowledge and skills (both general and subject specific) demonstrated by the students

(v)   the structure, organisation, design and marking of all assessments

(vi) the quality of teaching as indicated by student performance

(vii) the lessons of the assessments for the curriculum, syllabus, teaching methods and resources

(viii) any other recommendations arising from the assessments.

Source: University of Brighton Academic Registry

Responses by the examiners to this structured examination paper vary in quality! Taking the three main questions that press respondents to deliver comparative judgements (general standard and national comparability [i], overall performance in relation to peers

[ii], and quality of knowledge and skills [iv]) it is possible to grade the depth and adequacy of responses. For the 218 reports received in 1994/95 this has been done on a three point scale: 'not addressed' (not specifically commented upon); 'addressed' (coherent statement made); and 'addressed well' (using specific evidence). The results (in Table 9.5) are predictably mixed: positive features are the 85 per cent of reports including explicit statements about general standards and the 74 per cent expressing explicit judgements about the knowledge and skill levels of the students; negative features are the over one quarter evading the knowledge and skills question and the well over one half eschewing the opportunity to refer to national standards.

Table 9.5 Analysis of external examiners' reports

	Not addressed	Addressed	Addressed well
(i) the general standard of the work assessed and comparability with similar levels of work nationally			
(a) general standard	15.1%	68.3%	16.5%
(b) national comparability	49.5%	31.2%	19.3%
(ii) the overall performance of the students in relation to their peers in other institutions	55.5%	27.5%	17%
(iii) the quality of knowledge and skills (both general and specific) demonstrated by the students	25.7%	61.9%	12.4%

Source: Author

In addition to the use made of these reports by course teams and the committees to which they are responsible (course boards and faculty boards), and the ways in which they operate and responses to them form part of the official record of quality assurance in the institution, the reports are all read by working parties of the Academic Standards Committee and by the author as chair of the Academic Board. Notwithstanding the reservations expressed above, we have noted improvements in the incisiveness and value of reports, and that these have generally been correlated with course redesign, especially where courses have developed into modular and unit credit programmes. Here the needs of examination boards to read across, to ensure consistency of judgement between specialisms, and above all to operate equitably a set of programme regulations have all apparently had a positive effect.

The University of Brighton is not a fully modular institution. In institutions where flexibility of course delivery has been pushed further, using this device, there is even more evidence that modularity can serve to improve the performance of the external examiner system, and ironically return it more closely to its historical objectives (Scurry 1989, pp.74–90). To do so more generally will require explicit guidelines, intervention where necessary by institutional groups with responsibilities wider than for single subject provision, and an adequate level of remuneration (paid for possibly by the 'dividend' from the streamlined quality assurance systems).

Proposition three: the external examiner system has been helped not hindered by the development of modularity and Credit Accumulation and Transfer Schemes (CATS), and in adapting to these new conditions can recover and reinvigorate its original mission.

Futures

Recent anxieties about resources, overlaid onto those about the 'weight of accountability' and quality, have led to some almost apocalyptic statements about the future prospects of the system. From some perspectives it is almost as if a battle has been joined about the soul of UK higher education. Following such a Manichean line two types of future can be projected. The benign version builds upon institutional reciprocity, remaking the sector's commitment to standards and to quality in a much expanded and socially and economically more useful system. In this sense higher education is regarded fundamentally as a public service. This is not a simple proposition. Careful attention is needed for example to the 'fit' between educational attainment and employment prospects, especially as the national targets for education and training

(NETTS) imply up-skilling 'within' as well as 'for' work. The black scenario presents the antithesis of this vision. Higher education is regarded as a luxury consumer good, only regulated by what price the consumer is prepared to pay. Institutional reciprocity is replaced by a free market and as a result a wide spread of individual institutional reputations succeeds the controlled pluralism we now experience.

A manifesto

Building upon the analysis set out above and the three 'propositions', the personal recommendations for moving forward constructively will be repeated. They are predicated upon the assumptions (a) that the sector engages seriously with the 'limits to diversity' debate, rejecting the view that the concept means 'anything goes', and (b) that confidence can be established in a practical (what Middlehurst *et al.* call a 'cultural') solution to the standards issue (HEQC 1995, para. 2.3).

What could be moved forward:

- explicit institutional responsibility for setting and maintaining appropriate standards (the 'audit' legacy in 'quality assurance')
- evaluation of provision against clear aims and objectives (the 'assessment' legacy, in alliance where appropriate with professional bodies)
- a reinvigorated external examiner system (based upon a core job description, a revised and updated code of practice, and minimum, satisfactory remuneration) and
- a revival (in the context of the 'graduateness' debate) of the CNAA's principles for higher education awards, as set out in Figure 9.2 above.

For some this 'view from the sector' may appear anachronistic and backward-looking; I suggest instead that it supplies a responsible and worthwhile vision of the future.

References

Council for National Academic Awards (1991) *Handbook 1991/92*. London: CNAA.

CVCP (1984) *The External Examiner System for First Degree and Taught Master's Courses*. London: Committee of Vice-Chancellors and Principals.

Higher Education Funding Council for England (1995a) *Report on Quality Assessment 1992–1995*, M18/95. Bristol: HEFCE.

Higher Education Funding Council for England (1995b) *Analysis of 1995 Strategic Plans and Financial Forecasts, Circular 28/95*. Bristol: HEFCE.

Higher Education Quality Council (1995) *Graduate Standards Programme: Interim Report*. London: HEQC.

Robbins (1963) *Report of the Committee on Higher Education*. London: HMSO.

Royal Society (1995) *Peer Review. An Assessment of Recent Developments*. London: The Royal Society.

Scott, P. (1995) *The Meanings of Mass Higher Education*. Buckingham: SRHE and Open University Press.

Scurry, D. (1989) 'Assessment and examinations.' In D. Watson (ed) *Managing the Modular Course: Perspectives from Oxford Polytechnic*. Milton Keynes: SRHE and Open University Press.

Shephard, G. [Secretary of State for Education and Employment] (1995) Letter to Chairman of the CVCP on *Developing Quality Assurance in Partnership with the Institutions of Higher Education*, 21 September 1995. London: DfEE.

Silver, H., Stennett, A. and Williams, R. (1995) *The External Examiner System: Possible Futures*. Report of a project commissioned by the Higher Education Quality Council, May 1995. London: Open University Quality Support Centre.

Swain, H. (1996) 'Europe's students on the brink.' *Education Guardian*, 23 January 1996.

Watson, D. (1995) 'Quality assessment and self-regulation: the English experience, 1992–94.' *Higher Education Quarterly 49*, 4, 326–340.

Chapter 10

Power, Legitimacy and Academic Standards

Janet Finch[1]

Introduction

A concern with academic standards is buried deep in the historical development of universities in Western Europe, where it has always been linked with fundamental questions of academic authority and its relationship to political authority. As Scott has put it, 'the most important product of the medieval university was clearly the idea of itself as a university, and the separation of intellectual authority from the political power on which this depended' (Scott 1984, p.26). The ability of established and experienced academics to distinguish the good from the suspect or mediocre lies at the heart of the concept of the university as we understand it. At the same time, the authority of academics has always to be exercised within the context of a given political system on which universities depend to a greater or lesser extent for their continued existence. The fact that the separation of intellectual from political authority has been understood, and broadly accepted, since the middle ages does not mean that the relationship between the two is necessarily easy. Like all such relationships, it tends to be renegotiated and reformulated as circumstances change. In a sense therefore it is possible to see the present debate about academic standards as a phase of renegotiation of this historic relationship, rather than a set of issues peculiar to the 1990s.

---

1   The author would like to state that she is writing in a purely personal capacity.

Taking this rather long view of current issues in the UK, I hope to use this chapter to provide a particular perspective upon academic standards. The perspective is personal and draws upon my own academic background as a social scientist. My particular focus is going to be on the themes of power and legitimacy in the assessment of academic standards. I am going to relate this to both teaching and research, and compare the two. My analysis concerns the ways in which the authority of academics themselves is used to determine what is good and what is not good. This is not to deny that there are others – employers for example who have a proper role in making judgements about the quality of the product which higher education offers, whether that product be a graduate or a piece of research and development. But in this particular context, my focus is upon the role of academics themselves in the judgement of standards.

My reason for focusing on this issue is that it taps one of the most contentious issues in the whole current climate of debate about quality and standards. A key question which troubles academics themselves is whether the traditional authority of academics over their own subject areas is being compromised by systems of externally driven inspection, particularly of teaching quality and standards. Are agencies such as funding councils, professional accrediting bodies and the Higher Education Quality Council (HEQC) undermining traditional academic authority, vested in a deep knowledge of one's subject, and replacing this with external benchmarks which derive from some other set of priorities?

These are matters of deep concern to many in the higher education system. They are not merely about personal pride. They also concern the nature of intellectual and scientific authority in a deep sense. More generally, they can be linked to an analysis of social and political change which sees us as moving into an 'audit culture' (Power 1994) in which no individual or professional body is trusted for his or her competence and expertise, and everyone is required to give an account of what they are doing to people less knowledgeable than themselves. The hostility towards external assessments among academics can be regarded as higher education's version of resistance to the growing audit culture. But taking the longer term view, they can be seen as contemporary versions of the historic issue of how intellectual authority can be both separate from political authority, and yet related to it.

Judging academic standards: varieties of experience

This, then, is my starting point: the claim that academic authority is being eroded by externally imposed systems of assessment of quality and standards. One useful way of exploring this is to consider the range of circumstances in which such systems of external assessment do occur in academic life. I therefore decided that it might be instructive to subject my own experience to scrutiny, and Table 10.1 is the result. It is simply a list of all the different circumstances in which I personally have been involved in making judgements about matters related to the academic standards of other people's work. I have included in this list both teaching and research, and have encompassed assessments of subject content and also judgements about the more institutional-level questions of how programmes are managed and delivered.

Table 10.1 Judgements about academic standards: range and roles

Role	On whose behalf
Referee (articles)	Academic journal
Book reviewer	Academic journal and commercial publisher
Editor	Academic journal
Referee (book proposals)	Commercial publisher
Referee (grant proposals)	Various grant-awarding bodies
Board member/Chair	Grant awarding body
External examiner (students' work)	Various universities
Referee (staff appointments and promotions)	Various universities
External reviewer (departmental reviews)	Various universities
Panel member (course validation)	CNAA* and various universities
Academic auditor	AUU**/HEQC
Assessor (teaching quality)	Funding council
Panel member (research • assessment)	Funding council

Notes: *Council for National Academic Awards
        **Academic Audit Unit (of the Committee of Vice-Chancellors and Principals)

The table is drawn largely from my own experience as a practising academic. It lists the range of circumstances in which I have been asked to make judgements about the academic standards of other people's work. These do not include 'internal' judgements, that is to say, judgements related to equivalent matters within my own employing institution.

This exercise has proved very instructive. I found that there were no less than 11 different ways in which I personally had been involved in making such judgements. Two judgements below the line are examples of judgements currently being made within the system, in which I have never been involved directly as an assessor (though in the case of one, the teaching quality assessment (TQA), I was involved at the policy-making level). This amounts to a substantial amount of activity in which I have been involved in judging the standards of performance of other academics. I could equally, of course, have drawn up the table from the opposite perspective and listed the different ways in which I have subjected myself to the assessment of others. Those tables would be mirror images of each other, reflecting the overwhelming strength of the principle of peer review in the ways in which academic judgements are made in relation to both research and teaching. Being reviewed by one's peers means that each of us acts as both poacher and gamekeeper, and that we are expected to move between the two in order for the system to be sustained. One week you are making the judgement, the next week you are being judged, and the same person is equally likely to be on either side of the table.

There are many interesting conclusions which one could draw from the table. One which I find striking is that, under all the circumstances which I have outlined, the assessments which I have undertaken have always been on behalf of someone else. I have been commissioned to give an opinion on behalf of various institutions and agencies: a university, a journal, a publishing house, a grant-giving body and so on. I have always therefore been making judgements about academic standards as an advisor to someone else, never as it were purely on my own behalf. The outcome is that someone else, not me will take action based upon my judgement. The only exception to this is as a writer of book reviews, where the outcome of my judgement is not going to be acted on directly by the newspaper or journal which commissioned it. Even here however action may follow, albeit of a more diffuse kind: other individual academics in the same field deciding that they must buy and use the book which I have reviewed, or not, depending on what I have said.

This point about the combination of individual judgements and agency actions is important for the analysis which I want to develop. At this point I should like to refer to a very stimulating paper by John Brennan and his colleagues (1994), reporting work in progress which led me to start thinking along these lines. They are conducting a comparative study of the way in which a number of different countries are developing systems for monitoring the quality of teaching in higher education. The commonality of themes between different countries is remarkable but the differences, though subtle, are revealing. Amongst those sources of variation, they discuss the balance between what they call the 'moral' authority of the peers themselves and the 'bureaucratic' authority of the organisation which commissioned the judgement. They describe the authority of peers as 'derived from the expertise and shared values of (their) professional community', whilst bureaucratic authority is 'based upon the powers – rewards or punishments which may be consequential on the review – of the sponsoring body'. They argue that the authority of peers carries a clear legitimacy amongst the academic community whilst judgements based upon bureaucratic authority, and used for purposes pre-defined by the agency, are much less likely to commend legitimacy, even where the process has incorporated an element of peer review.

I think that Brennan is right to highlight the interplay between the individual and the agency in these exercises, but wrong to see it in terms of two different types of authority which vie with each other. Rather, what strikes me about the analysis of my own experience, and the variety of ways in which I have been involved in exercising my academic judgement, is that the agencies who have commissioned me are wholly dependent on me, and others like me. They do not have the capacity to exercise judgements about academic standards independent of asking the opinion of academics. In a sense bureaucratic authority does not exist separate from the authority of peers upon which it draws. If, for example, I act as a referee for a journal article and I say that it should not be published because its methods are flawed, or because it says nothing original, or whatever, the journal board has no alternative grounds on which it can decide to publish the article, even if it would like to for other reasons (perhaps because the topic is eye-catching). Certainly this would be true if three referees had been consulted and they all said the same thing. Similarly, if I am asked to review a particular university's teaching programme in my discipline and I say that it is out of date, or that it is not comparable with degree-level work in other universities, there is no basis for the university bureaucracy to give approval to the programme even if they might wish to do so, say for financial reasons. Having asked the question about quality and standards, there is no other legitimate way of answering it than to draw on the traditional sources of academic authority, that is the judgement of peers.

If I am correct, why is this so? Why is it that the institutions and agencies around which higher education is organised do not have sources of authority independent of academics' judgements? This would appear to be so even if they appear to hold all the powers, including the purse strings.

Power and legitimacy: some social science perspectives

At this point in the argument, it becomes necessary to think more systematically about the nature of power, authority and legitimacy in academic institutions. Some social science perspectives can usefully come into play. I find that one of the most classic discussions of issues in social theory – Max Weber's work *Economy and Society* (1924) – is extremely illuminating. Weber, who was writing about the nature of power in societies generally, contrasted two phenomena. These were, to paraphrase him, naked power and legitimate authority. The most obvious form of naked power is physical coercion, though Weber believed that the sources of power could be more varied than this. There is, however, a common theme in his definition (which has been very influential on subsequent social thought): the defining characteristic of power is the ability to realise one's will or aims despite resistance on the part of other people. This is his definition of what we could call naked power.

However, Weber believed that civil society could not be based on the exercise of naked power, since this would be an inherently unstable situation. He therefore argued that the stability of any society depends on the conversion of naked power into legitimate authority. In this analysis, legitimacy means that individuals treat certain rules and expectations as binding upon them; each of us recognises individually that it is right for those rules to command our assent and our obedience. For Weber this belief in social order is actually the basis of social order itself.

How does this help us to understand current relationships between the academic authority of academics and the organisational authority of the agencies who are in the business of maintaining academic standards? It seems to me that standards – whether in teaching or research – are the 'rules' of academic life, in Weber's sense. The whole of the academic enterprise depends upon there being a reasonably clear collective understanding between academics in a given discipline that a particular piece of work counts as good and something else as less good. Without that collective understanding, academic disciplines really do not exist. Were that to disappear, the resulting intellectual anarchy would bring down the whole edifice, since there would be no reason at all why taxpayers should pay us to educate the young, nor why sponsors should pay us to conduct research. It is therefore an absolute necessity of academic life that a collective understanding of standards does exist. This could be called – in Weber's terms – the academic social order. It follows therefore, again extending Weber's analysis, that we all have to believe in it, and that each of us individually assents to it. In practical terms, this means that we submit ourselves to the judgements of our peers and that we accept their judgements about our own work.

This is how academic life traditionally has operated, especially in relation to research. Though people may sometimes allege that a journal editor has selected the wrong referees, or that a book reviewer has not read the work properly, these complaints do not undermine my general analysis. Indeed, they reinforce my view that each of us does assent to the judgements of our peers as the basis of the academic social order, since such complaints are not against the 'rules' themselves, but merely assert that the rules have not been operated properly in my particular case. Thus it seems clear to me that the social order of academic life does depend upon each of us accepting the legitimacy of judgements made about us, and it is our academic peers in whom we have collectively vested the right to make those judgements. So where do agencies responsible for academic quality and standards fit into this picture? In a sense they represent the 'naked power' of academic life. That power comes from the formal rights vested in them (such as the professional bodies who can withdraw professional accreditation from a particular programme), or from their command over financial resources (funding councils or grant-giving bodies who can prevent academic activities from taking place by withholding money) or from their ability to make or break individual reputations and therefore ultimately livelihoods (for example, journals who publish book reviews). In that sense they do meet Weber's criteria of organisations which have genuine power – they have the ability to pursue their aims despite the resistance of others. However, by that very token, if they were to do so they would destroy the possibility of achieving their aims because the situation they would create would be totally unstable.

In other words, these agencies have no capacity to define and enforce academic standards in isolation from the academic community itself. In order for their work to be effective, they need each of us (at least most of us!) to accept the legitimacy of the decisions which they put into effect. How are they to create this legitimacy – remembering that in the Weberian analysis on which I am drawing, legitimacy is an active concept, since each of us must believe in its rightness and assent to abide by its outcome? It would seem as if the only way in which agencies responsible for standards can convert naked power into legitimate authority is to depend for their judgements upon the sources of legitimacy which academics already recognise, namely the opinions of peers. This is long established as practice in relation to judgements about research. Journals and grant-giving bodies, and of course the funding councils in their handling of the research assessment exercise, rely almost exclusively upon advice given through peer refereeing. Indeed when it comes to negative judgements, reliance on peer opinion is normally total. No journal editor or committee secretary would feel the need to bow to pressure from a disappointed applicant if all the referees have said no.

If we apply this analysis to judgements about academic standards in teaching, the picture is more mixed. In relation to the well established process of external examining, by and large there is an understanding that, in cases where the standard of an individual student's work is in dispute, the external examiner's decision is final. However even here there is probably more dispute than in relation to, say, journal publishing. When we come to the newer process of teaching quality assessment organised by the funding councils, what we see is a situation in which the relevant agencies have had to struggle to gain legitimacy. Partly of course this may be a matter of time: these processes are all much newer than those related to academic standards in research. However, in the light of the analysis which I am developing here, I would argue that it is not novelty *per se* which is the fundamental problem; rather it is the apparent difficulties experienced by the agencies concerned with teaching quality and standards, firmly embedded within the existing and recognised structure of academic authority. This is most obviously true of the teaching quality assessment. Debates about who the assessors should be, for example, and worries, certainly at the beginning of the process, that insufficient 'senior' people were putting themselves forward as assessors, demonstrate my point graphically.

Conclusion

What practical conclusions can one draw from this analysis? One conclusion certainly is that fears about the erosion of academic authority (the issue with which I began) are somewhat miscast. My analysis implies that, far from supplanting forms of authority based in intellectual skills and knowledge, external agencies in fact cannot operate without drawing upon those very sources of traditional academic authority, namely the judgements of peers. They cannot operate precisely because the standards which they reinforce must be accepted as legitimate by the academic community collectively and individually. They simply cannot operate on the basis of what I have called naked power. They must be able to operate in a climate where their authority is accepted as legitimate.

Academics therefore in a sense have nothing to fear from the establishment of external agencies charged with the oversight of quality and standards, as they cannot operate except with the active co-operative of academics themselves. At this point, those who are suspicious of all forms of external agency might draw the conclusion that withholding co-operation should be a very effective tactic: if they cannot secure co-operation, these agencies simply will collapse and academics will be left alone to manage their own affairs without interference. I believe that such a conclusion would be as misplaced as the view that any external scrutiny is a threat to academic autonomy. It is misplaced precisely for the reasons to which I referred in the introduction to this article. The great medieval achievement may have been to separate the idea of intellectual authority from political authority, but that is not to say that intellectual authority can operate in a vacuum. Certainly where intellectual life is vested in institutions which are in receipt of public funds, there is a perfectly proper interest in public accountability.

If one accepts this fundamental point, then external scrutiny will not go away, nor should it. The real issue is the precise form which public accountability will take, and the structures through which it will be expressed. If the creation of external agencies to oversee accountability is emerging as the preferred form for accountability in the late twentieth century, academics have all to gain by ensuring that they are actively co-operating with the development of these agencies at an early stage. To be involved sooner rather than later will mean that the academic authority on which these agencies must necessarily draw is embedded in structures which are appropriate for the purpose.

In the politics of the mid-1990s in the UK, the most urgent need is to form these alliances at the level of disciplines and subjects. It is these disciplinary communities who are the real guardians of academic standards. As the debate has shifted from quality to standards more explicitly, the need has become more urgent for disciplinary communities to be engaged directly. Their participation is essential if standards are to be defined and secured in a way which does indeed draw upon academic authority rather than attempt to supplant it. This must be part of the emerging settlement of the historic question about intellectual authority and political authority. The requirement for external guarantees of academic standards is proper and legitimate in a democracy where higher education is in receipt of public funds. But the agencies charged with securing those guarantees can only govern with the active participation and consent of academics.

References

Brennan, J., El-Khawas, E. and Shah, T. (1994) *Peer Review and the Assessment of Higher Education Quality: An International Perspective* (Higher Education Report No 3). London: Quality Support Centre.

Power, M. (1994) *The Audit Explosion*. London: Demos.

Scott, P. (1984) *The Crisis of the University*. Beckenham: Croom Helm.

Weber, M. (1978) *Economy and Society*. Berkeley, University of California Press. First published 1924.

Chapter 11

The Hunting
of the Gilt-Edged Degree

Tony Becher

Introduction

It is – and perhaps always has been – an interesting tendency of
policy-makers to focus on structural changes while paying scant
attention to the underlying processes. The two are of course interrelated: but changes on a macro scale are by no means always
reflected, at least in the way intended, at the micro level: grand
strategy and local tactics do not invariably form a perfect match.
There are countless cases where a lack of attention to the values
and practices of those targeted in a particular piece of reformist
policy results in its ultimate collapse. The notorious Poll Tax
debacle offers a recent case in point.

This is what is likely to happen in relation to the demand for
uniformity in academic standards, stemming from concerns on the
political front about comparability of degree awards. The irony
might be noted that many of those who fiercely resist the imposition of a common European monetary system seem to be equally
staunch advocates of a common currency in university qualifications. Be that as it may, the higher education system in Britain is
now faced with the challenge of responding to the requirement
that some sort of equivalence should be established between degree assessment across the multitude of different subject fields and
also throughout the now highly diverse range of academic institutions. The burden of that task has fallen to the Quality Enhancement Group of the Higher Education Quality Council (HEQC),
which – through its Graduate Standards Programme – is operating

in a way which merits the confidence of the university world (HEQC 1995). Many of the views to be put forward are indeed shared by those directly concerned in the Council (see Middlehurst 1996; Wright 1996). Nevertheless, it has been given an impossible assignment by its political masters.

In what follows, I reject the idea that all judgements are irrevo-cably subjective, and hence that any reference to standards is meaningless. I am nevertheless sceptical about uniformity, being concerned to emphasise the importance of contextual factors. In-sofar as standards can be established, they have to be seen as specific to a defined context. Within such a context, assessments can be reasonably objective: outside it, they are not directly meas-urable against other, similarly context-bound assessments. As has been remarked elsewhere, any pretence that they are is at best a polite fiction. (The claim for comparability of performance can also be seen as a politically convenient fiction, enabling central govern-ment to assert that its imposed mechanisms of quality assessment and control have succeeded in maintaining levels of academic excellence despite the budgetary cuts and structural changes to which higher education has been subjected.)

The very concept of standards is riddled with ambiguity. One might be referring, for example, to something laid down as a basis for comparison (as in British Standard Time); or to a fairly mini-malist pattern which is commonly followed (the standard pub lunch); or conversely to a measure of excellence (the standard bred horse). Or, in a rather different sense, one might regard a standard as a rallying-point, a mast to which to nail one's colours, something in which to invest one's values. It may be suspected that all these different connotations are involved in the unintentionally con-fused debate about academic standards.

To say that is not to imply that finding an improved verbal formula would solve all the problems. All of us are by now familiar with the phenomena of the equal opportunities policy and the institutional mission statement. Such mantras may give a sense of comfort, or even of achievement, while glossing over two common omissions. The first is to ensure that they do properly reflect a collective understanding and an accepted set of practices; the second is to confirm that they yield equitable results when applied to particular cases.

The first of these omissions – the failure to examine the appropriateness of a proper standard or set of standards – is neatly illustrated by the announcement, in January 1996, that over half the 11 year-olds in England and Wales had failed to reach the expected standards in mathematics and English (*Guardian* 1996a). The media made a great occasion of this: what is curious is that no one asked who it was who expected the basic standards to be much higher than even the average level of achievement turned out to be. Since these were new tests, introduced for the first time, one might conclude that the expectation was that of the educational psychologists who devised them. It is an interesting assumption that they cannot possibly have got their calibrations wrong. The mismatch was not, in the event, very substantially altered when it was found that there were numerous errors in the collation of the results (*Guardian* 1996b).

In the case of university standards, there is an even wider range than in primary schools of factors which operate to affect assessments of student performance. The existence, though not the nature, of such factors is indicated by some relevant statistics. Even at the level of the disciplines as a whole, rather than the individual students who follow them, there are some apparently bizarre differences in the distribution of grades. In the Higher Education Funding Council for England (HEFCE) assessment exercise, it is claimed that the assessors are given careful training to ensure, as far as is reasonably possible, a uniformity of judgement. Yet in the first round, 79 per cent of anthropology departments were rated as excellent, while the figure for engineering departments was 12 per cent (HEFCE 1995a, p.53). It is difficult not to believe that something more was going on here than a simple and straightforward judgement of quality.

Discrepancies – albeit not such spectacular ones – also arise in relation to examination awards in different subject areas. The data on degree classes in 1994 show that as many as 20 per cent of mathematicians graduating in that year earned first class degrees. The corresponding figure for mechanical engineers was 13 per cent; that for English graduates 12 per cent; and that for sociologists an even lower 6 per cent (Tarsh 1996). It might be thought that such divergences can be explained by the recent very rapid growth in student numbers and the great variety of institutions now included in the university sector – considerations which, taken together, might temporarily destabilise the established standards of academic performance. There is, however, little comfort to be had in this argument. In 1986, well before the period of dramatic expansion, the distribution of firsts between the four subjects mentioned above followed a broadly similar pattern: 18 per cent in mathematics; 12 per cent in mechanical engineering; 8 per cent in English; and 5 per cent in sociology (Tarsh 1988, pp.412–3, adjusted figures). And even in the much smaller, apparently homogeneous system of a generation ago, the statistics set out in the Robbins report showed comparable variations: in 1962, the percentage of firsts in mathematics was 14 per cent; that in mechanical engineering nine per cent; in English six per cent; and in social sciences two per cent. There is evidence of a similar pattern persisting between 1953 and 1959 (Robbins Report 1963, App.2a).

An optimist would take these figures to indicate a remarkable rise in standards – at least as measured by the highest levels of achievement – even though the student intake has broadened and resource levels have declined over the years. A pessimist would claim that such an implausible all-round increase in first class honours awards must surely mean that standards have been lowered. On either reading, there is a clear indication of the influence of factors not directly contributory to an identifiable and inbuilt concept of 'graduateness'. For the purposes of the present discussion, however, it is sufficient to note the long-standing pattern of differences between one discipline and another – the unchanging 'pecking order' in the way in which standards of excellence are deployed.

The strong inference from the various statistics quoted, for both quality assessment and degree awards, is that some underlying contextual differences are in operation. It is tempting to wonder, for example, whether in terms of their teaching competence the members of staff in anthropology are intrinsically better than their counterparts in engineering; whether their departments attract a better quality of student; whether the much smaller population of academic anthropologists is also more closely-knit and mutually supportive; or whether there is an amalgam of all three with yet other background factors. Again, one might ask whether mathematics students outperform sociologists because the former usually come to university with a long history of learning the subject in school, while the latter have more rarely taken an A level examination in sociology; or whether the signs of ability are easier to detect than in a qualitative and value-laden subject. Among the many other possible considerations, one might note variations in staff-student ratios, new patterns of modularity, and even perhaps an element of tradition: 'we only give firsts to about 1 in 20 candidates in philosophy, because the rest aren't outstanding enough'.

However, speculation on the causes of diversity is not to the present point. The proper identification of what is going on behind the scenes would call for quite extensive research time and effort – and to ameliorate the factors which are found to impede uniformity would almost certainly demand an unacceptably large investment of funds. The way forward, it would seem, lies in considering the implications rather than in pursuing the causes of inter-subject or even more intractably of inter-institutional variation.

If, as appears to be the case, contextual considerations play a large part in creating the differences between subjects, what can be said about standards? One possible reaction might be to argue that identifying and calibrating them is a pointless task – that academic awards are inherently arbitrary and unreliable. This sounds not only an uncomfortable conclusion, but one which seems to defy the experience of generations of students and teachers, who claim to know well enough what counts as a good and what as a mediocre academic performance.

Rather than going along such a path, it seems more constructive to argue that, while different contexts yield different patterns of assessment, when a particular context can be identified which is sufficiently stable in itself, the standards within that context have a coherent application. One of the conditions for such stability is the existence of a disciplinary culture within which the participants share broadly the same values, concepts and understandings (Becher 1989). It is admittedly the case that, in a number of fields, such cultures are becoming less coherent and less identifiable than they once were: and as they begin to weaken, close agreement on standards may become less easy to achieve. So too, in new disciplinary areas the values may still be only partially formed. But even in such cases of contention, there may well be agreement about the merits of specific pieces of work. Standards are nowhere near as arbitrary as the subjectivists would have us believe.

It remains to be considered whether, allowing that there is indeed scope for agreement on the assessment of quality, such agreement must necessarily be based on some form of measurement. For those who cannot accept that anything is objective unless it can be quantified, marking a piece of student work is a matter of assigning to it a number of some sort. But this is a false kind of quantification, because if the number assigned is challenged, its ascription has to be defended by qualitative reasoning. It is this ultimate dependence of assessment on reasoned argument that justifies the claim that standards are subject to rational procedures and are, to that extent, objective.

This claim for objectivity is supported rather than undermined by the existence of disagreement among examiners. Within a given contextual framework, two or more examiners may initially reach different judgements, though their areas of divergence will usually be confined to a relatively small proportion of the total student group. In the process of reaching a common assessment – which has eventually to be achieved if the students in question are to be given a mark at all – each examiner will draw attention to particular features of the work under scrutiny. One may contend, for example, that it is well-argued and clearly presented; another, perhaps, that it omits certain important elements of a well-constructed answer to the question posed. Eventually, agreement has to be established that the case in favour of a given judgement outweighs the case against, or *vice versa*.

The activity of deciding on the grades to be given to borderline cases offers a reminder to two important considerations. The first is that the process is reminiscent in some respects of a legal argument, and that it also has certain similarities to connoisseurship – the reaching of appraisals concerning works of art. In both such realms of discourse, it is the exercise of informed judgement that is called for: a judgement that is more than merely subjective, since it entails acceptability by other equally informed colleagues. Where it is questionable, the validity of a judgement in both fields can be tested, and on occasion negated, by appeal to independent expertise.

The second consideration is that it is misleading to present the assessing of academic work as an exercise which necessarily involves operating with standard criteria. Just as each work of art is unique, so at the university level each student is expected, within the limitations of his or her subject fields, to offer a personal answer rather than a routine or standardised one (this is true even in an apparently value-free subject such as mathematics, where the elegance of a solution is an important consideration). And in arguing the merits and demerits of a borderline case, in academic work as in connoisseurship, a pattern of considerations is brought to bear which reflects the particular character of that case. What is certainly not appropriate, and therefore not normally accepted practice, it to compile a list of criteria and to measure conformity against that. A checklist approach is inadequate because the same criteria can be seen to carry different weights in different cases, and because there will on occasion be found to emerge one or more new considerations not included among the already familiar criteria.

Insofar as a checklist modelled on the MOT test of road-worthiness for motor vehicles is a deficient *modus operandi* within a particular field of study, it is even more questionable if deployed in an attempt to conflate the processes of judgement across academic programmes as a whole. It is indeed curious that the possibility of such an exercise should be seriously entertained: none would want to spend much time and effort in ranking concert pianists on the same scale as playwrights, or in evaluating fourteenth century painters on an identical basis with impressionists.

Legal disputation in its turn offers a useful reminder that the process of forming a judgement is a disciplined one, in which precedent and analogy are strong determining factors. The appeal to decisions made in comparable cases can be an important element in reaching a final resolution, and case law provides the common ground on which debate can be conducted. In academic assessment, as in the operation of the law, it is legitimate in marking an examination script to argue by comparing the evaluation of one piece of work with that of another, as well as to refer back to established practice in conflating marks into an overall grade.

On this analysis, learning to be a fair examiner, and to apply the accepted standards within a shared framework, involves not merely a sound mastery of the subject-matter which is being examined but also an ability to deploy the related rules of connoisseurship and judicial procedure appropriate to the field in question. It is specific expertise of this kind which is required in any proper exercise of academic assessment. The epitome of such expertise is represented by the external examiner, who is appointed as an embodiment and upholder of the relevant academic culture (Silver 1995).

Academic standards, then, must in their very nature depend on a complex process of judgement which is sensitive to contextual as well as intrinsic considerations. Any attempt to standardise the standards – to impose uniformity on assessment procedures and the resulting ascriptions of merit across the whole range of academic enquiry – is doomed either to failure or to absurdity. One can meaningfully talk of shared notions of standards, and of comparability of judgements in history, and in physics, and perhaps – though with less certainty – in a newly-established field such as media studies. It makes no sense, however, to speculate about standards which relate indiscriminately to all three.

It may be replied that even if this is the case, there could nevertheless be common criteria which might be found to apply across the board; if not by detailed judgements related to the award to one degree class rather than another, then at least to what level of performance is acceptable and what is not. It is of some historical interest that in 1994 the Committee of Vice-Chancellors and Principals (CVCP), at the prompting of the then Secretary of State, embraced the notion that it might be possible to identify what they somewhat inelegantly termed 'threshold standards', but nimbly delegated the task of finding them to the Higher Education Quality Council.

What can be said with some confidence is that, even if a universally-applicable set of criteria could be found, they would necessarily be at such a high level of generality that they would add very little to the stock of existing knowledge. At best, they could only operate in a relatively symbolic way to supplement more localised and specific judgements: they could not themselves have a strong enough purchase on matters of academic details to be operationally effective in their own right. To say this is not in the least to denigrate the work of the HEQC's Graduate Standards Programme, which has launched a number of useful and interesting enquiries. It is only to predict that, with all the ingenuity it can muster, the Council will fail to solve the problem of standardisation in the terms in which it was originally set.

A current student handbook (whose provenance should remain anonymous) offers an example of the type of criterion which might emerge from any exercise attempting to define performance standards in general terms. It is admittedly an imperfect example, as it clearly relates only to the humanities and social sciences rather than to scientific and technological programmes – a more widely applicable formulation would have to be less specific.

The handbook in question describes what the various gradings – spanning the range A to F – imply. The description for Grade A reads: '[The essay] would have to be extremely well argued, fluently written and meticulously referenced. It would show a sophisticated and independent understanding of a wide range of literature, and engage with it in order to produce new insights…'. That for a C grade – which could perhaps be said to indicate a threshold standard – suggests that:

> A C-essay would show evidence of some structure and argument, but perhaps not too unevenly. The prose style would be generally competent, but might occasional lapse into awkwardness. References might be imperfect… [It might] err on the side of description rather than analysis, but it would have to show recognition of the need for critical engagement.

The criteria for the quality assessment exercises undertaken by the Higher Education Funding Council are set out in even less precise terms. Thus excellence (scale point 4) is established by the recognition, in respect of the various 'aspects of provision' to be examined, that 'this aspect makes a full contribution to the attainment of the stated objectives. The aims set by the subject provider are met'. A barely satisfactory grading (scale point 2) is to be allocated if 'this aspect makes an acceptable contribution to the attainment of the stated objectives, but significant improvements could be made. The aims set by the provider are broadly met' (HEFCE 1995b, p.22).

These instances suggest that what might be seen as a helpful guideline to those being assessed is in practice of relatively little use to those – such as employers of graduates or national agencies sponsoring overseas students – who want to know whether what is being judged is of an appropriate standard for their purposes. And certainly, definitions at this level of unspecificity can contribute little that is new and nothing that is important for those who have to make the assessment. It would have to be a naive examiner indeed to whom the definitions of A and C grades given above would come as a revelation, and a remarkable ill-chosen quality assessor to be unaware of the very general considerations cited for excellence and a threshold of satisfactoriness. In neither case would the formulae engage with, or make easier, the task of reaching a fair and well-informed appraisal. Terms like 'a sophisticated and independent understanding', or 'a reasonable range of reading', or 'an acceptable contribution' are not descriptive: their application depends on, and can in no sense bypass, the exercise of quite specific judgmental skills in relation to specific cases.

If, as I have argued, there is no realistic possibility of identifying a meaningful common standard for all first degrees – as against a series of worthy and high-sounding but relatively empty generalisations – we have to ask ourselves why the exercise is thought to be essential. Reference was made earlier to the statistics in the Robbins Report, showing the significant variations, apparently consistent over time, in first class honours awards between one type of institution and another. The Robbins Committee took a relaxed view of this, remarking (in §713) that:

> of course standards vary to some extent: such variations are in the nature of things. But an autonomous institution should be free to establish and maintain its own standards of competence without reference to any central authority (Robbins Report 1963).

Adam Smith could hardly have gone further. It is however one of the many paradoxes which those whose trade is education have learned to live with that exhortations about the need to embrace free market principles are frequently qualified by central regulation. It seems to be a source of current political – if not so clearly social – anxiety that individual institutions in what is now a much larger and more diverse university sector might be left free to establish and maintain their own standards of competence: as if the goal of uniformity has become more essential, even if hardly more attainable, with the advent of a mass system of higher education. An impartial observer might wonder at the origins of this apparently compulsive insistence on preserving a fictional gold standard backed by a depository of metals with such widely varied currency.

A well-informed comment from a knowledgeable transatlantic observer seems particularly apt in this context. As Martin Trow wrote in 1991,

> The concept of high and uniform academic standards is in British academic life something of a fetish or totem, the object of unquestioned and almost religious veneration and not of analytical scrutiny... It seems simply to be assumed that academic work at more modest standard offered to a broader student population must threaten the existing centres of excellence, as if Princeton were threatened by the standards of the state colleges or community colleges of New Jersey (Trow 1991, p.20 quoted in Eraut 1995).

More recently, Trow (1995) pointed out to the participants in a CVCP seminar on diversity in higher education that:

> if students gain their degrees or credentials with widely varying levels of proficiency and at different levels of difficulty, then the meaning of the degree itself must change; higher education leaves the gold standard, and degrees are increasingly assessed by the name (and reputation) of the institution where they were earned and the department in which the student took the degree (p.2).

To develop the point,

> in the United States there are no common academic standards maintained throughout the system...the meaning of a degree is established by learning where it was gained, and in what subject... Americans are comfortable with quite marked variation in the quality and difficulty and level of instruction in different parts of the same department...having a degree, or at least having spent some years in a college or university, is very important as establishing the probability that the individual has learned how to learn; but it is not very important for most of the ordinary occupations of life where that degree was earned or at what level of academic achievement (p.16).

To quest after a return to a gold standard – which, as Robbins reminds us, was a myth even in what traditionalists might call the good old days of elite higher education – is to pursue a romantic illusion. The currencies of degree awards depend, not on the vague promissory note of a general formula, nor even on the establishment of a clearly identifiable threshold, but on the determination of individual academics and their institutions to hold a shared expectation that a graduate is someone who 'has learned how to learn'. One may rightly regard the achievement of that goal as a reasonable and useful enough product of any degree programme: indeed, it could be claimed to constitute the hallmark of 'graduateness', and to signify the futility of the research for any more grandiose and all-embracing marker of academic acceptability.

Acknowledgements

I am indebted to Michael Eraut, Margaret McGowan, Robin Middlehurst and Martin Trow for their helpful comments on an earlier draft of this text.

References

Becher, T. (1989) *Academic Tribes and Territories*. Buckingham: Open University Press.

Eraut, M. (1995) *The Role of Standards in Academic, Professional and Vocational Contexts*, Mimeo. London: HEQC.

Guardian (1996a) 'Schooling setbacks for Tories,' 26 January 1996.

Guardian (1996b) 'Blunders over maths testing,' 13 February 1996.

HEFCE (1995a) *Report on Quality Assessment 1992–1995*. Bristol: Higher Education Funding Council for England.

HEFCE (1995b) *Quality Assessment Between October 1996 and September 1998*. Bristol: Higher Education Funding Council for England.

HEQC (1995) *Graduate Standards Programme: Interim Report*. London: Higher Education Quality Council.

Middlehurst, R. (1996) 'Degree standards and quality assurance.' In J. Brennan *et al*. *Changing Conceptions of Academic Standards Higher Education* Report No 4. London: Quality Support Centre.

Robbins Report (1963) *Higher Education: Report of the Committee Appointed by the Prime Minister under the Chairmanship of Lord Robbins 1961–63*, Cmnd 2154. London: HMSO.

Silver, H., Stennett, A. and Williams, R. (1995) *The External Examiner System: Possible Futures*. London: Quality Support Centre.

Tarsh, J. (1988) 'New graduate destinations and degree class.' *Employment Gazette*, 394–413.

Tarsh, J. (1996) Personal communication.

Trow, M. (1991) 'Comparative perspectives on policy.' In R. Berdahl, G. Moodie and I. Spitzberg (eds) *Quality and Access in Higher Education*. Buckingham: Open University Press.

Trow, M. (1995) *Diversity in Higher Education in the United States of America*. CVCP Seminar on Diversity in Higher Education, Mimeo. London: CVCP.

Wright, P. (1996) 'Mass higher education and the search for standards.' *Higher Education Quarterly 50*, 1, 71–85.

International Initiatives on Quality in Higher Education

In Part Three, we turn from national to international initiatives in the assessment of higher education quality. Within Europe, both the European Commission (EC) and the Association of European Rectors (CRE) have initiated development work in this field. The Organisation for Economic Co-operation and Development (OECD), through its programme on Institutional Management in Higher Education (IMHE) has a project which extends from Europe to America and Australasia. In addition, UNESCO has supported activity in this field at its European Centre for Higher Education (CEPES) and the various national quality agencies have formed an international body, the International Network for Quality Assurance in Higher Education (INQAAHE).

To a large extent, the interests of international bodies reflect those of their member national organisations: governments, universities, quality agencies etc. They also provide a mechanism by which policies and practice can be transmitted between countries. Above all, perhaps, they reflect the growing internationalisation of higher education, the growth in mobility of staff and students, and the need for institutions and others to understand better and to calibrate themselves against the academic work of institutions in other countries. This latter aspect is also reflected in the emphasis placed by several national quality agencies – and in some cases their sponsoring governments – on drawing upon foreign academic expertise in the quality assessment process.

The next three chapters describe the work of projects supported by the European Commission, the European Rectors and the OECD programme for Institutional Management in Higher Education. The projects differ sharply, in large part reflecting the interests of the sponsoring organisations. Thus, the EC project seeks to promote the extension of direct external assessment of academic work at a subject level as already practised by national quality agencies in several countries, generally, although with some important exceptions, at the behest of their national governments. The CRE project, conversely, places the focus at the institutional level, replaces direct quality assessment with an examination of the processes which institutions themselves use to assure quality, and seeks to reflect the interests of institutional leaders and managers in promoting institution-level autonomy. The IMHE project also reflects an institutional perspective but, unlike the other projects, is less concerned with methods of quality assessment and more concerned with their impact upon institutions.

The chapter by Barblan describes three pilot evaluations of the universities of Göteborg in Sweden, Oporto in Portugal, and Utrecht in the Netherlands. A three person review team visited each institution and, in the main site visit to each university, met with over 80 'witnesses' over three days. The focus was upon external constraints and institutional norms, and their influence upon the universities' capacity for change, or in other words, to quote Barblan, 'their autonomy'. The CRE project, therefore, is largely about the contribution which external quality assessment can make to the management of institutional change in higher education.

In their chapter, Thune and Staropoli describe the European Pilot Project for Evaluating Quality in Higher Education, sponsored by the European Commission but largely undertaken and co-ordinated by national quality agencies in France, Denmark, the Netherlands and Scotland (who constituted a management group for the project). All EU member states were involved plus Iceland and Norway. The focus was on the evaluation of teaching and learning in two broad subject areas: engineering sciences and communication/information sciences or art and design. The EU project reflects the interests of national governments and agencies in obtaining information about the quality of subject teaching in their national higher education systems. Thune and Staropoli emphasise the methodological consensus which appears to be emerging about how this task can be carried out.

The concerns of the IMHE project as described by Shah are somewhat different. The aims of the project are to examine both the declared purposes of different national quality agencies and the impact of the agencies, particularly on management and decision-making, as experienced by higher education institutions. As part of the project, over 40 institutions are conducting case studies of their own experiences of quality assessment. (The results of three pilot case studies are described in Part Four of this book.) As Shah points out, the interests of the IMHE project are in the ways in which quality assessment enters into broader relationships between higher education and the state and into internal relationships within institutions, effecting in both cases a shift in the balance of power and the locus of decision-making.

Chapter 12

Management for Quality
The CRE Programme of Institutional Evaluation: Issues Encountered in the Pilot Phase – 1994/95

Andris Barblan

The identity gap

For centuries, the leading universities in Europe have cultivated excellence and developed the necessary norms to test quality in teaching as well as in research. When combined, these standards expressed the academic culture that made the university a small and unique community dedicated to the development, transmission and conservation of knowledge. All members of that guild of scholars recognised that they were practising the same trade (even if in different ways) and sharing common values – i.e. a similar sense of truth and a common understanding of the ways and means to reach it.

After World War II, higher education underwent a massive expansion with new groups of people attending academic institutions: new teachers were appointed, new buildings erected, and new laboratories built. The demographic explosion coincided with an explosion of knowledge that led to the creation of many new specialisations asking for new expertise, new approaches to research and new ways of managing science. This trend fuelled the concept of interdisciplinarity.

The parallel growth of academic staff and ideas led to a diversification of activities, – old universities spawning new establishments (as in Finland, France, Italy, Spain or Turkey) or governments setting up specialised institutions to cater for specific groups or needs, as in Britain, Ireland or the Netherlands.

Massive growth in higher education made it difficult, however, to 'socialise' all newcomers to university life. Values and norms could not be transmitted as fully as before the war considering that new generations of teachers were often hired even before finishing their studies and presenting their PhD dissertation, the master-piece indicating that they had internalised the standards of the trade. The university's sense of purpose and identity was weakened by this expansion which rendered obsolete the elitist modes of academia: those were also challenged by the growing role of higher education as a gateway to upward mobility in a more open European society.

Today, the risk of fragmentation threatens academic norms and values: the self-image of the university profession is breaking up while members of the research and teaching community tend to ignore each other, not feeling that they can abide by the same rules. This situation is, paradoxically, being reinforced by the drive for intellectual integration in Europe: the lowering of national borders calls for a redefinition of a culture of excellence. But is there a shared understanding of quality underpinning knowledge development and transfer in Europe?

The responsibility gap

While intellectual democratisation was perceived as a tool for national development, governments in Europe footed the bill for expansion in higher education – leaving to the universities the level of scholarly autonomy that made possible their traditional quest for knowledge. In some countries, like Britain, academic freedom led to the strengthening of fully independent institutions; in others, such as France or Germany, universities were considered to be a public service and, as such, an integral part of national administration. Even if the taxpayers support the system everywhere, universities in the United Kingdom are accountable first to their customers while, on the continent, universities answer to public authorities.

In the 1980s, faced by growing deficits, governments re-assessed their various commitments and demanded value for money if subsidies were to continue. Universities were urged to take full account of their social and scientific responsibilities.

Their great independence – that is their organisational distance from national authorities – made the British universities an obvious prey to early government scrutiny. Were they delivering the goods they were paid to provide? If so, were they doing it efficiently or were national funds being squandered by an irresponsible elite? Thus, the quality debate first developed in the United Kingdom – a country that had developed a binary system of higher education where polytechnics further represented an alternative set of standards to traditional university norms or values.

A contrario, the quality debate is least developed in countries like Austria and Switzerland where universities are state services: as their detailed budget is referred to Parliament (federal or provincial), the official representatives of taxpayers can control their use of national finance. However, even in countries like these, where funds appeared readily available, economic recession has brought a revision of funding procedures. Universities have been given more leeway to use scarce resources to pursue their declared aims and objectives as a certain degree of autonomy is a pre-condition to responsibility.

Consequently, to justify the cost of their activities, universities look for common standards in terms of input or output. This implies shared norms and values that can be easily referred to, if one is to compare results and those processes used to achieve results. Such accountability to outside judges leads to the question already evoked by the internal fragmentation of the university system: in order to assess and compare, is there a shared understanding of quality underpinning knowledge development and transfer in Europe?

The CRE programme of institutional evaluation attempts to answer this question.

The credibility gap

Quality is a catchword of modern management techniques. In the academic world, it sums up the quest for excellence – as defined by the members of the intellectual community themselves – as well as its results, when they are deemed valuable by society. Hence, the loss of credibility suffered by many institutions of higher education, accused of practising a double language, one for insiders, the other for outsiders. The whole quality debate focuses on the harmonisation of these two concepts of excellence: how can an institution of higher education and research balance the *internal* and *external* requirements for quality in order to play its full role in social development? Over the years, different instruments have been created in order to assess quality, as seen from the internal or the external points of view.

Some tools help monitor processes of self-development when, for instance, control is exerted on the quality of the *teaching* staff – especially when people are hired. Faculties can also control the quality of *students* seeking admission. A system of peer review usually exists to control the quality of *research* and nearly everywhere there exist ways to check the quality of *instruction*. As a rule, the intellectual community initiates and develops these internal procedures for quality assurance that tend to *support* institutional development.

Other tools refer to standards determined outside of the institution in order to assess efficiency, usually on the basis of performance indicators. These indicators turn subjective processes of learning and innovation into objective, easy-to-measure, factual information, such as the number of publications or citations, the comparative cost of study courses or success rates of graduates in terms of income and employment. These procedures tend to *evaluate* institutional development, i.e. check whether the university provides social value in return for taxpayers' money.

On that basis, one can distinguish between *supportive* and *evaluative* approaches to quality assessment, and between *external* and *internal* initiations of the process. In a seminar given in Stockholm last year – in which Martin Trow was asked by the University Chancellor to survey quality evaluation procedures prevailing in the academic community around the world – Trow combined these four aspects to characterise four types of academic review (Trow 1994):

- *Type 1. The internal supportive* review is 'carried out within a university by its own staff in support of the work of the unit under review (p.23)'. It is based on recurrent peer reviews

- *Type 2. The internal evaluative* review is 'commonly initiated by institutional decision-makers who are forced

to make cuts in budgets and want to set priorities' (p.26).
It is usually carried out by a group responsible to the
institutional head using 'Type 1 reviews, supplemented
by such other indicators as student demand and retention,
time to degree, research productivity, quality of students
recruited, etc...' (p.26)

- *Type 3. The external supportive* review's 'primary function
  is the identification of academic strength and weakness
  with an eye to confirming the former and amending the
  latter' (p.28). It is not tied to funding and is entrusted to
  outside operators who tend to base their assessment on
  Type 1 reviews

- *Type 4. The external evaluative* review, as it is 'linked to
  funding, is powerfully coercive. It conveys the lack of
  trust by government in the intrinsic motivations of
  academics or in their own internal processes of quality
  control. It operates as an instrument of management and
  control over the reviewed institution' (p.32).

CRE's Pilot Programme of Institutional Evaluation

The model

The Association of European Rectors (CRE) aims to develop an
external supportive review system. To quote Martin Trow further 'this
type of review is relatively rare, perhaps because "external" usually means "government" or "the state", institutions that are more
likely to be concerned with the "efficient" use of public funds than
with helping universities strengthen themselves'.

In our case, the assessor is a university organisation, CRE, whose
European dimension ensures a clear distance from those institutional and disciplinary interests that could be important in traditional peer reviews.

Obviously, CRE has no power to guide its members' funding,
finances for higher education and research being organised at
national or regional levels. As the association of European universities, CRE can however propose to its members a mirror reflecting
their strengths and weaknesses and making apparent their management of quality development. Thus, a CRE audit represents a

clearly *supportive* type of review although, like Type 2, it is often initiated by university leaders interested to know how they could better steer their institutions through periods of change. To answer leadership needs, the CRE programme has thus some elements of evaluation that are usually discussed with the governing group of the reviewed institution. 'For governments and the larger society', such assessments 'have the legitimacy of being external to the units reviewed, and are thus presumably free from the constraints of collegiality that are inherent in internal reviews'. 'Type 3 reviews are more likely than Type 4 reviews to gain the trust of the units being reviewed, and of having their inquiries answered truthfully and with candor' (Trow 1995, pp.28–29).

> More compatible with their self-defined mission, Type 3 reviews have the large advantage over all others of being able to carry news and information about good practice from one institution to another. In the process of doing reviews in different institutions, a central reviewing body [like CRE, *author's comment*] becomes a repository of special knowledge and expertise about educational reform and innovation – about what characterises strong academic units, and how weaker ones can become stronger. This capacity to learn and then to teach about academic quality across institutional boundaries, free from the constraints of guild loyalties and jealousies within universities, is surely the greatest contribution Type 3 reviews can make to academic life (p.29).

The chief risk of external supportive reviews is their superficiality as 'they are further removed from the units under review than internal reviews'. Martin Trow adds that this drawback, however,

> is much reduced if what they are assessing is the quality of self-assessment procedures – i.e. if they are conducting *audits of procedures* rather than evaluations of the quality of academic units. A secondary risk – diminished by the fact that they are *ad hoc* events – is to become more 'evaluative' in order to answer the needs of governmental funding agencies (p.29).

Although this model was unknown to CRE when it entered the field of academic assessment in 1993, it does describe well the programme of the association and its ambitions to *reveal, evaluate, advise* and *educate* in order to spread anew a European quality culture in which most institutions of higher education and research would recognise themselves and test their *knowledge* contribution to the development of their social environment. It also pointed to the qualities required from CRE reviewers, university leaders with a personal understanding of academic institutions, of their members – be they professors, students or technical staff – and of their modes of government.

The practice

CRE as a revealer

Three institutions were proposed to be evaluated during the pilot phase of the programme: the Universities of Göteborg, Oporto and Utrecht. All three are classical universities, covering most fields of knowledge from arts to medicine and from science to law. All three have more than 20,000 students and are key employers in their region. They are mainly urban institutions, although, in Oporto and Utrecht, a growing part of academic activities is being moved to campus sites on the edge of the city. These common features were deemed important as they allowed for some kind of comparison to be made at a European level.

With the help of CHEPS (the Centre for Higher Education Policy Studies) at the University of Twente, self-evaluation guidelines were sent to the three institutions. They proposed a SWOT analysis, i.e. a study of institutional strengths and weaknesses on the one side, and an understanding of the opportunities and threats to be met in further institutional development on the other. Such an analysis is a pre-condition for strategic management, a tool for institutional government which, for CRE, makes sense of quality as a target to be reached.

The three universities were given a free rein to organise this self-analysis according to their own consultative and decision-making structures and using material already gathered through internal routine assessment procedures or external evaluative processes. It was thus hoped to keep the self-study exercise light. CRE also underlined that each institution had its specific routines and traditions, usually rooted in local constraints and culture. A call for trust and openness was made from the outset.

During the self-evaluation process, preliminary visits were organised with two members of the evaluating team. These visits were most useful in order to give visibility to the process inside each institution and to define the expectations of the university under review as well as those of the review panel. The resulting self-study represented the main activity for the university, in terms of effort – and, as has been discovered, in terms of importance to the institution itself. All three pilot universities offered a candid, truthful account of the role quality plays within the university and how quality is nurtured.

In fact, considering that most documents used in the three universities were in Swedish, Dutch or Portuguese, the three institutions had to make an early choice about the type and quantity of information they would make available in English to the review panel. Such a synthesis exercise was made all the more exacting by the fact that the self-study report was not to exceed 25 pages – excluding annexes.

Moreover, as the three reviewers were coming from different systems of higher education – Britain, France and Germany – the three universities had to make clear which systems of decision-making and types of financial or organisational idiosyncrasies they live with, i.e. they had to explain those daily requirements usually implicit in the national context. The obvious could be questioned and brought into international perspective.

Thus, through guided self-analysis, the three universities made apparent the critical processes they had developed to steer institutional development in terms of teaching, research and management. For its part, CRE's revealing role was to present a mirror to the institutions in which the differences between image and self-image were made meaningful. The three universities agreed that the difference between what they thought they were and how others perceived them to be was illuminating, as it called for adaptation to change and triggered ideas for new action among staff and outside partners.

CRE as an evaluator

CRE asked three well-known academics to constitute the review panel. All of them had had experience of auditing procedures, usually in their own countries, and were keen to test their evaluation tools in foreign environments. For the sake of comparability, they accepted to visit the three pilot universities in less than a year. These reviewers were Hinrich Seidel, President of the University of Hanover and then President of the CRE, David Smith, former Principal of Edinburgh University and now President of Wolfson

College, Oxford, and Pierre Tabatoni, former Chancellor of the Universities of Paris and then President of the Institute for Education and Social Policy in Paris.

They focused their preliminary visits to the reviewed institutions on the latters' capacity to elaborate internal structures and external links in order to respond to their development needs. This helped them to understand the universities' management framework, that is, indirectly, their institutional culture and, in particular, its influence on quality management. The purpose of preliminary visits was to have a still picture of the universities' institutional machinery while that of the main visits was to understand the dynamics of the institutions' development, i.e. to assess how the machine is working.

In order to comprehend the forces at work in the development of the three universities, reviewers centred the main visit on external constraints and institutional norms, as they condition the universities' capacity for change, i.e. their autonomy. In each case, more than 80 witnesses were met by the experts in less than three days. They came from the various boards and committees in charge of the institution as a whole as well as of faculties and departments. They represented students, teaching and research staff – or administrative personnel. Outside viewpoints were welcomed too, members of local authorities, regional policy-makers, representatives from competing colleges, related research institutions or the media also being interviewed.

Over the last few years, the three universities have been developing step-by-step the conditions of their autonomy as the Dutch, Portuguese and Swedish governments started to devolve more and more responsibilities to the institutions of higher education. In 1993, the Higher Education and Research Act allowed Dutch universities to develop their own institutional profile and made them responsible for the quality assurance of their activities. The same year, in Sweden, power had been devolved from the Ministry in Stockholm to the various universities in the country but under strict rules that made quality an obvious point of reference: thus, financing was to be based on results, i.e. on the assessment of previous performance, the number and achievement of students finally enrolled, or the success of PhD students. In Portugal, at the end of 1994, Parliament adopted a law on quality assessment that indicated how universities were to report to public authorities about the success of their activities.

Faced by impending change, the three universities adopted a pro-active stand and decided to 'mark their territory'. This was particularly true of Oporto, where the rectorate in 1992 organised a national seminar in order to compare provisions for evaluation in Britain, France and the Netherlands. The meeting led to the development of a quality assessment system for Portugal emphasising quality improvement (a policy modelled on the Dutch experience).

To forge the conditions of their growing autonomy was also the reason invoked by the three universities when asked why they volunteered to join the pilot phase of CRE's programme of institutional evaluation. They wanted to define better the boundary to be drawn between state and institutional responsibilities – an effort welcomed by public authorities that need solid partners. Indeed, a growing autonomy implies a sense of purpose shared by the whole institution. This requires good co-ordination of activities and programmes so that the university as a whole develops a profile that can be referred to by all units. As in continental universities personal allegiance is usually placed in the department or the faculty; increased autonomy calls for a leap in loyalty from the faculty to the university level if the institution is not to break up into its constituent parts. Consequently, present academic leaders have to facilitate a change of behaviour among staff and students that induces a feeling of belonging to the university as a whole.

In terms of structure, how far should the university be centralised or decentralised as an institution? Should co-ordination come from units that discover their common needs or should it be stimulated by central management as they are well aware of institutional constraints that affect all departments? In other words, how strong should the rector and other members of the university leadership be – in the context of national university structures and culture?

This question was important as, in all three universities, faculties have high profiles. In Utrecht, the university defines itself as a federation of autonomous faculties. At institutional level, this entails a shared awareness and explicit understanding of the university's encompassing role based mainly on the consultative process linked to the elaboration – every two years – of four-year development plans. In the two other establishments, where institutional coherence is left implicit, the achievement of general aims is left to the responsibility of the faculties, schools and departments.

To reinforce institutional identity, the three universities used similar strategies by proposing targets for development that could be referred to by all sectors of the establishments. In Göteborg, – where teaching and research units have often had a long history as independent schools – the rector, after the change of organisation in 1993, indicated some priority fields for development that could evoke interfaculty co-operative efforts and underlined the importance of interdisciplinary projects. In Oporto, a first planning exercise was launched in 1991 when the rectorate asked the schools to prepare strategic plans outlining their desired development over the next years. In 1994 these plans were integrated into a university development plan (1994–1999). In Utrecht, the university first made known in 1988 its long-term perspectives for growth based on five institutional goals. This document represented the framework within which four-year institutional development plans have been drafted. On an operational basis, their implementation is regulated through a yearly Planning and Control Cycle.

Identity reinforcement of course varied and was a function of the maturity of internal dialogue, still experimental in Göteborg, already well-accepted in Utrecht – where it is helped by a clear mission statement. In all three countries, however, reviewers felt that the mission of the institution could be re-stated, usually to take better account of the needs of the region.

At present, these documents tend simply to recall the importance of the university as a centre of knowledge and thus to reaffirm the basic consensus existing among European academics on the role of their institution: in Oporto, the self-evaluation committee went so far as to enquire about academic self-understanding in the university. It received very congruent answers, most professors accepting the fundamental rules of their trade and most of them considering that they were doing their utmost to obey them.

For the reviewers, however, to become a reference for action, the mission statement should go further and define the institution through its social aspirations as a knowledge centre, *hic et nunc*; it should target areas of commitment in response to general demands coming from the community at large, a community for which the university represents an important partner. Thus, the mission statement should propose the image of an ideal university in society – to be realised as time passes.

Such a sense of mission leads to the definition of focuses of development that inform institutional goals and norms taking into account the legal, financial and political constraints prevailing in the local situation. When the reviewers were looking for a clear vision of the future able to shape decision-making processes inside and outside the institution, they felt that the creative link between mission and goals could be strengthened in the three universities. The simple addition of converging aims can help design a vision of the future but does not evoke among staff and students a sense of belonging to academic communities which are more than the sum of their parts, that is institutions whose identity allows for autonomous decision-making.

From this point of view, a mission statement is more than a preamble to university statutes. It is the foundation stone of identity processes that give a common ethos to institutional policies when they are translated into strategies, i.e. when decisions are being made to commit specific resources to the achievement of specific objectives. As a result, the university evolves towards new balances in its activities, and these equilibria determine the profile of the institution for its external partners, its public presence in society. CRE's role is thus to evaluate the strategic planning cycle as it moves from one set of identity characteristics to another – a set that is deemed better considering existing constraints.

That is why reviewers started from a discussion of constraints – as variously understood by the different actors – in order to make sense of the strategies adopted in each institution and see their development towards the desired university profile.

In terms of resources, the three universities, to various degrees, are suffering from funding restrictions – although not for the building and equipment programmes in which they are all engaged to reduce the geographical dispersion of campuses scattered over wide areas. Apart from ensuring better working conditions to staff and students, bringing closer classrooms and laboratories from different faculties could be a way to increase interdisciplinary co-operation. However, reviewers, when interviewing concerned staff, were often told that not much was made of that opportunity:

indeed, departments were more interested in the organisation of their new premises than in developing collaborative action with formerly distant colleagues. They considered such an eventuality as a second stage of development and not as a pre-condition of their reorganisation. Thus a chance to use a break in working routines to induce long-term change was not used to the full for lack of a policy aiming explicitly at global institutional coherence by requiring faculties and schools to assist one another.

In the three pilot universities of the CRE programme for institutional evaluation, research funding – all or in part – comes from sources other than the Ministry that provides for higher education. In Portugal, the Ministry of Planning is in charge while in Sweden, funding is allocated to individual projects presented by university staff to national and international agencies. In the Netherlands, if some of the central funds from the Ministry of Education still provide for a part of the research costs, most of the money comes from research agencies and from private contractors. From the institutional point of view, this implies that the university can become dependent on outside research priorities.

As a rule, flexibility is the key word for the strategic management of change. However, when faculties manage financial resources themselves, they tend to fund what already exists, especially if they are to take into account future restrictions. Moreover, to enforce accountability from the various units, the trend is to give them full responsibility for all costs – in Göteborg, they rent their premises and in Utrecht, since 1995, they have had to take into account the depreciation of facilities. Such a process could close the faculties in upon themselves – or entice them to re-organise. Hence the importance of a stimulation fund at the disposal of the university central authorities in order to encourage new initiatives, reward good practice and steer action towards the desired institutional profile. In Utrecht, this university fund represents 2 per cent of non-earmarked funds while, in Göteborg, the faculties had to be persuaded to redirect some monies to a strategy fund – of their own free will – also some 2 per cent of the budget. In Oporto, a quality development fund is still to be created.

In terms of human resources, flexibility means questioning the concept of tenure, at least *de facto* when temporary contracts are preferred to indefinite employment. Over the last few years, for instance, in Utrecht where faculties can hire staff in proportion to their earning capacity, the number of temporary contracts has increased to 50 per cent of all university employees – including research assistants. In Göteborg, the university's main tool for staff management could consist of the re-deployment of personnel imposed from outside by new funding criteria: as 40 per cent of governmental support for educational activities is channelled through student vouchers – redeemable on the basis of actual enrolment – there is a clear link established between the supply and demand of courses. Empty classrooms could lead to a redistribution of teaching obligations! Re-deployment also plays a key role in Oporto as the Ministry recently defined at national level student/staff ratios for every discipline: thus, some faculties are now considered overstaffed and there should be redistribution of positions towards understaffed areas. To develop a margin of manoeuvre in the process, qualified staff are often contracted on a private basis using the income generated by university/industry co-operation, a policy also followed in Utrecht. However, to exploit to the full such opportunities for change, the three institutions, while planning human resources development, could take better account of the desired staff profile in terms of age and specialisation as needed to reinforce the university as a whole.

Re-organising present human resources and hiring new staff can also be complemented by out-sourcing policies in order to increase the institution's potential for change. In Utrecht, the university has launched Topselect, an innovative broker scheme helping redundant staff – academic and non-academic – to develop personal profiles fitting the need of today's labour market. On average, job-seekers are accompanied in their search for some nine months or more: in less than two years, more than 140 people have found new positions.

In terms of development, the three universities have little or no control over the intake of students. In some fields, they have to abide by national quotas; in others, they must accept all students who apply. The overall situation is still one of growth as, in Oporto, a 47 per cent increase is expected from 1992/93 to 1998/99 while in Göteborg, the intake has already grown by one third between 1991 and 1994. To keep open disciplines in which the state provides support for only a limited number of candidates, some flexibility has been found in Göteborg by addressing local and regional authorities: in specific fields, like medicine and odontology, they agreed to make up for the scarcity of funds coming from central authorities, thus keeping a critical mass of students, allowing for high-level teaching and research. Indeed, in Göteborg, there is great freedom in curriculum development and, without referring to national regulations, be they governmental or professional, the Faculty of Medicine has thus decided to stress student-centred learning and to take advantage of renovated facilities for testing new teaching processes; other schools reform graduate studies, renovate pedagogical concepts or develop interdisciplinary course offerings.

Do all these initiatives coming from departments combine into an institutional policy? In other words, can the university guarantee the values of all its services? Indeed, the three universities do stress quality as a key concept for their global development. But do they have the means to stimulate institutional strategies for quality?

In the Netherlands, a national system of external quality assurance is managed by Vereniging van Samenwerkende Nederlands Universiteiten (VSNU), the collective organisation of the 13 universities in the country. Thus, in Utrecht, a programme is assessed *internally* on a yearly basis, and *externally* every three, four or five years (for research), or every five years (for teaching), all these assessments becoming part of the yearly planning process for future activities. Moreover, a growing number of staff go through an appraisal system that culminates in an annual discussion with a superior when targets for future personal achievement are being defined for the coming year. After some ten years, the evaluation culture has become an integral part of the Dutch university culture – particularly in Utrecht, where most management tasks have already been devolved to faculties and departments – in anticipation of the coming recommendations to be negotiated by VSNU at national level. This pro-active attitude is typical of Utrecht University which seeks to pre-empt the imposition of possibly rigid rules – even if the planning and control cycle, in its yearly regularity, could also turn bureaucratic.

Inspired by the Dutch model, a new law is to develop course evaluation in Portugal while, in Sweden, there is also a long tradition of quality assessment, but still on an experimental basis as far as the national comparative assessment of disciplines is concerned. The three universities also try to take into account the assessment of courses by students, but the procedure is organised at faculty or department level. If the university as a whole were to benefit from student evaluation of courses, it would need to develop shared references, i.e. transparent common guidelines in terms of quality assurance.

Reviewers also noted that student assessment usually leads to some kind of didactic training offered to the teaching staff. In Göteborg, such courses tend to be extended to all faculties. In Utrecht, the university has created a centre for the training of teaching staff that develops special programmes and provides didactic mentors. The course is compulsory for the training of teaching staff who develop special programmes and it provides didactic mentors. The course is compulsory for newly appointed staff and sanctioned by a special certificate. This service to university members leads to new criteria for educational achievement: teaching as a career is then proposed by four faculties next to the traditional research-based career. Teachers are able to choose between 20 per cent of research against 80 per cent of teaching organisation of their time – at one extreme – or 20 per cent teaching against 80 per cent of research, at the other. As time passes, they should be able to change these proportions without losing status or responsibilities. Four other faculties are now interested in the scheme, a clear success for a strategy of incremental change and personal mobilisation.

Fragmented audits, be they external or internal, do not make an institutional strategy for quality development. In each university, the CRE reviewers discussed the strategies proposed for quality as the adequation of existing means to chosen ends. At which level of authority should such an adequation be found? In Göteborg, one of the committees appointed by the University Board to co-ordinate transversal university needs – i.e. those problems affecting all members of the institution – takes care of quality development whereas, in Oporto, the committee set up for the self-evaluation requested by the CRE could prefigure a structure of a similar type. In Utrecht, the Board – i.e. the executive triumvirate in charge of the institution – is responsible for quality.

Regarding capacity for change, two main questions were asked by the reviewers. The first concerned the consultation process about quality: is there in each institution a forum where the university interest groups can negotiate how existing means should meet chosen ends? In other words, is there a place where university members can develop a sense of belonging to the same institution because they share the same vision of the future? Consequently, is there an arena safe enough for the dissemination of good practice from one sector of the institution to another? Reviewers met members of the Senate in Oporto and of the University Council in Utrecht: as representatives of the teaching staff, students and administrative personnel, they vote the budget and approve the annual reports. In Göteborg, the majority of the University Board comes from the outside. Can such bodies go beyond the interests of the groups they represent to take full account of the quality that should be the institutional trade mark for teaching and research? Or is quality the domain of the professionals, i.e. the academics who usually define it, that is the members of the College of Deans in Utrecht or Göteborg, and of the Scientific Council in Oporto?

Indeed, the reviewers wondered if some kind of academic take over were not happening in the visited institutions, for instance in Göteborg where the once powerful position of university director had been suppressed after 1993, or in Oporto, to a lesser degree, where the Scientific Council – reserved to the professoriate – had become *primus inter pares* in relation to the administrative and the pedagogical councils. This trend was perhaps less apparent in Utrecht, although the weight of academic advice brought about some integration of academic and administrative processes, simply because teaching and research are the basic activities of university institutions. In any case, there seems to be a blurring of boundaries between academic and administrative streams of power. Although professors are usually amateurs in the field of administration, deans, where they exist, are more and more given full managing responsibilities that reflect the large – and often growing – decentralisation of universities.

The second question touched on the power of the structures responsible for quality. Can they provoke change? In Göteborg, although somewhat marginal in its status, the Quality Development Committee manages a small fund to support initiatives presented by the various units; in Utrecht, the Board can channel monies from the stimulation fund to encourage new developments. In Oporto, the rector is the final referee and can use his personal influence to develop an area.

If the trend in Europe is towards a greater emphasis on quality management, the first conclusions of the CRE evaluation project – based on a very small sample of universities – underline that there is place for improvement as quality strategies vary from 'not institutionalised yet' to 'pragmatic' or 'pervasive'. A quality focus leads to a global approach of university development which implies some concentration of power at the centre. Indeed, the strategic choices of universities imply a reconciliation between the quality of their processes and products, and the level of satisfaction of their constituencies. Reconciliation of purpose is made easier when centre and periphery agree to move in the same direction.

Both can gain from such a course of action as is shown in the Netherlands where quality is the key to research capacity – at department, faculty or university level. Since the early eighties, researchers have been encouraged to develop their activities within the framework of larger programmes, often on a faculty basis, i.e. to foster centres of excellence that can rival work done in other universities, either in the country or outside. This is achieved by the clustering of lesser projects into common thematic fields. By suggesting the creation of research schools, the government recently induced researchers to go one step further in collaboration activities by organising inter-university co-operation in key areas of innovation, thus considering the Netherlands as one pool of expertise placed under the 'supervision' of the Royal Academy of Sciences – which grants the status of research schools to those initiatives and networks presenting the most promising programmes. In Utrecht, the long-standing investment in research quality supported by the institution as a whole has led many departments to assume the secretariat of such national initiatives, indeed to take up responsibility for the development of 14 research schools (at the time of the evaluation visit) – thus justifying the university's claim for excellence.

In brief, CRE's role as an evaluator has been to look into the external and internal constraints that affect university development and to assess the way they have been taken into account by institutional decision-making processes in order to foster change.

CRE as an adviser

The CRE programme of institutional evaluation also helps member institutions to focus on their strategic, future-oriented choices.

As strategic choices are the purview of academic leaders, CRE chose the team of reviewers among present or former academic heads, not only because they had experience of audit procedures in their own context but also because they would have a direct experience of universities as complex organisations and, as a result, recognise the problems met by their counterparts in the reviewed institutions. Advice from peers is usually well received and provides a kind of collegiate control that transfers from one individual to the next, from one institution to the next, the common values of a quality culture often implicit in European universities.

Thus, in the three pilot universities, the reviewers opened and closed the evaluation process with the institutional leader and his team. The latter were asked at the beginning why they proposed their establishment for an evaluation. Did the process dove-tail with existing decision-making routines concerning university development? What were the results expected? Were there special points that needed attention? They were also asked at the end about what they had learned from the process. Had the evaluation been accepted in the institution, at the centre and in the faculties or departments? Was the institution *as a whole* more aware of its strengths and weaknesses? How would the evaluation be used to meet necessary changes in the organisation?

In other words, the CRE programme should be part of the university development policy and the more it is integrated into the institution's decision-making process, the more it can influence the future of the university. By bringing an outsider's viewpoint, it supports internal impetuses for adjustment to new social and financial requirements.

Thus, referring to the mission of the institution and its explicit goals, the review panel discussed how these aspirations might materialise in the daily routines of the organisation, that is, how to reinforce the academic presence in the community by profiling better its potential role in society. Have the institutional leaders the means available to steer change and create new balances among people, programmes and activities in the university? These new equilibria express the strategic choices that will shape the future.

In Göteborg and Oporto, for instance, the review panel thought it important to re-state the mission of the university in order to have a document that could become a reference for action. This statement should indicate whom the university is to serve, in the

region and the city (as both institutions play an important economic role that could be stressed *vis-à-vis* public opinion). The
same goal should also be made more explicit in Utrecht.

Consequently, to express the unique identity and role of each
institution, such a statement should define specific balances:

- between training and research activities
- between graduate and undergraduate education
- between educating the young and training the adults
- between regional and international commitments
- between scholarship and service to the community
- between disciplinarity and inter-disciplinarity
- between fundamental and applied research
- between public funding and private financial support.

Once the strategic context is clear, constraints can be viewed as
potential opportunities. As the role of academic leadership is to
seize these change opportunities, reviewers spent some time with
the three rectors and their collaborators to discuss if and how
quality could become a lever for new developments within the
institution. For instance, in Sweden and Portugal, government
envisages contracting the universities for various services to be
carried out over a three or four year mandate respectively. Taking
these external constraints into account, a new round of discussions
on possible scenarios for development could be initiated in Göteborg or in Oporto. Thus, a redefined institutional role could be
embodied in clear political objectives for the institution, in terms
of its staff (human resources policy), its students (clientele policy),
its teaching (curricular patterns and learning policy), its research
(innovation policy) and its finances (funding policy). After all,
these fields are core elements of university autonomy.

Advice was the key to the oral report of the review panel
presented at the end of the three-day visit. On the basis of the
equilibria desired by the institution, it underlined the institutional
goals that needed specific support if the expected profile of the
university was to be reached; it also reviewed the means available
for academic accountability and their potential for improvement
in terms of internal decision-making procedures; finally, it
summed up its findings on quality management, that is on the

stimulation and dissemination of good quality practice in and around the university.

This oral report was then completed by a written document setting the advice in its institutional context and conveying the views of the panel through an analysis of the evaluation process in the university. This written document was confidential and for the use of the institution. Of course, the university could decide to make it public and use it as a tool for change, if it so wished. In fact, the leaders of the three pilot universities chose not to keep the institutional report confidential: it became part of the internal and external consultation process about change. In other words, it turned out to be an *external* and *supportive* element of evaluation procedures (to use Martin Trow's typology).

CRE as an educator

Etymologically, *e-ducere* means to 'lead out', i.e. to move away from a situation that can be considered unsatisfactory. That is also the role of an institutional evaluation when it points the way to improvement. However, to be educated, that is to agree to go out, one has to become aware of present insufficiencies. This represents the motivation for change.

The self-evaluation exercise proposed by CRE is the key to transformation processes as the institution is asked to assess its strengths and weaknesses with regard to its norms and values, its quality culture and its capacity for further development. In other words, the university is asked four strategic questions: What is it trying to do? How is it trying to do it? How does it know that it works? How does it adjust in order to improve?

Each university agreed not only to answer these questions but to start a process of enquiry inside the institution – for some matters, at the level of the faculties in Göteborg, or the departments in Oporto – in order to present a well-founded SWOT analysis. As this document was to be read by outsiders – and foreigners – an effort was made to look at oneself from a distance so that institutional problems could be understood by the CRE reviewers. Moreover, as mentioned already, the whole exercise had to be boiled down to some 25 pages of text.

These constraints were an integral part of an educational process for the members of the institution. During the interviews, they often mentioned how difficult the procedure had been – especially in Göteborg and Oporto – but also how rewarding it had proved as they had learned a lot about the organisation and their role in it – by uncovering implicit rules of institutional behaviour and questioning the explicit ones. Sometimes, it was just a matter of stating the obvious that too often was taken for granted. In other instances, the unexpected came from a change of perspective on the daily routines. That changed awareness of the university opened the way to the dissemination of good practice because the SWOT analysis was calling for adjustments to a new situation, i.e. some kind of improvement. The proven success of one department or faculty, inside or outside the institution, could then be referred to and adapted to innovation needs.

With such a self-study prepared in the institution, CRE visits turned out to be more a way to accompany a process of change – set up in its wider context by the reviewers – than an auditing procedure supposed to validate institutional policies. Indeed, the educational process went on during the visits themselves as the institutional leaders, the initiators of the process, discovered new situations they had not necessarily expected when they asked CRE to intervene. Their identity, responsibility and credibility were questioned as much as the identity, responsibility and credibility of their institution. So were those of their collaborators – clear evidence that the university is nothing more than the people who inhabit the organisation!

The future success of the CRE programme will be measured by the capacity of reviewed institutions and their members to move from one situation to a new one, viewed as more relevant to its academic potential in society.

Envoi

Martin Trow suggests that external supportive review systems can suffer from superficiality and instability. CRE's first round of evaluation visits tends to show that reviews can be precise and deep even if they are removed from the immediate daily practice of quality management in departments and faculties. Indeed, the aim of the process was not to assess academic products but to evaluate those modalities set up to ensure quality. As CRE is interested in organisational structures and the dynamics of change in member universities, the review panel obtained direct access to the data and people supporting management. They could discuss with the university opinion leaders and official decision-makers their understanding of the institution and its future. Moreover, the preparation of the visits made inside by organisational units gave depth to the process of peer evaluation made by the CRE reviewers, academic leaders themselves who could quickly judge the value of the many testimonies received, either verbally or in written statements. The diagnostic presented by the reviewers was based on subjective and partial impressions, but they still contributed to determining the relative weight and validity of their conclusions. The representatives of the three pilot universities were indeed surprised by the rapid understanding of their problems that was manifested by the panel.

The pilot phase did set up an *ad hoc* process of evaluation. There is no proposal to repeat the process in the future in order to establish whether, and how, recommendations have been used for the development of the institution. The follow-up of the exercise is in the hands of the visited universities. If the supportive element of the evaluation has proved important, there should be no reason to refuse the conclusions of the panel. On the contrary, they could help boost institutional adjustment to conditions that were presented in a new light by intensive discussions with external experts. Although a single operation, the evaluation can and should have long-term effects if it becomes part of an organic process of growth: the stability of the process is linked to its acceptance by the institution.

For other members, CRE intends to make use of the experience accumulated in the review visits by publishing booklets, information hand-outs or handbooks of good practice material that should help universities in Europe to develop management strategies furthering their institutional development. Seminars could also be organised on specific change policies.

At a later stage, once the experimental phase of the programme is closed, CRE should examine whether it should go one step further and propose to its members a consultancy service in institutional quality management to accompany the transformation process initiated by the evaluation programme. This would represent the logical development of the desired spread throughout Europe of a quality culture that should foster a sense of belonging in the academic community around the same quest for identity, responsibility and credibility.

This will be discussed in the next report presenting the issues encountered in the experimental phase of the CRE evaluation programme – the report summing up the results of reviews now being conducted in another ten universities throughout the continent.

References

Trow, M. (1994) *Academic Reviews and the Culture of Excellance.* Universitetskanslern: Sweden.

Ministry of Education and Science (1993) *Dutch Legislative: Everything you always wanted to know about the Higher Education and Research Act (but were afraid to ask).* Zoetermeer: Ministrie van O and W.

Chapter 13

The European Pilot Project for Evaluating Quality in Higher Education

Christian Thune and André Staropoli[1]

Introduction

In 1991, when the European Commission undertook the first step to initiate the European Pilot Project for Evaluating Quality in Higher Education, issues of quality in higher education were at the forefront of the debate in Europe but few European countries had developed systematic evaluation procedures for their higher education system. Thus, the goals of the project were to enhance awareness of the need for evaluation in higher education in Europe; to enrich existing national evaluation procedures; to further the transfer of experience; and to impart a European dimension to evaluation.

It is important to point out that the project did not aim at comparing or ranking the institutions involved, nor did it intend to develop a single evaluation structure in Europe. Instead, it aimed at developing simultaneously, in each country, an evaluation culture, by testing a common method that was open to national adaptations.

The project involved 17 countries – the 15 European Union Member States, Iceland and Norway. It focused on the evaluation

---

1   This paper is based on the European Report (November 1995) – the final report for the European Pilot Project – which was written jointly by the two authors of this paper as well as Dorrte Kristoffersen, Marie-Odile Ottenwaelter and Andrée Sursock.

of teaching and learning – while taking into account research activities in so far as they affect the educational process – in two broad subject areas: engineering sciences and communication/information sciences or art/design. It involved the university and non-university sectors. Each country, depending on its size and following criteria set by the Commission, was asked to select two or four volunteer institutions in these two fields and two sectors, for a total of 46 institutions which were evaluated simultaneously, from November 1994 to June 1995.

In a year, it resulted in:

- 46 self-assessment reports and a corresponding number of evaluation reports at the institutional level

- 18 national reports (the French-speaking and Flemish-speaking Communities of Belgium having produced one each) which analyse the experience at the national level

- a final report at the European level (November 1995). The European report which is based on the national reports, presents and analyses the experience with the Pilot Project and offers suggestions as to procedures for future collaboration and follow-up activities.

Organisation of the project

The organisation of the project was multi-layered and collegial. The project demonstrated the efficiency of this collegial structure which benefited from the qualifications, experience and commitment of a small group of experts who worked closely with national leaders in each country.

The European Commission and its Advisory Group were assisted by a Management Group who provided the technical leadership for the project, designed its methodological framework and ensured the transfer of experience among participating states. The Management Group consisted of six experts from the evaluation agencies of Denmark, France, the Netherlands and the United Kingdom – along with one representative each from Germany, Portugal and Norway.

The Management Group delegated the responsibility for the daily management of the project and the drafting of the major documents to a secretariat – shared between Evalueringscenteret (Denmark) and the Comité National d'Évaluation (France), each establishing the liaison with a number of participating countries. Their practical experience and technical expertise shaped their relationship with the National Committees (which were formed by each country to implement the project at the national level): contacts were frequent and were intended to support and help, prod and encourage.

The method

The methodological guidelines

The goals, method and organisation of the project were described in the 'Guidelines for Participating Institutions' (1994), designed by a small group of experts from the four countries with an established and functioning evaluation system at the time the project was set up (Denmark, France, the Netherlands, United Kingdom). The group consisted of: Jim Donaldson from the Scottish Higher Education Funding Council, Edinburgh; André Staropoli and Marie-Odile Ottenwaelter from the Comité National d'Évaluation, Paris, Christian Thune from the Evalueringscenteret, Copenhagen and Ton Vroeijenstijn from the Vereniging van Samenwerkende Nederlands Universiteiten (VSNU), Utrecht. The Guidelines set out instructions regarding the self-assessment and the peer review processes, as well as the composition and responsibilities of the various groups in charge of the project nationally.

The project design rested on the four principles which were common to the evaluation systems in the aforementioned countries, namely:

- autonomy and independence in terms of procedures and methods concerning quality evaluation both from government and from higher education institutions
- self-assessment
- external assessment by a peer review group and site visits
- publication of an evaluation report.

Conclusions on the method

The main body of the European Report (European Commission 1995) synthesises and analyses the recommendations made by the countries regarding all phases of the evaluation process. This article focuses on a few key issues.

The European Project had to overcome two difficulties: the diversity of disciplinary areas and the variety of evaluation experiences among the participating countries. Thus, the Guidelines needed to be sufficiently specific to help inexperienced countries, and also sufficiently general to be applicable to different national contexts and to a wide range of disciplines.

Since the project did not intend to design an evaluation model that would be generalised to all participating states, the implementation of the four aforementioned principles varied. In fact, Chapter 2 of the European Report presents a brief but complete overview of the status of evaluation and an acknowledgement that even the application of common principles will vary according to national differences.

Based on the national reports, it is possible to say that the four principles adopted for the project were validated by all participating states:

- The autonomy of the evaluation process was guaranteed by the National Committees. It is important that each participating state establishes a national coordinating body which will ensure the legitimacy of the peer review and prepare all aspects of an evaluation: the design, the planning, and the process of adapting the method to the specifications of the evaluation undertaken.

- A good self-assessment process requires wide participation within a department or institution; it should be a recurring practice based on ongoing data collection and analysis.

- A good external evaluation requires a competent and balanced peer review group that includes academic and non-academic members; the participation of an international expert gives an added perspective. The peer review group must be supported by a national coordinating body and a professional staff.

- The major purposes of the evaluation report are to assess strengths and weaknesses and suggest improvements. The final judgement should take into account the context and, particularly, the department's (or institution's) stated mission and goals. The evaluation report must be published.

Conclusions and future developments

At the conclusion of the project, it is possible to say that its goals have been reached.

The project did enhance awareness of the need for evaluating higher education. All countries agreed to participate in the evaluation process – a new experience for many of them. Several reports noted that the value of the evaluation became even more evident at the end of the process than at its beginning.

In many countries, the project triggered a debate on evaluation. Some states have indicated explicitly that they are working on establishing a regular evaluation process. The project ensured that government, institutions and experts gained a significant evaluation experience which the countries can draw upon in the future. For example, Spain's participation in the project was a contributing factor leading to a vote in September 1995 that led to the establishment of an evaluation agency, the *Consejo de Universidades*.

In addition, several countries have asked for a follow-up of the project at the European level arguing that it would be interesting to build on the current experiment in a second phase. The proposal presented in the European Report is as follows: the method for Phase 2 would retain the basic four principles of Phase 1, integrate the recommendations given in the national reports, and develop the European dimension further.

- The pilot project has demonstrated the need to define more precisely the evaluation: the scope should be enlarged to include both research activities – since they affect the curricula – and an institutional analysis; the boundaries must be narrowed to strengthen the process while maintaining feasibility. Therefore, a single discipline might be chosen, as suggested by several countries.

- At the European level, the method should be 'customised' to fit the discipline while each participating state should 'customise' it further to adapt it to its national context. It is essential to emphasise that the customising process should be included as an explicit step instead of simply mentioned as an optional process in the project that just ended.

- Thus, the design would introduce a comparative dimension, not in terms of departments but in terms of the state of the art in each country as well as the national objectives that will be developed as an outcome of the evaluations.

- It would be worthwhile to maintain the presence of the international experts in the peer review groups.

Similarly, experience transfer did take place and enhance national practice. That the countries with little or no prior experience were enriched by the process was to be expected. But even some countries with a regular evaluation process noted that they learned from this experiment.

The process did add a European dimension since it occurred simultaneously in 17 countries and was managed in a collegial manner. Multiple occasions for European collaboration and exchange were provided through the training sessions, the working meetings of both the National Committees and the Management Group and the circulation – among National Committees – of all the national reports in three languages.

Given the common Guidelines can never be fully exhaustive and applicable to every situation, the training of self-assessment teams must be introduced, while the training of peer review groups and the preparation for the site visits must be strengthened. Based on recommendations from several countries, the European Report argues that training be envisaged at the European level.

To benefit from the momentum that has just been created, many reports asked that the collaboration that has been started should continue in the form of regular meetings to ensure experience transfer with an ongoing dissemination of relevant experiences and methodological developments. This collaboration would include not only the leaders of the established and embryonic European evaluation agencies, but also the presidents of the National

Committees for those countries who are not yet at the preliminary stage of establishing a systematic evaluation programme. In addition, it would be worthwhile to open these exchanges to other European countries as well.

References

Donaldson, J., Staropoli, A., Ottenwaelter, M.-O., Thune, C. and Vroeijenstijn, T. (1994) *European Pilot Project for Evaluating Quality in Higher Education: Guidelines for Participating Institutions*. Brussels: European Commission.

European Commission (1995) *European Pilot Project for Evaluating Quality in Higher Education: European Report*. Brussels: SOCRATES/European Commission.

Thune, C., Staropoli, A., Kristoffersen, D., Ottenwaelter, M.-O. and Sursock, A. (1995) *European Report: Final Report for the European Pilot Project*. Brussels: European Commission.

Chapter 14

Quality Management, Quality Assessment and the Decision-Making Process
The IMHE Project on Institutional Impact

Tarla Shah

Introduction

In recent years the creation of national systems for the assessment of quality in higher education has been a major feature of developments in many countries. There are now over 70 quality assessment agencies around the world which have responsibility for undertaking a review of the quality of higher education provision in their respective countries.

There are some common features in most national systems of quality assessment, for example self-evaluation and peer review visits, but there are significant differences in the purposes and methods between different systems. These are reflected in the balance of objectives between accountability and improvement, the focus of review (i.e. whole institution, subject level, teaching, research or a combination of these), and the ownership of the system (i.e. state owned, institution owned or independent).

There have been several projects and much debate about systems and methods used in quality assessment, but there is much less information available and remarkably little discussion about the real purposes of quality assessment (beyond general statements of public accountability and improvement). Virtually no information is available about the impact that external quality assessment is having on higher education institutions themselves.

These two issues (purposes and impact) form the basis of the project being undertaken for the Institutional Management in Higher Education (IMHE) programme of the Organisation for Economic Co-operation and Development (OECD). The project is entitled 'Quality Management, Quality Assessment and the Decision-Making Process'.

The IMHE Project on Quality Management, Quality Assessment and the Decision-Making Process

This project, funded by the Institutional Management in Higher Education (IMHE) programme of the OECD, commenced in 1995 and is due for completion in early 1997. The aims of the project are two-fold:

(i) to clarify the purposes, methods and intended outcomes of different national systems of quality assessment, and

(ii) to investigate their impact on institutional management and decision-making.

The project involves *two main phases*:

(i) a conceptualisation and review of national systems of quality assessment in terms of their purposes and contexts

(ii) a series of institutional case studies of the impact of quality assessment on institutional management and decision-making.

The *first phase* – a review of national quality assessment systems – formed part of the work undertaken during 1995. Since detailed descriptions of quality systems in many countries were already available, it was decided not to replicate this work but instead to undertake a conceptualisation and review of existing available material. The review of national systems addressed the following features:

- context of external quality assessment (how, when, why set up, historical and environmental factors)

- who undertakes quality assessment (meta-agency, ownership issues, scope of review)

- purposes of quality assessment (accountability, improvement, rubber-stamping exercise, ranking of institutions)
- methods used (self-evaluation, peer review visits)
- intended outcomes (public report, links to funding).

The *second phase* of the project was undertaken during 1996. This involved a series of institutional case studies. The purpose of the case studies was to investigate the impact of external quality assessment upon institutional management and decision-making. These case studies were undertaken by staff within the case study institutions within a common framework which provided guidance on content and focus.[1]

The focus of the institutional case studies was on the following:

- the *contexts* for quality assessment e.g. national system features, government policies, external quality assessment requirements, institutional characteristics
- the *internal quality assessment methods* that are in place in institutions e.g. external examiners, student feedback, regular review and monitoring of courses
- how quality assessment (both internal and external) affects the *management and decision-making processes* e.g. relationship to planning and resources, curriculum development
- the *impacts* of external quality requirements upon the institution at structural, cultural, curriculum and governance levels
- where possible, institutions would undertake internal case studies (within the overall institutional case study) *of recently evaluated departments or disciplines*
- the *interpretation* of outcomes from quality assessments and how the *future* of an institution's mission, policies, structure and culture are related to this.

---

1   Three pilot case studies were undertaken in institutions in Australia, Denmark and Sweden during the first phase of the project in 1995 to test the framework document. This was amended as a result of the pilot case-studies. The reports of these studies are published in Part 4 of this book.

Authors of the case studies were asked to address all of the above in the context of institutional and system change.

Examples of issues which the case study authors were asked to examine were: how quality assessment enters into the management and decision-making process; the impact on governance; impact upon the nature of academic work and the distribution of academic and administrative staff time; the relationship between quality assessment and educational outcomes; where the aim of quality assessment is improvement/enhancement, does it work?; the relationship between accountability, value for money and quality improvement.

Over 40 higher education institutions in over 15 countries (both OECD Member States and non-OECD Member States) participated in the project. The countries ranged from Europe to Australia, Canada and Mexico.

Complementary to the institutional perspectives on impact of external quality assessment are the perspectives of the national quality assessment agencies themselves. Some agencies have recently commissioned or undertaken evaluations of their activities. It was, therefore, decided to extend the project to involve case study reports of the impact of national quality assessment agencies as seen from the perspectives of the agencies themselves. As with institutional case studies, a framework providing guidance on the focus for national agencies was devised.

Key elements in investigating the impact of quality assessment

The IMHE project has taken the view that quality is a useful concept with which changes at the macro level of systems and policies of higher education can be linked with changes at the micro level concerned with curriculum, teaching, student learning and assessment. At the macro level quality assessment is about power and control. At the micro level it is about student experience and achievement. With the growth in the demand for higher education, the micro level processes have become more visible, more important and more costly to society. External quality assessment is, therefore, used as a means to subject higher education institutions to greater public scrutiny.

New external quality assessment systems are now being established in many parts of the world and existing systems are changing their mode of operation to meet the requirements of the changing higher education environment. At the same time, individual higher education institutions are devoting more attention to internal assessment and evaluation. To some extent, these two trends are connected: institutions are looking at their internal quality *because* of the expectations of external quality bodies. But they are also doing so because of reasons to do with growth in demand for higher education, with diversification and with financial cutbacks. These changes in the external environment pose questions of choice and decision-making for institutions and internal assessment and evaluation processes can inform these decisions.

Until recently 'exclusiveness' of entry to higher education had been the traditional form of quality assurance. Admission to higher education was restricted, socially and educationally, not just for students but also for staff. Today, there are more students and more staff than was the case, say, even ten years ago. This move from 'elite' to 'mass' higher education has lessened the reliance that can be placed on exclusiveness of entry to higher education as the main guarantor of quality.

This growth in the demand for higher education has led to students being admitted from varied backgrounds, with different abilities, needs and ambitions. This has led to increased diversity of course content, delivery methods, forms of student assessment, and a diversity of types of institutions. This diversity implies increasing choice which, in turn, implies that adequate information should be provided to inform consumer choice.

Another development has been in the forms of control which are exercised in higher education. There is considerable variation between higher education systems in the extent to which matters are decided at the level of the state (government departments and their agencies), at the individual institutional level, or at the level of departments and faculties of institutions. Debates about autonomy are often about the extent to which the level of the state puts constraints on actions at the institutional level. But there is also considerable debate about the autonomy of departments and other basic units within institutions and of individual staff members. Quality assessment is central to many of these debates.

There are also differences in the way in which matters are decided at the different levels. At the system level there is considerable variation in the balance which is struck between political, bureaucratic and what Clark (1983) has termed 'system-wide academic oligarchy'. At the department and faculty levels different mixes of autocracy and collegiality are found. At the institutional level collegial, bureaucratic and managerial forces compete for power.

Differences also exist in the relationship between higher education and the wider social environment – a relationship which is increasingly characterised in many countries by market conditions. Higher education institutions are today increasingly finding themselves competing for students, funding, staff and reputation.

Purposes of quality assessment

The changes that are currently taking place in higher education systems around the world are reflected in the purposes of external quality assessment. A combination (but not always the same combination) of the following seven purposes has been identified from the national quality assessment systems that have been looked at so far in the IMHE project:

- to ensure greater accountability for the use of public funds
- to improve the quality of higher education provision
- to stimulate competitiveness within and between institutions
- to undertake a quality check on new (sometimes private) institutions
- to assign institutional status
- to transfer authority between the state and institutions
- to make international comparisons.

There is, of course, some overlap between the purposes. Accountability and improvement are most commonly stated. In addition, by linking assessment to rewards of funding or reputation, quality assessment is frequently claimed to increase competition between institutions and between departments, providing incentives and encouraging responsiveness. The role of quality assessment (generally developed into a system of accreditation) to impose a 'quality check' on new institutions or to assign status to existing institutions tends to be a feature of higher education systems in transition and growth, for example countries of central and eastern Europe, the Caribbean, parts of Africa. Its importance in the transfer of authority from the state to institutions is often held to be a feature of continental European systems where relaxation of government legislative controls has been accompanied by an emphasis on accountability through quality assessment. However, in the United Kingdom, traditionally lacking close government control over higher education, the introduction of quality assessment has generally been seen as strengthening such control. The emphasis upon international comparison is particularly strong in countries in central and eastern Europe (reflecting a long period of perceived isolation) but is also a feature in many smaller countries, in part reflecting the limited possibilities for within-country comparison.

Purposes reflect national contexts but they also reflect differences in emphasis between state, institutional and market forms of regulation and decision-making. Accordingly, even with a single system, different interest groups tend to emphasise different purposes.

A model of quality assessment

The IMHE project has indicated that there is considerable variety in the methods and practices of existing quality assessment systems (this is sometimes confused by differences in interpretation of terminology). However, there are common elements and these can be shown through the 'general model' of quality assessment that Van Vught and Westerheijden proposed (1993). The model is based on a survey for the Standing Conference of Rectors, Presidents and Vice-Chancellors of the European Universities and the European Commission. The model consists of the following five elements:

- *A meta level agency* with responsibility for co-ordinating the quality assessment system. This role entails the formulation of procedures and formats for use by universities and colleges in the development of mechanisms for the assurance of the quality of teaching and research. Examples of such meta-level agencies are the Higher Education Quality Council (HEQC) in the UK and the Association of Universities (VSNU) in the Netherlands.

- *Institutional self-evaluation*: based on procedures and formats laid down by the meta-level agency.

- *External peer review*: external peers visit the department/institution to discuss the self-evaluation report and plans for the future.

- *Reporting*: a published report is the outcome of the peer review visit.

- *Links to funding*: there should be no direct relationship between the outcomes of quality assessment and decisions about the funding of higher education. Van Vught and Westerheijden argue that such direct relationships undermine the purposes of the quality assessment process. However, there has been considerable debate about this issue, with government pressures in several countries to introduce such links.

However, the work of the IMHE project suggests that this model may be less universal than its authors supposed. Firstly, there is much quality assessment taking place without any reference to a meta-level agency and where such agencies exist, they are frequently unstable with regards to both constitution and methods. Second, the activities which occur under the headings of self-evaluation and peer review are so varied as to require extremely broad definitions of these terms. 'Self-evaluation' is sometimes nothing more than collecting information and 'peers' can be almost any kind of outside visitor. Third, reports are not always published (see, for example, accreditation practice in the US) and when they are, they may refer to either subject, institutional or system levels. Fourth, as we have already noted, the question of a link to funding is hotly disputed in several countries.

Impacts of quality assessment

Quality assessment can impact upon higher education at all of the levels of decision-making identified earlier. Quality assessment may be the basis of intervention by the state – through funding or course approval decisions; it may cause changes in policies and procedures at institutional or department levels; it may generate changes in attitudes and behaviour of individual staff members. The balance between these varies and depends on the traditions of different higher education systems and institutions and on the methods of quality assessment used.

The first phase of the IMHE project included three pilot case studies (at the University of Monash in Australia, the University of Aalborg in Denmark and the University of Uppsala in Sweden). A small number of case study reports undertaken as part of the second phase of the project have also been received. Some of the reports come from institutions in countries with well-established quality assessment systems; some are from countries where national external quality assessment systems have recently been introduced; some are from institutions in countries where the introduction of national quality assessment is still being discussed and where institutions are preparing themselves by undertaking self-evaluations in anticipation; some are from institutions which have developed internal quality assessment processes solely to meet institutional needs and with no pressure from an external agency.

An initial analysis of some of these reports suggests the following:

- impact takes a very different form in each individual institution and the nature of this impact is related to the distribution of authority in the higher education system, i.e. what is typically decided at what level

- overall impact of quality assessment is greater where it achieves legitimacy at the basic unit (department/faculty) level, i.e. individual staff members accept the conclusions and the processes on which they are based

- impact at the institutional level results in more centralisation of procedures and greater managerialism.

Conclusion

It is unclear at this stage of the project to what extent external quality assessment on its own has any impact upon institutional management and decision-making processes. Maybe impacts do not become apparent immediately and the real effects of any changes introduced as a result of external quality assessment will become visible only in the longer term. However, it appears at this stage of the project that other, more important external forces (relating to funding, expansion and diversification) are forcing institutions to change. To quote one of the case study authors:

> The recent changes within this university reflect the tremendous changes in culture within higher education itself: a heightened awareness of the use of and, in some instances, the mis-use of league tables; the public's perception of higher education provision; and the national and international raising of consciousness about quality in higher education institutions. The changes form part of the university's response to the 35 per cent increase in student numbers in the last five years, the process of modularisation, and raised expectations on the part of its students.

Thus, a major difficulty for this or any similar study is to isolate the impact of quality assessment from the impact of the many other changes which higher education institutions are experiencing.

In a recent paper, Martin Trow (1996) has questioned the compatibility between internal evaluation processes which are designed to address internal needs and problems and internal evaluation processes which feed into the requirements of external quality bodies. The first type he describes as being primarily about *learning* and the second type primarily about *persuasion*. Trow questions whether the two functions can be achieved within the same process.

The picture which is beginning to emerge from the IMHE project is that it all depends on context and that the three crucial elements of context are (i) the general state of relationships between higher education and government (including the level of trust between the two), (ii) the methods adopted by the external assessment agency (including the extent of standardisation and whether rankings or league tables are involved), and (iii) the character of the higher education institution itself (with factors such as reputation, pace of change, external threats all important).

References

Clark, B.R. (1983) *The Higher Education System: Academic Organisation in Cross-National Perspective*. Berkeley: University of California Press.

Trow, M. (1996) *On the Accountability of Higher Education in the United States*. Paper presented at The Princeton Conference on Higher Education, March.

Van Vught, F. and Westerheijden, D. (1993) *Quality Management and Quality Assurance in European Higher Education*. Enschede: CHEPS.

PART FOUR

Institutional Experiences of External Quality Assessment

The final three chapters of this book describe the experiences of external quality assessment of three universities from different countries. They are experiences of relatively recently established quality assessment systems – Sweden, Denmark and Australia – two of which have been described elsewhere in this volume. But here the focus in on the institutional experience of these systems and many of the issues which are discussed in other chapters in general terms appear here in a more practical and specific context. Issues such as the balance between improvement and account-ability, the relationship between quality issues and other factors affecting higher education, the relationship between quality as-sessment and institutional change, and the implications for the locus of power and decision-making in higher education, are all raised in the accounts of institutional experiences which follow.

The Swedish University of Uppsala, the Danish University of Aalborg and the Australian University of Monash have all been exposed to the quality assessment requirements of their various national agencies. At Uppsala, the university was required by the Swedish national body (at the time, the Universities' Chancellor's office) to initiate quality evaluation although the national body was not prescriptive about the form that such evaluation should take. In the case of Aalborg, departments are subject to national reviews undertaken by the Centre for Evaluation and Quality Assessment but commissioned by subject 'councils' on behalf of the ministry. Monash had been subject to a form of institutional audit undertaken by the Committee for Quality Assurance in Higher Education (now disbanded), the results of which linked to funding decisions made by the federal government.

These are three different universities in countries with different traditions of higher education, with different and changing meth-ods of political steerage, and with very different approaches to external quality assessment at a national level. Therefore, their experiences provide us with some useful indications of the extent to which generalisations about the impact of external quality processes on institutions are possible and how much depends on context and institutional and national circumstances.

In his chapter, Engwall describes how Uppsala University responded to the requirement from the Chancellor's office to introduce quality evaluation. Uppsala is Sweden's oldest university, a prestigious institution with powerful faculties. It is perhaps not surprising, therefore, that the main work of responding to the requirements of the Chancellor's office was undertaken within the faculties, nor that the faculties responded to these requirements in quite different ways. An understanding of the impact of quality assessment at Uppsala, therefore, is primarily a story of what happened in the faculties.

A somewhat contrasting experience is described by Rasmussen in his chapter on Aalborg University. For Aalborg, the results of national subject reviews are contained in system-wide reports which are then considered by the commissioning subject councils at a national level. Arising out of a review of history, a recommendation was made for the history course at Aalborg to be closed down. The grounds for the recommendation appear to be complex and largely unrelated to quality considerations; and in any case the recommendation was eventually rescinded. Nevertheless, the Aalborg experience is a reminder that the impact of quality assessment can in some cases be through decision-making outcomes at a national level.

The experience of Monash University, as described by Baldwin, appears to be of a strengthening of institutional-level authority as a result of recommendations made by the external assessment for greater centralisation through the introduction of new and more effective institutional procedures.

Common to all three universities is an increase in the attention given to teaching and learning issues, involving more time and resources devoted to internal quality assurance matters. All three authors are fairly positive about the benefits to their universities of this.

The university experiences described in these three chapters were case studies for the international project 'Quality Assessment, Quality Management and the Decision-Making Process' which was described by Shah in Chapter 14. For the main part of this project, around 40 other universities from different parts of the world are preparing similar case studies. The results of these studies should provide us with a much fuller picture of the nature and the scale of the impact on higher education institutions of external quality assessment.

Finally, it should be noted that in only one of the cases described in these three chapters has the national quality assurance system remained unchanged since the institutional case studies were prepared. There is an instability in current national arrangements for quality assurance in many countries which suggests that the issues and debates contained within the various contributions to this book are far from resolved.

Chapter 15

A Swedish Approach
to Quality in Higher Education
The Case of Uppsala University

Lars Engwall

Introduction

Quality management and quality assessment in the modern sense are fairly recent features of the Swedish system for higher education. Although external evaluations of research in the natural sciences were started in the 1970s (see e.g. Natural Science Research Council (NFR) 1981), even spreading to other areas as well (see e.g. Engwall 1992 and Öhngren 1994), they have been less common in higher education. However, it should be added that local student evaluations have a long tradition, although it was not until the early 1990s that government policy started explicitly to include quality management and quality assessment as strategic features of educational policy. The story that can be told from the Swedish scene is therefore rather short. It is also a story characterised by instability, due to changes in the political power in Sweden.

The present paper starts with a brief summary of the Swedish system for higher education, followed by a look at the general structure of the system and a description of the development of the governance structures. It is against this background that the quality activities at Uppsala University will be focused, with a description first of the local governance structure and then of the organisation of the quality work.

The Swedish system for higher education

The general structure

In the academic year 1993/94 Sweden had 73 institutions for higher education. However, only one-sixth of these (12) had regular resources for research. The rest were regional university colleges (18), art and music colleges (9), schools for the nursing profession (29) and theological colleges (5). (This information on the present state of the system is based on the annual report for universities and university colleges (Årsrapport för universitet and högskolor 1993/94). In the figure for the university colleges the education provided on Gotland has been included, although the institute is not formally a university college.) Among the institutions with regular resources for research, six are universities. They are, in the order in which they were founded: Uppsala, Lund, Stockholm, Göteborg, Umeå and Linköping. In addition there are six other institutions with research providing a professional education: Karolinska Institutet (a medical school in Stockholm), the Royal Institute of Technology, Chalmers Institute of Technology, the Stockholm School of Economics, the University College of Luleå, and the Swedish Agricultural University. With the exception of the private Stockholm School of Economics and the recently privatised Chalmers Institute of Technology, these institutions are run by the state. (In 1994 Chalmers Institute of Technology was turned into a semi-private organisation, after part of the resources from the wage-earner funds had been transferred to a foundation to finance Chalmers. Its mission is governed by a contract with the Ministry of Education.) This is also the case for the 17 university colleges and eight of the art and music colleges. The remaining 35 institutions are run by municipalities (27) or by foundations (8). Needless to say there are big variations between the more than 70 institutions of higher education. The old universities of Uppsala and Lund with a large number of different faculties and with student bodies corresponding to around 20,000 full-time students are at one extreme, and the small specialised colleges, like the University College of Opera in Stockholm with about 20 students, at the other.

Altogether there were 256,400 students in the system during the academic year 1993/94. Of these the majority, or 64 per cent, studied at the 12 institutions with regular research resources, while 26 per cent were students at the university colleges. Enrolment in the system as a whole has increased every year since 1986/87, with the growth in student numbers occurring particularly in the university colleges. However, this is not necessarily an indicator of student preferences, as access to higher education has been restricted by *numerus clausus* since the late 1960s. Student selection is based mainly on school grades, but a general aptitude test (*Högskoleprovet*, i.e. 'the university test') provides an alternative chance for predefined quotas of students. Entry requirements vary considerably between different types of education. As a result of great excess demand, some institutes take only top students. This is particularly the case for the professional schools like the schools of journalism and medicine.

The national governance structure

In the late 1960s a reform was introduced in the Swedish system for higher education, involving the standardisation of educational programmes throughout Sweden. The reasons for this were an ambition to achieve equivalent quality in all institutions, to facilitate movement between institutions and to provide 'the most adequate' education for different sectors of society. For this purpose national planning boards were created to co-ordinate and develop the different programmes. Resource allocation was originally based on the number of positions in a department, and later came to be linked to the number of incoming students.

Another effect of the university reform was a division between education and research. Resources were allocated by way of separate grants for the two tasks. However, even more important in this context was the introduction of lecturer positions to help professors to meet the expansion in student demand. The occupants of these lectureships were expected to teach full-time, and not to be involved in research. This arrangement with parallel career tracks has been repeatedly criticised by foreign evaluators (see e.g. Dixit, Honkapohja and Solow 1992, pp.145–158).

A few years ago the centralised system, which by the 1990s had been in operation for almost 25 years, was challenged by the centre-right government which took office in the early autumn of 1991. The new Minister of Education immediately set about initiating reforms. From the summer of 1992 Swedish colleges and universities were given greater freedom of operation. The new legislation governing higher education introduced far-reaching decentralisation, allowing each university and college to design its own programme. Universities could now also appoint their own professors. Part of the resource allocation began to be based on productivity.

The basic idea behind these changes was to introduce an element of competition between the institutions for teachers, students, resources and prestige. However, such competition requires some form of external assessment. The government therefore appointed a secretariat for evaluation, the director of which bore the title of Chancellor of the Universities and Colleges. After roughly one year the secretariat changed its name to the Office of the Chancellor (*the Kanslersämbetet or KÄ*).

This organisation has sought to initiate quality and evaluation programmes at all Sweden's universities and colleges. Each one has been asked to delegate a liaison officer. These representatives have met with *KÄ* staff members, who are responsible for groups of colleges and universities. In the first phase these *KÄ* staff members and their colleagues served as advisers. Later they were also expected to act as evaluators of the quality assurance efforts (cf. below). This latter arrangement was a result of a decision by the Resource Management Commission (*Resursberedningen*), which after lengthy negotiations arrived at a system whereby 5 per cent of the resources available for basic education would be allotted according to the institution's success in terms of the quality assurance. The system was planned to come into effect in 1995. However, the government that took office in the autumn of 1994 has decided not to adopt the system. It has even changed the system of governance for institutions of higher education by re-establishing a government authority (*Högskoleverket*) for this purpose, which started its operations on 1 July 1995. The former *KÄ* has become part of this new organisation and the former head of *KÄ* has been appointed chairman of the board.

It should be evident from what has been said above that the Swedish system of higher education and research has been going through a turbulent period. After decades of centralisation a new decentralised structure was introduced. Then, a few years later, a change in the political power meant that some of the reforms were abolished. The attitude of the new Minister of Education to quality issues has been uncertain. However, although he first labelled quality management as 'consultants' chatter' he has subsequently expressed a more positive view. However, the new government authority (*Högskoleverket*) will definitely be evaluating the quality work in all universities and university colleges over the next three year period. A pilot study was undertaken in the academic year 1994/95 and the first regular round will take place in 1995/96. Uppsala University will be among the institutions under scrutiny in this project.

Uppsala University

General information

Uppsala University is the oldest of the institutions for higher education in Sweden. Founded more than five hundred years ago, in 1477, it is in fact the oldest university in Northern Europe. However, it should be added that the activities of the university in the sixteenth century were limited. Reinauguration therefore took place four hundred years ago, in 1595. Seventy-three years later a second university was founded in Lund in southern Sweden. Uppsala and Lund then remained the only two Swedish universities until 1954, when the private university college in Göteborg was turned into a university.

Uppsala University is thus an institution with a long tradition which over the centuries has attracted a large number of students from all over Sweden. It offers a relatively full range of educational programmes with faculties of arts, theology, law, social sciences, medicine, pharmacy and natural sciences, and a teacher training programme. It does not have odontology or any programmes in the practising arts. On the other hand Uppsala University has the only faculty of pharmacy in Sweden.

The total number of students in 1993/94, measured as full-time equivalents, was 17,643. Of these almost two-thirds are below 25 years of age (Årsrapport 1994, Table 5). Their education and the research at the university required the equivalent of 4,544 full-time employees, of which about one-third were teachers (professors, lecturers, etc.) (Årsrapport 1994, Table 6). For the academic year 1995/96 the government allocated about SEK 900 million (approximately GBP 78 million) for the educational programmes, and a similar sum for regular research resources. Additional research resources will be obtained by applying to various research foundations.

Governance structure of the university

The top decision-making body of the university is the University Board (*Konsistoriet*). It is chaired by the Vice-Chancellor, who is appointed by the government for five years after an election procedure inside the university. Members of the board are of three kinds: seven representing the general public, three professors and two students. The representatives for the general public are appointed by the government, while the professors are elected inside the university. Student representatives are chosen by the Student Union. Local trade unions have the right to be represented by observers, who may also take part in the discussion.

The Board, which meets approximately once a month, essentially takes the overall long-term decisions for the university. The preparation for these decisions and their implementation is the responsibility of the Vice-Chancellor. The Administrative Director in charge of the University Administration works in close co-operation with the Vice-Chancellor. Other units associated with the Vice-Chancellor's office are the capital and property administration, the university library and the data centre; the task of the capital and property administration is to manage endowments to the university. A large part of these date from the seventeenth century, when the university received land grants from King Gustav II Adolf. Earlier the revenues from these assets were the main source of income for the university. To-day they account for a small percentage only.

Below the Vice-Chancellor the university organisation consists of the various faculties. These are headed by deans appointed by the Vice-Chancellor after elections among the members of their faculties. In order to deal with issues of concern to the Vice-Chancellor and the deans, the two parties meet regularly in the Council of Deans.

The deans chair the faculty councils, which consist mainly of elected teacher representatives and a few students; an earlier system with representatives for the general public was abolished a few years ago. The faculty councils take the overall strategic decisions on resource allocation and policy issues within the faculties. These decisions then have to be implemented by heads of departments (*prefekter*), who are normally appointed for three years. In addition to responsibility for day-to-day operations they also chair the department boards. Members of these are elected inside the departments.

Quality work at Uppsala University

Background

The various colleges and universities in Sweden have adopted different models in their quality work. This is only natural inasmuch as the institutions differ greatly, as has been made abundantly clear in discussions between the Chancellor of the Universities and Colleges and the appointed liaison officers. The course chosen at Uppsala was to appoint a Committee on the Quality and Evaluation of Education in the autumn of 1993. However, evaluation was nothing new to Uppsala University even before that date. For many years the university had central units for pedagogical projects and the competence-development of its staff. Course evaluations, too, had a long history in the university.

In the early 1990s the university administration initiated an evaluative project to prepare for the transition to new steering and financing systems. The appointment of a working group to evaluate progress to date was a natural step in this context. The working group, chaired by a professor of education, proposed changes in the university's statistical routines, measures to encourage evaluative activities at the departmental level, and the analysis of certain strategic variables. The group also drafted a proposal as to how a future organisation for evaluation and quality control might be organised. The comments submitted showed that whereas the faculties were favourable to the idea of working to ensure the quality of their work, they were clearly sceptical of the proposal to establish an organisational unit charged with monitoring and improving the quality of education. In concrete terms, the results of the evaluation during the academic years 1991/92–1992/93 were a refinement of the university's statistics and a series of seminars for heads of department and directors of undergraduate studies on questions relating to evaluation.

The Quality Committee

The decision to form the above-mentioned Committee on the Quality and Evaluation of Education was taken by the university board in the spring of 1993. Composed so as to ensure a broad interface with the university, the committee includes representatives of the various faculties, two representatives of the student union and two members representing staff who are not attached to any specific faculty (Figure 15.1). (Originally the committee only included one student representative. In the autumn of 1994 an additional student joined the committee.) A natural division of labour has been adopted, whereby the faculty representatives serve as liaison between the committee and the respective faculties, the students communicate with student organisations, and the two other members focus on auxiliary services and teacher education, both of which transcend faculty bounds.

The main task of the committee is to assist the Office of the Vice-Chancellor with work relating to the quality and evaluation of education in the university. Such assistance was given, for example, when the Ministry of Education requested the submission of a programme for quality assurance (University of Uppsala 1993) and when the university submitted comments on the proposals of the Resource Management Commission. The committee has also been involved in judging various requests for the funding of projects designed to improve the quality of education, and with regard to planning the future organisation of quality efforts.

For the coming academic year the central role as a result of a decision of the University Board. It has been decided that 5 per cent of the grants given to the different faculties should be used for quality work. As a result of this decision the Quality Committee is conducting consultations with the Faculty Deans over the use of these resources. These discussions will also provide the basis for the self-evaluation part of the evaluation by *Högskoleverket* of the quality work at Uppsala University mentioned above.

In order to establish external points of reference the Vice-Chancellor has appointed, at the committee's request, an international advisory board. It consists of professors Erik Allardt, Helsinki; Tony Becher, Brighton; Helga Nowotny, Vienna; and Martin Trow, Berkeley. The task of this group is to follow the university's quality work and in this way provide ideas on possible improvements. The group has visited Uppsala twice so far.

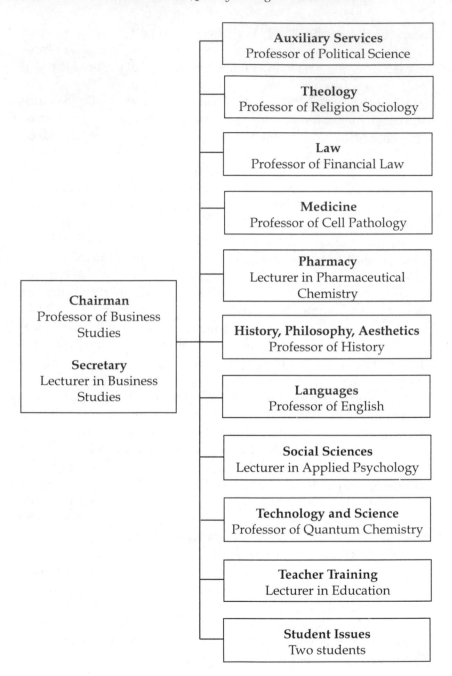

Figure 15.1: The Uppsala University Quality Committee

The philosophy of the committee

The basic idea behind the quality work at Uppsala is that evaluating what comes out of a system is not enough; it is equally important to analyse the conditions under which the outcomes are achieved and how the work is organised. Another important consideration is the need to evaluate results in a longer-term as well as a short-term perspective (see Figure 15.2).

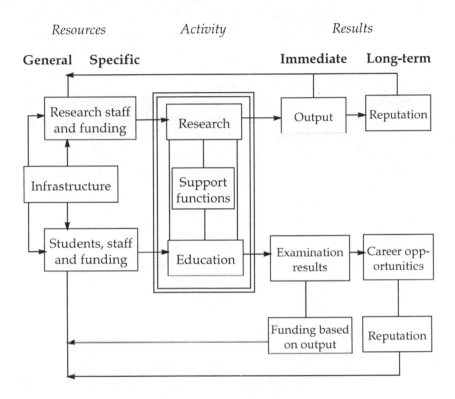

Figure 15.2 Basic model for the Quality and Evaluation Project at Uppsala University

In terms of resources it thus appears important to take into consideration not only the specific resources (staff, students and funding) but also the general resources (infrastructure of the university). With respect to activities it is crucial to consider the interplay between different tasks of the university staff (education, research and support functions). Immediate results in terms of research output and examination results provide the basis not only for funding in the short run but also for long-term reputation and the university's attraction for students and financiers.

Another point of departure for the committee's work is a conviction that quality is best assured, and evaluations have the greatest effect, when the activity is well-established locally. The activities of the Quality Committee have therefore been presented in a variety of contexts: to the deans, to the heads of departments, to the University Board and in the staff magazine.

However, at the same time it is also of the utmost importance to convey the message that quality work is an inescapable activity in a modern university. This was also the theme for the second publication from the Quality Committee, which was distributed to key persons at various levels in the university in the autumn of 1994. By way of introduction this publication summarised some of the arguments behind quality work. It was pointed out that quality development requires open and systematic self-criticism and that this is particularly needed at a time when rapid advances in knowledge are taking place. It was also stressed that the university needs a joint quality development programme:

> The need for a concerted approach to quality issues…stems from our mutual dependence in the face of outside appraisal of our activities, and from the importance of an effective exchange of ideas and initiatives between the different parts of the university.

> It is Uppsala University in its entirety that may be rewarded or penalised via the funding system. In this context it is undeniably true that a chain can be no stronger than its weakest link… Just as one success story is a boost to us all, so too are we dragged down by shortcomings and mistakes, in whatever part of the University they occur (University of Uppsala 1994, p.8).

The joint programme, it is argued, has to be based on a dialogue between various actors. Among them students play a particularly important role. In this context the committee declared the importance of regarding students not as customers but as 'co-workers':

> The tendency to view students as customers, which has become widespread in recent times, must be resisted in whatever form it assumes. The role of students in shaping

the education they receive must not be reduced to that of passively absorbing knowledge and subsequently, if it suits them, moving on to the next education provider. The Swedish tradition of students playing an active part in improving the quality of teaching is one that better befits a university (ibid., p.10).

Finally, it should be stressed that the committee is a relatively independent body in relation to the Vice-Chancellor's Office and to his administration. Although the members of the committee have been appointed by the Vice-Chancellor, the committee does not constitute his 'extended arm' but an intermediary with a relatively open mandate between the central administration and the faculties.

Quality development in the different faculties

The approach chosen for tackling quality issues at Uppsala University implies that faculties and departments are expected to find the most appropriate organisation for their quality work. In a survey during the spring of 1994 it was found that many faculties had chosen to create special working groups. This study also indicated certain variations between these. Special working groups have been set up by the language section, the faculty of social sciences and the faculty of science and technology. Their tasks vary somewhat. In the language section the group:

> has been entrusted with encouraging and supporting the departments in their quality work, for example by arranging meetings of directors of undergraduate studies to discuss quality development and follow-up, taking section-wide initiatives on teaching methods, and organising training seminars for the section's teaching staff. The group also has a mandate to propose models for self-assessment and quality assurance, including methods for evaluating entire one-term courses and shorter modules, and to promote external evaluation of the section's departments, for example by means of peer reviews. In addition, it is expected to identify any problem areas and recommend suitable action (University of Uppsala 1994, pp.22–23).

In the faculty of social sciences the group has 'arranged a conference, for all the faculty's directors of undergraduate studies, on teacher development, student recruitment and the link between undergraduate education and the employment market'. And in the faculty of science and technology the specially appointed group has been asked 'to find out what 'quality' actually entails, in undergraduate academic education in general and within science and technology in particular'. It has also 'been entrusted with drafting a quality-based system of resource allocation, reflecting the principle that merit should be rewarded' (ibid., 1994).

In the two above-mentioned faculties certain other steps have also been taken. The faculty of social sciences has allocated SEK 1 million for quality projects, and the faculty of science and technology 'has drawn up a programme for change, based on an earlier list of 117 points aimed at ensuring the further development of the Faculty' (ibid., 1994).

The Faculty of theology has chosen not to set up any special group. Its philosophy has been that quality issues should be an integrated part of normal responsibilities. However, it does not exclude the possibility of establishing such a group in the future, since 'there is a risk that long-term quality development could be overshadowed by more pressing day-to-day issues' (ibid., 1994).

Needless to say these different solutions to quality management are not final. Many measures were taken just a few years ago in response to government signals of a quality bonus and to the activities of the University Quality Committee. The recent decision requiring 5 per cent of the grants to be used for quality improvements is very likely to influence future measures taken by the faculties (cf. above).

Areas of priority

Introduction

The above account of approaches to quality management in the different faculties is based on an inventory of the various faculties, made with a view to identifying problem areas and noting current activity and plans for quality assurance and evaluation. This inventory indicates that even though the faculties differ widely with respect to working conditions and the nature of the work they do, they nonetheless share many problems. Seven areas in particular proved to require special attention:

- departmental self-assessment

- departmental management
- conditions for students
- equal opportunities at the university
- the potential of information technology
- postgraduate research training
- international relations.

Since the committee regarded further work in these areas as a step towards achieving the university's priority goals and as a tool for the co-ordination of the university's quality and evaluation efforts, it has continued its work by making in-depth studies in these seven areas. Committee members have been working in pairs to prepare meetings of the committee and to follow up these meetings with publications in the series. So far reports have been published on departmental management, departmental self-assessment and conditions for students (University of Uppsala 1995a, 1995b, 1995c). Two additional publications are under way. They deal with postgraduate research training and international relations.

On the advice of one of the members of the International Advisory Board, Professor Martin Trow, particular attention has been devoted to the first two of the above-mentioned issues. In his own words, in a letter (4 November 1994) after the second visit of the International Advisory Board to Uppsala, he suggested that special consideration be given to:

> the governance arrangements, the way decisions are made in the university, especially in the light of the reforms in university governance initiated by the last government; and…the forms and procedures in place in the university for monitoring, assessing and improvement of the quality of academic work, as administered by the university itself.

Departmental self-assessment

In dealing with departmental self-assessment course evaluations and external follow-ups are important means. On the subject of *course evaluations* the students expressed very clear views:

> Course evaluations provide one of the best opportunities for students to influence the education they receive. […] A university cannot develop and flourish if the views and perspectives of its students are not integrated into the evalu-

ation process, e.g. by means of course evaluations (University of Uppsala 1995(c), pp.12–13).

The views of the departments and faculties are more varied. A number of more or less formalised systems are in operation. The faculty of medicine has established a course evaluation centre, and evaluates all courses. As a result 'staff in charge of courses are then informed how their own courses have been assessed in relation to others, both in general terms and as regards specific issues such as supervision of students, small-group tuition etc.'. Similarly the faculty of pharmacy has long had close co-operation with its students in evaluating all courses. However, in recent years response rates have been somewhat worrying.

Another faculty where course evaluation is a standard procedure is the faculty of law. There it has been considered particularly important in view of the restructuring of the Master of Law programme. The evaluation is undertaken with the help of a standard form for all courses in the programme.

Scepticism towards course evaluations is more noticeable in the faculty of arts and in the teacher training programme:

> Several departments in the historical-philosophical section consider course evaluations in their present form to be of limited use. Response rates are often low, and students' perceptions of course quality are not always particularly mature: often an entertaining lecturer is rated more highly than one with an analytical approach.

> Within the section for teacher education, course evaluations used to be regarded as being of fairly limited value. One explanation for this may be that they were rarely related to other information about entire programmes or specific aspects of them, and thus produced fragmentary knowledge which staff were unable to use (ibid., pp.12–13).

However, in the language section department boards have adopted evaluation programmes. Lecturers are required to undertake student evaluations after each course module is completed, and to summarise the results in a report to the director of undergraduate studies.

Regarding *external evaluations*, the survey of the faculties referred to several such activities. Examples are:

- an evaluation of the faculty of science and technology by a group of Nobel Laureates

- evaluations of the MSc and University Certificate programmes in pharmacy
- in the language section national tests are used. In addition reviews by peers from other universities have been undertaken.

Efforts in the historical-philosophical section to set up joint examination with other institutions, however, have so far been in vain.

Despite the efforts for self-evaluation described above, it seems to be an urgent task for the Quality Committee to increase such activities, in particular the comparisons with other comparable institutions. A basis for such projects has been provided by the committee in a recent publication on self-evaluation (University of Uppsala 1995b), which presents both the scientific foundations for such evaluations and a case study demonstrating how they can be carried out.

Departmental management

On *departmental management* the inventory pointed out the need for improvement. The views of the faculties can be exemplified by the faculty of science and technology's submission to the Quality Committee, which suggested that 'many departments have now become overgrown and are performing rather poorly, partly owing to inadequate management'. Further it expressed the view that:

> management at the departmental and faculty levels must be more subject to evaluation and more accountable than it has been up to now: 'If staff lack confidence in their management, they will feel less enthusiastic and less inclined to make an extra effort'. Furthermore, communication between managers and other staff needs to be improved. It is important to inform staff about what is being planned and what decisions already taken will mean in practice.

A publication from the Quality Committee (University of Uppsala 1995a) discussed this issue further and provided a platform for future work. It stressed the importance of paying attention to the distinctive character of universities and the special requirements of university management. It also discusses the meaning of academic leadership, the recruitment of leaders and the working conditions of department heads. This publication is now being followed up by a study of a selection of departments in the univer-

sity. The hope is that this project will provide the basis for constructive reforms.

Conditions for students

As regards conditions for students, four issues were found to be of
particular importance: the working environment, the linking of
undergraduate teaching to research, third-term courses and teaching staff. It is concluded that 'ensuring a good environment...is a
crucial responsibility of the university, and an important factor in
ensuring the quality of the education it provides'. It is also found
'that the link between teaching and research could be significantly
developed'. In this context the third-term courses provide a particular opportunity for Uppsala University with its heavy emphasis on research. An example of how to handle this is provided by
the language section, which 'has set aside project funds to co-ordinate the development of a new type of undergraduate dissertation'. This implies that:

> supervisors at different language departments are working
> together to elaborate suitable forms for such dissertations,
> attaching equal weight to language proficiency and theoreti-
> cal content. Striking a balance between proficiency in and
> general theoretical knowledge about the language studied is
> a problem specific to these departments.

On the subject of the teaching staff, several of the faculties have
discussed different types of training in teaching methods. One
example is a recently created education unit in the faculty of
medicine to implement change, follow-up and quality assurance,
and to provide courses in educational methods.

Another sign of a greater emphasis on teacher qualifications can
be seen in the measures taken in the faculties of social science,
pharmacy, and science and technology. For appointments in the
faculty of social sciences requirements regarding the documentation of teaching qualifications and experience have been made
more stringent. In the same vein the two other faculties have now
decided to attach greater weight to teaching and managerial qualifications in future appointment decisions.

Needless to say the question of the conditions for students is
likely to remain important. A contribution to future discussion and
action appears in a report produced by the two students in the

Quality Committee, which has just been published (University of Uppsala 1995c).

Equal opportunities

With respect to equal opportunities, it is generally a fact that the relatively equal gender balance at the undergraduate level is replaced by a predominance of men at the higher levels. For different reasons Uppsala University has a particularly low proportion of female professors: while the average for Sweden is 7–8 per cent, the figure at Uppsala is 3 per cent. Several steps are being taken in the different faculties to address this problem, for instance:

- the historical-philosophical section is taking measures to increase the number of female teachers and of works by women on the reading lists
- the faculty of law has adopted an equal opportunities plan
- the faculty of theology has made a long-term financial commitment to research on women and religion
- the faculty of social sciences has a special research fellowship in women's studies.

In addition, for a number of years the university has had a special committee dealing with equal opportunities issues. The Quality Committee has therefore found it appropriate to collaborate with this body on equal opportunities issues.

Postgraduate research training

Crucial problems in postgraduate research training, particularly in the 'soft sciences', are recruitment, admissions, supervision of students and completion rates. Several faculties have therefore taken steps to improve the efficiency of their research training programmes. The following measures are mentioned in the report:

- efforts being taken, for instance in the faculty of theology, to reduce the number of doctoral students working less than half-time
- new screening procedures, such as the use of a preparatory term and interviews

- a project in the historical-philosophical section to find ways of accelerating the rate at which postgraduate students complete their doctorates

- tutor and mentor systems in the faculty of theology and the historical-philosophical section

- more systematic range of courses in the faculty of pharmacy.

A report on issues and possible measures for improving the efficiency of postgraduate research training will be published during the autumn. Among other things it emphasises the crucial role of postgraduate research training for equal opportunities in the university. The report may be followed by a project in this area. It should also be noted that last year, at the suggestion of the Quality Committee, the university financially supported projects in the various faculties to improve the supervision of doctoral students.

Information technology

The Quality Committee has stressed the importance of exploiting information technology in the university's efforts to improve performance. Needless to say there are big variations between the faculties here. The faculty of science and technology is naturally the most advanced, but other faculties are making progress in their use of modern information technology for both research and educational purposes. A very important step has been the development of the university's computer network, which means that most employees now have access to electronic mail, world-wide web, the university library's electronic services and other literature searches. A project is now under way to link student accommodation to the university network.

The committee has devoted a seminar to information technology. This was followed by an official letter to the Vice-Chancellor of the university stressing the need for action. As a result a special group for information technology issues at the university has been created. However, it is the intention of the committee to check continuously that the university is maintaining appropriate standards in information technology.

International relations

International relations in education and research are an important way of assessing the activities of a university. It is therefore a great advantage for Uppsala University to have been involved for some time in different types of international exchange. Because of the university's research orientation, many of its employees take part continuously in international activities through guest appointments, publications and conference attendances. In this way university employees, and the university itself, obtain constant feedback on activities. Likewise a large number of visiting scholars from other countries add external perspectives.

However, it is not only in research that Uppsala University has a strong international orientation. Over recent decades the exchange of students in undergraduate and graduate programmes has been expanding rapidly. The university thus now has a great many agreements with its foreign counterparts. Some of these arrangements are at the university level but many others are between departments at Uppsala and their counterparts in other countries. In several instances these bilateral agreements are combined with arrangements within the European exchange programme ERASMUS (now SOCRATES) and the Nordic exchange programme NORDPLUS. In connection with these exchanges, the participating departments have started courses taught in English.

The department of business studies and the faculty of law have been particularly prominent in these exchanges. Their experiences so far seem to indicate that the education provided at Uppsala maintains a standard at least as high as that of their partners. Needless to say comparisons are rather difficult, due to differences in the systems. However, both incoming and outgoing exchange students seem generally satisfied with their experiences.

In connection with student exchange, the university also participates in the exchange of teachers. This provides yet another opportunity for obtaining feedback on the standards at Uppsala. It also provides information on alternative teaching methods.

It is the conviction of the committee that this international exchange is a valuable asset in the university's quality work. It is therefore extremely important that these programmes are maintained and developed.

Conclusions

It should be evident from this paper that the Swedish system for higher education has been and still is in a period of turbulence. After a long period of stability within a centralised system, where quality was assumed to be the same in all institutions, a market-oriented system was introduced in the early 1990s. This implied that output in terms of examination results was favoured. This in turn called for output control and the associated quality management. However, the means for achieving this quality control were not self-evident. After much debate it was decided that the institutions of higher education should be rewarded for their systems of quality assessment. The various institutions then chose their own solutions for achieving this. These are generally still in operation, although a change in government has cancelled the earlier decision to give the institutions a bonus on a basis of their quality work.

At Uppsala University the approach has been to appoint a Quality Committee with representatives from the various faculties. In view of the wide range of activities in the university this committee found it appropriate to adopt a decentralised way of working, i.e. to base the quality system on initiatives on the faculty and department levels rather than on central directives. However, it has also proceeded in dialogue with faculties, in the course of which seven areas of priority for future work have been identified: (1) departmental self-assessment, (2) departmental management, (3) conditions for students,(4) equal opportunities at the university, (5) the potential of information technology, (6) postgraduate research training, and (7) international relations. With the help of seminars and publications the committee has looked carefully at each of these areas. It is now planning various projects within them in order to improve the performance of the university. In order to stimulate research about universities as organisations, a special interdisciplinary seminar has been started.

The committee's work has met with varying degrees of enthusiasm. Several faculties have started ambitious projects. Most of these are projects initiated by individuals who had been eagerly awaiting an opportunity to discuss quality issues. Another aspect that should be considered in connection with the way quality projects are 'anchored' locally concerns the different departments' relations with other departments in the same discipline. Several participants have found it strange to be collaborating with rival departments in the quality project, inasmuch as they are competitors on the Swedish 'market'. The committee has responded to such sentiments by stressing the value of maintaining the greatest possible degree of openness within the project. It has argued that such openness will benefit both the project and the respective departments much more than if they were to try to keep their quality initiatives a 'business secret'.

As regards the long-term effects of the committee's work, it is difficult to make any predictions. So far, we can see that collaboration between departments has been a vital and highly productive feature of the project. In its present form the project may be considered a comprehensive effort to develop the organisation with a view to achieving better resource utilisation. As the initial enthusiasm dies down, it is important to maintain continued momentum.

The possibility that the project may have to pay greater attention to the constraints of available resources cannot be excluded. If and when this comes about, it will probably put a strain on interdepartmental collaboration, unless the departments can reach consensus concerning a comprehensive rationale for the distribution of resources. Such a consensus is especially important in view of the fact that there is an inherent contradiction between schemes aimed at raising quality and others aimed at generating a greater volume of resources. In the former case it is natural to highlight shortcomings and point out the need for improvement, whereas in the latter it is often more expedient to mention only merits and past successes. If the documents emanating from the evaluation adopt the rhetoric of budgetary documents, they are not likely to be very productive.

Postscript

The above text was finished in early October 1995. Since then the quality work at Uppsala University has been dominated by the preparations for an evaluation by the National Agency of Higher Education (*Högskoleverket*). This project is part of a larger commission to be undertaken by the agency, to evaluate the standards of quality work at the universities and university colleges over a three-year period. In a first round Uppsala University and five other institutions were selected for evaluation. The evaluation team for Uppsala consisted of the former Vice-Chancellor of Stockholm University (Chairman); the Dean of the Faculty of Odontology, Lund University; the Dean of the Faculty of Science, Göteburg University; the Director General of the Swedish National Board for Industrial and Technical Development; the Vice-Chairman of the National Swedish Union of Students; and a University Administrator from Lund University (Secretary).

At a first meeting in late November 1995 with the Chairman and Secretary of the team, it was decided that the university should deliver a self-evaluation report by mid-February 1996, that a site visit should take place in late April, and that a preliminary report from the team was to be presented in late May. In order to produce the self-evaluation report the Quality Group visited all the faculties during the autumn term. On the basis of these site visits and the collection of documents from the faculties, a first version of the self-evaluation report was drafted by the Quality Committee. This draft was sent to all heads of departments, deans, directors in the university administration, the Vice-Chancellor and members of the University Board. After feedback, the report was completed and submitted together with eight folders containing supplementary material.

The site visit lasted for three days, during which the evaluation team visited all the faculties. At each one they had separate discussions with deans and administrators, a selection of directors of studies, and a number of students. The site visit also included the university administration, the university library, the Student Union and the Vice-Chancellor's Office. On the basis of observations made during the site visit and of the submitted material, the evaluation team delivered a preliminary report four weeks after their visit.

The evaluation report contained three parts: (1) a description of the work undertaken by the evaluation team; (2) assessments of the quality work at the university overall, and in the different units; (3) conclusions. Essentially the report endorsed the Uppsala approach to the handling of quality issues. However, it also indicated certain measures which could appropriately be taken by the different faculties and the Quality Group. In conclusion the report thus indicated areas which the evaluation team considered to be particularly worth attending to in the future work, namely relations between the university and the society at large, the systematic exchange of ideas within the university, and further action within the identified areas of priority.

A week after its delivery, the preliminary report was discussed at a meeting attended by the Chairman and the Secretary of the evaluation team, representatives of the National Agency of Higher Education, the Vice-Chancellor, directors of the university administration and the Quality Group. At this meeting the representatives of Uppsala University expressed a fundamentally positive attitude towards the report although a number of points were also raised, particularly regarding the description of the contacts between the university and society at large. After the meeting the report will be finally adjusted and made public by the National Board of Higher Education. The task of the Quality Group will then be to start a new round of interactions with various members of the University, in order to enhance quality. The endorsement of the evaluation team regarding the general direction of the quality work and their suggestions for further action will certainly both be important to these future activities.

References

Årsrapport för Universitet and Högskolor 1993/94 (Annual Report for Universities and University Colleges), Stockholm: Verket för högskoleservice.

Dixit, A.K., Honkapohja, S. and Solow, R.M. (1992) 'Organization of research.' In L. Engwall (ed) *Economics in Sweden*. London: Routledge.

Engwall, L. (1992) (ed) *Economics in Sweden*. London: Routledge.

Uppsala Univeristy (1993) *Kvalitetsutvecklingsprogram* [Quality Development Programme], Meddelanden från Kvalitetsgruppen 1 [Reports from the Quality Committee 1], Uppsala University.

Uppsala University (1994) *Uppsala måste bli ännu bättre!* [Uppsala has to Become Even Better!], Meddelanden från Kvalitetsgruppen 2 [Reports from the Quality Committee 2], Uppsala University.

Uppsala University (1995a) *Ledningen av universitetsinstitutioner* [The Management of University Departments], Meddelanden från Kvalitetsgruppen 3 [Reports from the Quality Committee 3], Uppsala University.

Uppsala University (1995b) *Självvärdering – vad ska det tjäna till?* [Self-Evaluation – What is the Use?], Meddelanden från

Kvalitetsgruppen 4 [Reports from the Quality Committee 4], Uppsala University.

Uppsala University (1995c) *Studenterna i kvalitetsarbetet* [The Students in the Quality Work], Meddelanden från Kvalitetsgruppen 5 [Reports from the Quality Committee 5], Uppsala University.

Natural Science Research Council (1981) *International Evaluations of Research Projects Supported by the Swedish Natural Science Research Council. Summary of Reports, Achievements and Criticisms, 1977–1980*. Stockholm: Swedish Natural Science Research Council.

Öhngren, B. (1994) *Utvärdering av Svensk Forskning Inom Humaniora och Samhällsvetenskap. Kommentarer Kring HSFR:s utvärderingsprogram 1985–1992*. Stockholm: HSFR (MIMEO).

University of Uppsala (1995) *Katalog 1995. Nämnder, institutioner, anställda m m* (Catalogue 1995, Committees, Departments, Employees, etc.). Uppsala: Uppsala University.

Chapter 16

A Danish Approach to Quality in Higher Education
The Case of Aalborg University

Palle Rasmussen

In this paper I look at the impact of external quality control in one institution, Aalborg University in Denmark. This is seen against the background of the development and present state of external evaluation in Danish higher education. The paper was written as a pilot study for a project on 'Quality Management, Quality Assessment and the Decision-Making Process', which has been initiated by the programme of Institutional Management in Higher Education (IMHE) of the OECD.

The political and institutional context
International level: rise of the evaluative state
External evaluation and quality control has spread rapidly in the higher education systems of most Western European countries during the last decade. This is a fact reflected in the everyday experience of people working in higher education, but it is also documented in cross-national analyses. External evaluations of study programmes and departments have certainly been used earlier, e.g. for handling budgetary cuts and staff reductions during the eighties, but they have now been generalised and have acquired a more strategic function.

This is not a development confined to higher education, or even to education. The forms of controlling public activities and institutions are changing in many areas, and systematic procedures for evaluation are increasingly being used as an integral element in public policy. This represents a shift towards monitoring the 'output' rather than the 'input' side of policies, and is accompanied by the strengthening of new competences and discourses. Whereas public policy was earlier dominated by juridical discourse, other kinds of social science discourse (e.g. sociology) have now gained a definite foothold.

In an early but still valid analysis of these phenomena, Guy Neave (1988) summarised these developments as the 'rise of the evaluative state'. This term certainly seems relevant to the situation in Danish higher education.

National level: developments in Danish higher education

The development in Danish higher education since the mid-eighties is marked by some distinctive changes in policy and discourse. These may be characterised as three interrelated movements.

First, a movement *from participatory institutional democracy to legitimate leadership*. During the 1970s and 1980s, management and decision-making within Danish universities were regulated by an Act of Governance introduced to democratise the university power structure, not least in response to demands made by the student movement. Power lay mainly in the hands of the scientific and teaching staff (tenured professors) rather than in the hands of small groups of professional leaders or senior professors. There was a considerable amount of organised student influence. This meant that many different groups, among students as well as teachers, had a good chance of having their criticisms and demands heard and negotiated. The act on university governance has been an object of much political controversy, and in 1993 the liberal-conservative government finally succeeded in introducing significant changes. The system of elected leadership has been preserved, but election periods have been made longer, and authority has been placed more clearly with individual leaders on different levels, rather than with commissions. The overall authority of the rector has also been strengthened.

Second, there has been a movement *from planned economy to quality management*. During the 1970s, higher education was increasingly characterised by centralised distribution and control of resources on a national level, including the study programmes to be maintained at each institution, the number of students to be admitted to each institution, and the allocation of resources for the study programmes. The allocation of resources was made mainly on the basis of each institution's recent activities, e.g. the number of students passing exams. As a result of this, the institutions of higher education paid a good deal of attention to their internal efficiency. It was increasingly argued, however, that efficiency was not identical to quality. For instance, some years ago internal memos from a department head at the Technical University of Denmark caused a public debate on this issue. The memos could be interpreted as suggesting that teachers should lower the demands on students in order to have more students pass exams, and thus secure the allocation of more resources to the university. The centralised resource system has also been criticised by the universities, because it left little room for institutional priorities and strategies, and because it made institutions vulnerable to budgetary cuts dictated by fiscal policy.

Partly in response to such criticisms procedures for resource allocation have been undergoing changes. While institutions earlier had to follow centrally-decided norms in the distribution of resources (e.g. national resource standards for different study areas, and a balance between resources for research and for teaching), institutions are now allowed a much more free hand in the use of grants. The universities have been promised (through parliamentary settlement) more long-term stability in the size of their grants. It is intended that the availability of resources will be less dependent on the productivity (in terms of number of exams) of the individual institutions, and also less vulnerable to general public sector cuts. The government has emphasised, however, that the increased institutional freedom should be used to increase the quality of study and teaching. To support and secure this the Ministry of Education has established a formal system for evaluating the quality of higher education. An independent evaluation centre has been set up, and the ministry has announced that all major higher education study programmes are to be evaluated at five year intervals.

Third, and at a more general level, Danish higher education seems to be moving *from German to American ideas about universities*. This may be seen for instance in the introduction of the bachelor level in Danish universities, and the official policy of differentiating strongly between the bachelor, the master and the graduate levels of study. It has also become official policy, especially under the conservative-liberal government of the late 1980s, to promote a 'free market' within higher education, with a stronger element of competition among educational institutions.

But although the inspirations and the aims of policy have changed considerably, Danish higher education is still very different from American higher education, not least because it is funded almost exclusively by direct state grants. In a recent analysis of higher education policy in Denmark, Bache and Maassen (1994) found that while the Ministry of Education had taken a number of steps to increase institutional self-government, the institutions and their staff still felt subjected to a centralised regulation from above. Bache and Maassen offer several explanations for this, but seem to overlook the obvious one: that centralised control is still a very real element in Danish higher education. The greater institutional freedom allowed in the intake of students, the use of resources, and other areas, must be seen against a background of harsh reforms of educational structures. In the years around 1990 central educational authorities decided that no study programmes could have a duration of more than five years, demanded specific forms of examination and grading for all study programmes, and dictated that all programmes should be adjusted to a bachelor/master structure. The freedom left for institutions under these conditions is in fact limited, especially if the institutions try to uphold the previous standards in the study programmes. Also, the Ministry of Education continues to control which study programmes can be taught at which institutions.

The persistence of a strong element of central control may reflect the fact that the Ministry of Education has built up a 'control culture', which changes slowly. But at a more fundamental level, institutions which are funded exclusively by public grants will often encounter bureaucratic control.

So, although some barriers have been moved and new strategies are being pursued, Danish higher education has still not definitively moved towards the 'American' model. Rather, it has become an uneasy mix of principles from different models.

The institutional level: Aalborg University

Aalborg University is the most recent Danish university, established in 1974. Together with Roskilde University Centre, which is two years older, Aalborg University was the product of an expansive and innovative strategy for higher education. This aimed at:

- establishing new institutions of higher education to cope with rapidly rising educational aspirations of young people

- integrating higher vocational education (which had previously been located at separate institutions) with the traditional university subjects and faculties. In this way it was hoped to make more efficient use of resources and to avoid premature specialisation among students

- renewing the organisation of research, teaching and learning at the university. This reflected ideas about interdisciplinarity and problem-centred learning which were at the time being promoted by agencies like CERI, but it was also an attempt to break away from elitist conceptions of higher education.

The result was the so-called 'university centre' model, in which study programmes in different areas and at different levels are tied together in one institution. This principle had a strong impact at Aalborg University. Study programmes like engineering, business studies, business languages and social work, which are elsewhere taught in specialised schools of higher education, account for roughly half the students (and more than half the teaching staff) of the university. This has probably contributed to the strong pragmatic element in the internal culture of the university.

Studies start with a common 'foundation year' programme (one for each faculty), and only in the second year do the students choose more specialised study programmes (Rasmussen 1991). All studies more or less adhere to a common pedagogical model emphasising students' independent work. Time is generally divided equally between seminars and lectures on the one hand and project work done in groups of students on the other (Kjersdam and Enemark 1994). Departments have an interdisciplinary profile, and the organisation of teaching often rests on a high degree of co-operation between academic staff from different departments.

The innovative educational and pedagogical model became a key element in the 'identity' of Aalborg University. It is often referred to in staff and student discussions, and it is invariably mentioned in public presentations of the university. Still there have been noticeable changes, especially in the academic staff's attitude towards teaching. During the first years of the university's existence, teachers were very much preoccupied with introducing and developing interdisciplinarity and project study. Frequent discussions and adjustments meant that there was a strong, if informal, element of internal quality control and assessment. Gradually, however, teaching has become more systematic, partly because stable forms of good practice have evolved, but also because staff interest focuses more and more on research.

The shifting priorities of academic staff are a logical development, because a visible and recognised research effort is still the main criterion of academic status, both for institutions and individuals. While the establishment of Aalborg University focused on teaching, its consolidation must focus on research. This has not led to a general retreat from the innovative educational principles, but it means that educational quality is less easily secured through informal procedures. Around 1980 many students reacted to this situation by demanding formal procedures for internal quality control, especially evaluations of teaching and pedagogical courses for teachers. These demands were also encouraged by the educational rhetoric of the liberal-conservative government, which emphasised the student's role as user or consumer.

Quality assurance

The development of quality control in Danish education

There are few examples of systematic evaluation activities in Danish higher education until the mid-1980s. By this time, the Ministry of Education was developing a more comprehensive planning of higher education, and this implied evaluation procedures. One example of this was the 'institutional visit' procedure, which meant that a delegation from the Ministry of Education visited the main institutions of higher education. Before the visit, each institution was asked to prepare a document on its situation, problems and priorities. After the visit, the representatives from the ministry wrote up the results in a report, which also included recommendations, e.g. on the closure or expansion of specific study programmes.

In the late 1980s, the advisory bodies in higher education, especially the so-called educational councils, began to use evaluations of institutions or study programmes as part of the basis for their recommendations. This was not a systematic practice; it was mostly used to support decisions on whether newly established study programmes (e.g. programmes in business law studies) should be discontinued or made permanent. The evaluation reports were of varying quality.

In 1988 the Danish Ministry of Education established a quality development project. This can be seen as an attempt to focus thinking and activity at all levels of the educational system on the theme of quality. The project turned out to be a specific kind of quality assessment, namely evaluations of individual subjects at different levels of education. For instance, a recent report evaluates the teaching of geography in the Danish educational system. It describes and discusses the form and content of geography in the primary school, in the different forms of general secondary school, in the teachers' colleges and in the universities. Criticism and recommendation tend to focus on coherence within the subject, through clearly defined transitions from one level to another, through identical content in primary schooling and teacher training etc. Almost all school subjects have by now been scrutinised in similar reports; and almost all the report-producing commissions have argued that 'their' subject should have more resources and more teaching time to function properly. The quality development project addresses itself to primary and secondary education rather than to higher education.

Around 1990, many higher education institutions also engaged in different forms of internal quality assessment on their own initiative. For instance, the Copenhagen Business School initiated regular course evaluations through questionnaires; Aalborg University undertook a broad survey of student satisfaction with study structures and teaching; and several institutions joined international collaboration on quality assessment, often through peer group procedures. The motivation for these activities was mostly defensive: the institutions wanted to demonstrate that they could manage quality assessment without interference 'from above'. But the evaluation activities were often fruitful.

In 1990 the Minister of Education announced his intentions to establish a national centre for quality assessment in higher education. Although the universities did not like the idea, the centre was established in 1992. Its work is described in more detail below. Since 1992 the question of quality control has mostly been linked to the work of the evaluation centre. However, one other development has occurred. In the three latest years, a major Danish newspaper has commissioned an independent investigation (done by a private consultant firm) of the quality of the different universities and their major study programmes, and has published the results up to the deadline for study applications. An unofficial rating system for institutions has thus been established.

Internal quality assurance in Aalborg University

Like other Danish universities, Aalborg University has no strong tradition of formalised evaluation of courses or study programmes. Both teachers and students seem to have trusted the effect of informal contacts and feedback. Following the increased focus on quality control, more formal procedures are now being used in many study programmes, sometimes following guidelines laid down by study boards. The results are mostly used by the teachers themselves for improving the content and form of teaching.

At the central institutional level, Aalborg University's rector has been a strong proponent of the view that institutions should develop their own measures for quality assessment and quality development rather than depending on national assessments and the evaluation centre. During recent years the Ministry of Education has earmarked special funds for quality improvement, and the rectorate of Aalborg University have taken pains to channel a good deal of these funds into evaluation projects. Several study programmes, for instance humanist information science, have been evaluated. Some evaluations have focused on special features of the university, the integrated foundation year programmes and the project study method. In 1994 the rectorate also set up an educational development centre, with special responsibility for the pedagogical training of teachers, but also with a more general mission of quality development.

In sum, Aalborg University has made considerable efforts to evaluate its own teaching and study programmes. On the other hand, many members of the teaching staff do not engage in these activities, and even regard them with scepticism ('just another of the rector's ideas'). And the fact that all study programmes will have to produce self-assessment reports as part of external evaluations (see Section 3 below) makes it harder to define the rationale of internal evaluation projects.

External evaluation and the evaluation centre

As mentioned above, the Ministry of Education announced in 1990 its intentions to establish an independent agency for systematic evaluation of higher education. The idea met some institutional and political resistance, but the decision was confirmed, and the 'Danish Centre for Quality Assurance and Evaluation of Higher Education' (which I refer to as 'the evaluation centre') commenced its work in 1992. The centre has already finished 26 comprehensive evaluations of higher education study programmes, and expects to have evaluated all study programmes by 1999.

The establishment of the centre was closely connected to the work of the Committee of Chairmen of the Danish Educational Councils. The educational councils are advisory bodies within each of the major subject areas (humanities, social sciences etc.), and although their members are appointed individually by the Minister of Education, most of them have roots in the institutions of higher education. In some ways the councils function as buffers between the ministry and the institutions. Towards the end of the 1980s, when quality control became a major policy issue, the educational councils began to experiment with systematic evaluation of disciplines across institutions. And the chairmen of the educational councils produced a report on general questions of quality development and quality control. The work of the chairmen was mainly inspired by the forms of quality monitoring institutionalised in the Netherlands, and the report contained a separate presentation of the 'Dutch model'. While the Standing Conference of Rectors (composed of leaders from the universities and other institutions of research-based higher education) generally opposed the establishment of an independent evaluation agency, the chairmen of educational councils supported it. In the end, the committee of chairmen came to function as the board of the evaluation centre, and Christian Thune, who had chaired the committee of chairmen around 1990, became director of the centre.

This strong link to the educational councils helps to explain the fact that the work of the evaluation centre focuses not on institutions, but on subject-defined study programmes across institutions.

The evaluation centre also has roots in the policy of promoting an 'open market for education', launched around 1990 by Mr Bertel Haarder, who was at the time Minister of Education in the liberal-conservative government. The idea was to give students more freedom to choose between institutions. This would lead to increased competition between institutions, and the government assumed that quality would be a key criterion in students' choice. Market mechanisms would then force institutions to improve the quality of their study programmes and teaching. In this perspective, an important purpose of an independent evaluation agency is to inform students' choices with authoritative knowledge on the quality of study programmes and institutions. The 'open market' programme actually states that evaluations are to serve as 'consumer guidance for students'. It would seem a hard task to combine this kind of consumer guidance with well-documented and comprehensive evaluations, and this aspect has in fact been downplayed in the actual work of the centre.

The evaluation centre is an independent agency funded by the Ministry of Education. The purpose of the centre is:

- to initiate evaluation of higher education in Denmark
- to develop appropriate evaluation methods
- to inspire and guide institutions in matters of evaluation and quality development
- to compile national and international experiences on evaluation and quality development in higher education.

The ministry decided from the outset that the centre should evaluate education and teaching, not research. Because of the close interaction of research and teaching in universities, this is in fact a difficult mandate. Evaluation is not voluntary. The institutions of higher education are obliged to submit their activities to evaluation. It should be noted, however, that the institution itself has no authority to request evaluations. This authority rests with the ministry and the educational councils. These have formulated a policy of cyclic evaluation of study programmes. All major study programmes are to be evaluated before 1998, after which time a new cycle will start. As mentioned above the centre's evaluation activities focus on all study programmes within a specific discipline. The centre does not evaluate whole institutions (except in cases where an institution is identical with a study programme, as for instance the Danish School of Pharmaceutical Studies). This means that evaluations often have a strong element of comparing practice at different institutions.

The evaluations of the centre follow (with some minor variations) a standard method. This method is an attempt to draw on various kinds of documentation and assessment, and integrate them in a robust framework. The method contains the following phases:

(i) *The planning phase*, in which a steering committee and a project secretariat are established. The secretariat is responsible for the actual work, and is staffed by the centre. The steering committee usually has four members, of which one acts as Chairman. The committee members, and especially the Chairman, should be '...perceived by all concerned by the evaluation as credible and authoritative' (Thune 1995, p.9), but on the other hand they must of course be independent of the study programmes being evaluated. As the evaluations usually cover all national study programmes within a given subject, the recruitment of relevant members for the steering committees is not an easy task.

(ii) *The self-assessment phase*, in which each institution assesses its own study programme on the basis of a general set of questions formulated by the centre and the steering committee. Much of the self-assessment work is descriptive, but the institutions are also asked to define their own goals for the study programme, and to point out strengths, weaknesses, and possibilities for improvement in the study programme. In the centre's own words, 'The self-assessment is the standard against which the institution can measure itself. It provides a framework for building up a definition of quality, it helps the institution decide how far it is achieving its strategic mission and goals, and it allows it to build an action plan for development' (Thune 1995, p.11).

(iii) *The survey phase*, in which the experiences and opinions of
different groups of users are documented through
surveys. Three groups of users are most often
investigated: students, recent graduates, and employers
of graduates from the study programme. In this phase the
centre also asks for a report from the group of external
examiners attached to the study programme. The external
examiners are in fact obliged to comment on the quality
of programmes in annual reports, but the centre may also
obtain an *ad hoc* report for the evaluation.

(iv) *The visiting panel phase*, in which each institution involved
is visited. The visiting party consists of the Chairman and
perhaps other members of the steering committee,
supplemented by experts in the subject under evaluation.
The experts should have a 'thorough understanding and
knowledge of the subject matter under scrutiny' (Thune
1995, p.12), and they represent an unbiased approach to
the subject. This points towards the use of non-national
experts. In order to avoid complicating language
problems, the centre has turned to using a mixture of
Danish and Nordic experts. The visiting party has had
the opportunity to read the self-assessment report, and
will use it as a starting point for further questions.

It is worth noting that the centre's description of phase four
has changed since the establishment of the centre. In
early presentations the 'visiting panel' phase was called
the 'peer review' phase. This change of terminology may
indicate that the centre now places less emphasis on the
competence and the legitimacy of peers, and more
emphasis on the steering committee.

(v) *The reporting phase*, where the steering committee writes
up the final report. The preparation for this usually
includes an evaluation conference of one day's duration,
where the steering committee presents preliminary
material for the report, and all parties involved take part
in the discussions. In the final report, the steering
committee summarises and draws on the material
produced in all phases of the evaluation. But the

committee itself has a clear responsibility for lines of argument, conclusions and recommendations.

The final report is submitted to the agency (most often an educational council) which has commissioned the evaluation. The evaluation centre itself has no responsibility for subsequent policy decisions or follow-up procedures. But if the report prompts institutions to start some kind of continuous quality monitoring, the evaluation centre may advise on this.

In my opinion, the evaluation centre has developed a professional and fairly convincing evaluation model, and is using it to produce a steady stream of evaluations. In this way, the centre is clearly fulfilling its explicit purpose. A more open question is whether the evaluation activity plays the expected role in higher education policy. In this context I see several problems.

(1) Follow-up procedures and policy consequences are not the responsibility of the centre, but they are nevertheless crucial to the usefulness of evaluation. In some cases the completed evaluations have prompted the educational councils and the ministry to make visible changes, but often the follow-up has been reduced to a formal demand that institutions should describe their efforts to implement the recommendations in the evaluation reports.

(2) It is clear that the evaluations do not give the 'consumer guidance' to students which Mr Haarder intended. Actually, it is hard to see how this could have been done. A related question is whether the evaluation reports provide the political decision-makers with a reliable source of information. This has yet to be seen.

(3) The evaluations are to make well-informed and neutral judgements on the quality of study programmes. However, because the focus is subject-defined study programmes across institutions, it is hard to avoid comparing institutions, which in turn makes it hard to avoid involvement with inter-institutional differences, conflicts and settlements. In this situation, the emphasis placed on the steering committee (which is not a group of peer reviewers, and whose authority is not

counterbalanced by the limited element of peer review) may undermine the neutrality of the evaluations.

Impact of external quality assessment at Aalborg University

The fact that external quality assessment in Danish higher education consists almost exclusively of cross-institutional evaluations of subject-defined study programmes means that the activities involve many institutions. Aalborg University has participated in or is currently engaged in about 15 external evaluations. In the next section of the paper I shall describe in some detail the process and content of two of these, in order to estimate their impact on internal structures, cultures and decision-making at Aalborg University. The two cases have been chosen because they were some of the first evaluations undertaken by the evaluation centre; both were completed during 1994. The fact that some time has passed since the completion should make it easier to obtain a balanced picture of the impact.

In presenting and discussing the evaluations, I rely mainly on two sources. One is the written reports from the evaluations (which contain summaries in English), the other is interviews with the persons who have had the main responsibility for Aalborg University's involvements in the evaluations, i.e. the heads of study for the two study programmes.

Framework for analysis

Institutions of higher education are complex organisations, and assessing the impact of specific interventions or policies is a difficult undertaking. It will seldom be possible to demonstrate clear-cut causal relationships, and in a limited study such as this the ambition must be humble. What I will try to do is to (a) locate changes which have probably been caused by external quality assessment, and (b) to classify these changes into different types.

In judging the probability that changes have been caused by the influence of external evaluations, there are some elementary criteria. The changes should generally occur after the evaluations, and the changes should concern areas and activities which have logical links with the issues treated in the evaluations. These criteria still leave the question of probability very open, and in practice I shall have to rely on the statements and interpretations of the actors involved, e.g. of the heads of study boards.

As to the types of changes, it seems reasonable to distinguish between different levels or areas of institutions. To limit the number of categories, I shall distinguish between:

- changes in *decision-making* and governance (e.g. the establishment of new committees, the discontinuation of old committees, the establishment of new chains of command)

- changes in the study *structure*, curriculum or resources of studies (e.g. the establishment of new study levels or new possibilities of study specialisation; the reduction of the number of external examinations, and the allotment of more teaching resources to specific subjects)

- changes in study and teaching *culture* (e.g. increasing student demands on the entertainment value of lectures; shifting of staff identification from teaching roles to research roles).

However, it is also necessary to distinguish between different 'channels', through which external evaluation may influence educational institutions. Some changes occur because the participation in evaluation makes them logical and desirable for the institutional actors, while other changes occur through policy interventions based on the outcomes of evaluation. I find it reasonable to distinguish between three channels of influence:

- influence through participation and consensus (e.g. when the local study board implements new and innovative teaching methods, because participation in the evaluation procedure has convinced the board and most teachers of the possibility and desirability of this)

- influence through policy intervention (e.g. when national educational authorities close down a study programme, because evaluation has shown that it is badly managed and taught)

- influence through status allocation (e.g. when published results of external evaluations show distinct differences in quality and labour market value, and this causes students and teachers to migrate from some institutions, departments or study programmes to others).

The dimension of areas and the dimension of channels may be combined in a matrix, as follows:

Area: *Channel:*	*Decision* *making*	*Structure and* *curriculum*	*Study* *culture*
Participation and consensus			
Policy intervention			
Status allocation			

In the following, I will try to use this matrix to describe the impact of two external evaluations in Aalborg University.

Case study: history

Local background

From its start Aalborg University operated a MA programme in history. While the subject of history has in Denmark generally been regarded as a part of the humanities, Aalborg University placed it in the social science faculty, and placed most of the teaching positions in a department of 'Social Development and Planning'. During the 1970s and early 1980s, history was one of the most popular study programmes in the social science department. However, in 1985 the Ministry of Education closed down the MA programme in history at Aalborg University. This was not based on a criticism of the quality of the study programme, but was part of a programme of selective reduction of university studies in areas of rising unemployment. Rather than reducing the allowed number of history students at all universities, the Ministry chose to close down the study programme of one university. The reasons for picking Aalborg were not specified. The university was allowed to keep a minor study programme in history (one and a half years, for MAs who had majored in other subjects), but this did not attract many students. So since 1985 Aalborg University has been downscaling the teaching of history, one measure being the discharge of two full professors. The university has of course protested against the closure of the MA programme, and has several times proposed that it should be re-established.

The evaluation

The external evaluation of study programmes in history was one of the first undertaken by the evaluation centre after its establishment. It was commissioned by the National Educational Council for the Humanities in November 1992, and the final report was published in March 1994. The evaluation comprised study programmes at all five universities, and also at the Royal School of Educational Studies (which offers a degree-awarding study programme for primary school teachers, qualifying them for work in teacher training colleges).

Initially the evaluation was received with considerable scepticism by the participating institutions and their scientific staff. There was fear that central authorities would use it to enforce an increased division of labour in the study of history in Denmark. The Humanities Council, on the other hand, maintained that the evaluation aimed only at a clarification and documentation of the state of the subject, and that all partners could benefit from such clarification.

The evaluation followed the general model developed by the evaluation centre. The steering committee, which had the general responsibility for the study and the recommendations, had four members and was led by the Director of the Danish National Archives. The evaluation was done in four phases:

- planning
- documentation through self assessment and user surveys
- peer review
- reporting.

In the documentation phase, each of the institutions involved prepared a self-assessment report on the basis of a framework provided by the evaluation centre. The reports were to contain not only factual information, but also discussions of strengths and weaknesses of the study programmes, their scientific basis and their institutional environment.

The report prepared by Aalborg University assessed that the supplementary study programme generally functioned in a satisfactory way, but that it was not easy to preserve a broad basis of scientific competence for such a small programme. The teachers involved in the evaluation generally feel that preparing the self-assessment report was stimulating and fruitful, but also that the considerable workload strained the limited staff resources in history too much.

The other parts of the documentation consisted of: a survey of the present job situation of a sample of graduates from the study programmes, including graduates' assessment of the labour market relevance of their study; a register-based analysis of the labour market situation of history graduates; an assessment of the study programmes from a number of external examiners (i.e. persons from outside the individual university appointed to participate in exams); a survey of the precise content of the degrees of chosen graduates, i.e. which sub-disciplines they had studied, and the literature they had used. The Aalborg history staff feel that this material contained much useful information, though the small size of the Aalborg study programme meant that the surveys were mostly relevant to the other institutions.

The peer review part of the evaluation was done by a group of four historians, three of them from other Scandinavian countries. The participating institutions were invited to suggest members for this group. The review group made visits to the participating institutions and had discussions with staff responsible for the history study programmes. In the opinion of the Aalborg staff, the peer review group did good work; they took pains to learn about the specific conditions for and considerations behind the Aalborg study programme, and gave fair assessment.

The report and the assessment of the Aalborg study programme

The general assessment of the history study programmes in Denmark is a positive one. To quote from the English summary of the report:

> The evaluation leaves the steering committee with the impression of a discipline and of study programmes where the standard of quality is satisfactory. This is the case whether

the comparison is with corresponding study programmes abroad or with other liberal art study programmes in Denmark... This positive attitude of the steering committee towards the academic standard of the discipline corresponds to the opinion of the external examiners, the visiting panel of experts and the graduates (Danish Centre 1994a, p.117).

The report contains a number of more specific recommendations, but none of them reflect serious criticism of the work done by the staff and the institutions running the study programmes. However, the report objects strongly to the structural framework of the study programmes, a framework laid out by the central educational authorities in 1985. The framework stipulates that the study period for a two-subject arts degree must be no more than five years, with three and a half years for the major subject and one and a half for the minor. The steering committee especially emphasises that the one and a half years of study is not enough to provide 'a satisfactory quality' (p.119) for teaching history in secondary schools. So if the minor subject is to have this function (and this is in fact the predominant function of the two-subject degree), the study of the minor subject should be no less than two years.

This argument does not imply criticism of the institutions. It has in fact been presented to the Ministry of Education by the universities and the secondary school teachers many times during the last ten years. However, the general criticism of the structural restrictions on the quality of history as a minor subject leads the steering committee to discuss the situation at Aalborg University, which as mentioned above manages only a minor subject study programme. The steering group acknowledges that the Aalborg study programme seems to be of good quality under the circumstances, but repeats that a study time of one and a half years is unsatisfactory, and concludes that:

> If Aalborg University is to continue managing a minor subject study programme, the time frame should be extended in accordance with the general recommendations in this report (pp.74–75).

The steering group goes on to cite a formulation from Aalborg University's self-assessment report, in which the university points to the difficulties in maintaining a 'history environment', when the history programme is small, and the history staff have to do much of their teaching in other study programmes. The steering committee is aware that these difficulties could be solved by re-establishing the MA history programme in Aalborg, but in view of the employment prospects for history graduates, the steering committee will not recommend this. So the recommendation is that the history study programme in Aalborg should be closed.

This is the only specific recommendation made in relation to the Aalborg study programme. It is not based on any criticism of the work done within the programme; in fact, in the discussions preceding the finalisation of the report, the peer review panel explicitly said that their impressions could not support a discontinuation of the Aalborg study programme.

When the evaluation report was published, it was made public. As it was one of the first evaluations to be finished, it had some news value, and it was immediately covered in some major newspapers. At this time, Aalborg University had still not received copies of the final report. It turned out that the press treatment was misleading; it indicated that the Aalborg study programme was of low quality and had been badly managed. This was later corrected by members of the steering committee, but as usual this could do little to change the public impression originally created.

The impact

The most important impact was made of course at the level of educational policy. Aalborg University protested against the recommendation to close the study programme, maintaining that the steering committee had exceeded the limits of the task originally set up for the evaluation. The university also felt that when the MA study programme was closed, the university had been promised that it could keep the minor study programme, if it wished. The university renewed its proposal to re-establish the MA programme in Aalborg.

About a year after the publication of the evaluation report, the Ministry of Education gave Aalborg University permission to reopen the MA programme in history. The political interests and negotiations behind this are complicated, and outside the focus of this paper. The role of the evaluation report is also difficult to assess, but two facts are worth mentioning. When the Humanities Council discussed whether to recommend a reopening of the MA programme in Aalborg, several members based their reservations on the fact that the evaluation report, which the Council itself had commissioned, had recommended closure. On the other hand, there is little doubt that the evaluation report forced central educational authorities to make a decision in the matter of history studies in Aalborg. If not for the evaluation report, the ministry might have continued stalling the issue.

Some other effects of the evaluation can also be identified:

- The work on the self-assessment report seems to have been a fruitful process for the Aalborg history staff. However, the positive impact of this must be weighed against the fact that the production of the report was very demanding in time and effort. For a small staff it was a heavy burden.

- As the report contained virtually no other comments on the Aalborg study programme than the suggestion to close it, there has been little chance to discuss or implement such suggestions. When the Ministry of Education demanded (about a year after the publication of the report) that the institutions should describe their efforts to implement the recommendations, it was felt by the Aalborg staff as an unnecessary measure, perhaps even an unclear political signal.

- The press coverage of the report, which reported that the Aalborg study programme was of low quality, had a clear effect on the attitude of students towards the programme. Several students stopped studying history in the weeks afterwards, and the number of applications for the programme fell.

There were no negative effects on the relations to the other institutions managing history programmes. On the contrary, these institutions indicated that the treatment of Aalborg was unfair.

I shall try to summarise these effects, using the framework outlined in section 3.1.

Case study: social work

Local background

Denmark has two different kinds of study programmes for professional social work: full-time study programmes of three to three and a half years' duration, and part-time study programmes which

Area: Channel:	Decision making	Structure and curriculum	Study culture
Participation and consensus	Slightly better links to other educational institutions		Both positive and negative effects of self-assessment and peer review
Policy intervention		Reopening of MA programme	
Status allocation			Short-term loss of student confidence of study programme

enable people already employed in public administration to qualify for social work. The full-time study programmes are mostly managed by schools of social work, which are independent institutions located in major Danish towns. Aalborg is the only place in Denmark where the study of social work is part of the university. This is because Aalborg was created as a university centre, which was to integrate existing institutions of higher education.

The content of the study programmes is much the same across institutions, because it is regulated by a relatively tight framework set up by the Ministry of Education. But because it is part of the university, the Aalborg study programme differs in several respects from the study programmes at the schools of social work. Most social work students do the first year of their study in the common social science foundation year, along with students in economics, business studies, public administration etc. The staff of the social work programme are employed on the same basis as most other university teachers, which means that they do research alongside teaching. And the programme is managed through the university system of governance, which means that although there is a head (elected) of social work studies, this person has limited authority and has to consult the social science dean or the rector on important matters. The schools of social work, on the other hand, each have their own rectors.

The evaluation

The evaluation of the study programmes in social work was started in September 1993, and the final report was published in November 1994. The evaluation was commissioned by the Conference of Rectors of the schools of social work. The Ministry of Education had announced that all institutions and study programmes in Danish higher education were to be externally evaluated sooner or later, and the Rectors' Conference wanted it to be sooner. The reason for this was that they wanted to examine and if possible improve the quality of social work education. At the time when the evaluation was initiated, there was some unofficial speculation that the schools of social work wanted to use the evaluation as a lever to secure for their graduates the title of bachelor, which has only recently been introduced in Danish higher education, and which is generally restricted to the university study programmes. But this has not been confirmed.

It should be noted that the initiative came from the rectors of the four schools of social work, and that the Danish School of Administration (which manages the part-time programmes) and Aalborg University only joined the evaluation after it had been decided. The social work staff at Aalborg University did not agree with the idea. This was because another quality assessment and development project (initiated by the professional association of social workers) had been finished the year before, and the Aalborg staff felt that it would be fruitful to digest and follow up on the conclusion from this study before another was initiated. However, once the external evaluation was decided, Aalborg University felt it natural to participate.

The evaluation followed the general model developed by the evaluation centre. The steering committee had four members and was led by a senior official from the Ministry of Social Welfare. The evaluation was done in three phases: planning; documentation and visits to institutions; reporting.

There is no distinct peer review part or phase in this evaluation. This means, of course, that the burden of professional credibility is placed more clearly with the steering committee.

The documentation phase encompassed a number of activities. The most important was probably the preparation of *self-assessment reports* by each institution. At Aalborg University the staff members involved found this the most fruitful and stimulating part of the evaluation. Preparing the self-assessment report made it necessary to explicate and reflect on problems and experiences, which were usually handled in more structured ways. But it also demanded a lot of work; for instance, finishing the report meant that the head of the study programme had to leave aside a research project, which she had been preparing for some time.

The other parts of the documentation consisted of: a survey of the present job situation of a sample of graduates from the social work study programmes of the different institutions, including graduates' assessment of the labour market relevance of their education; a survey, where leading staff members in offices of social work were asked to assess the competence of graduates in social work; interviews with 12 'experts', who had broad experience within the area of social work, but without being professionally involved in social work education. They were asked to formulate their ideas and visions of social work education.

The head of the Aalborg study programme found these parts of the documentation of little value. The two surveys provided some factual information, but the general tendencies were well known. The 'expert' interviews contained many interesting viewpoints, but their value was limited by the fact that the 'experts' had little concrete knowledge about the social work education. So when the report cited the views of the 'experts' on the present state of educational practice, the result was misleading.

After the self-assessment reports and the other documentation was finished, the steering committee visited each educational institution to discuss questions raised by the documentation. The written reports from these visits were part of the basis for the final report.

The report and the assessment of the Aalborg study programme

The assessment of the study programmes is generally positive. To quote from the English summary:

> The fact that the institutions have seized the opportunity to have an external evaluation of their study programmes is positive, testifying to a willingness of change that is absolutely essential to further development in quality... The comprehensive documentation gives the impression of an area of higher education, where graduates and employers generally express their satisfaction with the programmes

and the qualifications imparted to the graduates (Danish Centre 1994b, p.122).

But the steering committee also has some clear reservations.

- It seemed to be difficult for the institutions to formulate the basic ideas in the social work study programmes. This lack of overriding, central categories led to a multitude of subjects and compact study programmes.

- The institutions had developed a management style based on the mutual recognition of various specialist groups, and this made it difficult to implement general changes.

- The element of practical training, and thus the relationship between theory and practice, should be strengthened.

In addition to these general concerns, the steering committee makes many more specific comments and recommendations. There are few specific comments on the Aalborg study programme, but most of them are positive. For instance it is pointed out that the Aalborg programme has a good distribution of examinations during the study period, and that the university environment seems to foster a more independent student approach to learning than at the schools of social work.

More important than these specific comments are the relationship between the Aalborg programme and the general recommendations in the report. The steering committee proposes that the established division in 10 disciplines, which is part of the framework prescribed by central educational authorities, should be broken up and reorganised in three main disciplinary fields, of which the core field should be social work methodology. This reorganisation should be supported by the formulation of new 'visions' for social work education and perceptions of professional identity. It should also be supported through research, especially research in social work methodology. The steering committee finds '...the lack of possibilities of research in social work a great weakness', and it strongly supports an initiative from the Ministry of Social Affairs to establish a centre for research in social work.

As mentioned earlier, the staff of the Aalborg social work programme do in fact have the opportunity (and the obligation) to do research. The head of the Aalborg programme finds it curious that the report does not discuss this. The report only makes the brief comment that in spite of the research opportunities, Aalborg University '...has not established research in social work as a distinct field' because teaching staff 'are not placed with the study programme, but with different departments' (p.85). The last part of this statement is a misunderstanding; but the main point is that the steering committee does not want to discuss the connection of teaching and research in Aalborg, probably because it does not want to undermine the argument for the proposed new research centre. This interpretation is supported by the fact that the Chairman of the steering committee is also one of the originators and main sponsors of the idea of the research centre.

In the view of the head of the Aalborg study programme, many of the recommendations in the report have little relevance for this programme. For instance, the report recommends that theory and methodology of science should be important areas during the first year of study. This is exactly the case in the social science basic course at Aalborg University. The report seems mostly to focus on problems and strategies which are relevant for the four schools of social work, whose rectors also initially requested the evaluation.

The impact

At the level of educational policy, two recommendations in the evaluation report have been implemented: the proposed centre for research in social work has in fact been established, and it has decided to issue a new formal framework, common to all the social work study programmes. Aalborg University, which up to now has had its own formal framework (combining university legislation with the general rules for social work education) had in fact earlier suggested a reform of the framework, and this can now go ahead. It is difficult to say how much the evaluation influenced these decisions; both were more or less under way already. The consequences for the Aalborg study programme are difficult to predict, because the decisions focus mostly on the situation at the schools of social work.

Later the Ministry of Education has announced that the new common framework will be based on a maximum study time of three years. The evaluation report had actually recommended a maximum study time of three and half years, which would have meant extending the study time at the schools of social work. The ministry has chosen instead to shorten the Aalborg study programme. This has naturally led to dissatisfaction among social work staff and students at Aalborg University.

Preparing the self-assessment report seems to have been a stimulating experience, not only for the few teachers participating in the evaluation, but also for other members of the social work studies staff. But it has demanded too much work.

As yet, there has been no noticeable effect on student orientations towards the Aalborg study programme. Nor have there been any negative effects on relations to the other institutions managing social work study programmes. Competition seems not to have increased. The continuous contact during the evaluation period seems rather to have improved the mutual understanding of the institutions. The same can be said about the relationship between the social work staff and the administrative staff of the university.

Finally I shall try to summarise the effects of the external evaluation in the matrix developed earlier.

Area: Channel:	Decision making	Structure and curriculum	Study culture
Participation and consensus	Slightly better co-operation with other educational institutions		Positive: experience of self-assessment. Negative: much extra work
Policy intervention		New general framework for study programmes to be issued. Reduction of allowed study time.	
Status allocation			

Conclusion

The two cases described above raise some general questions about the effects and the rationale of the form of external quality assessment currently practised in Denmark. To conclude, I shall discuss these questions in relation to the background of the political, institutional and political developments which I outlined in the first part of the paper.

Systematic measures of quality control have been institutionalised or are emerging in most western European countries. Probably they are here to stay, at least for some considerable time. But it should be remembered that this development is fairly recent. External quality control has been launched as part of new policies for higher education, but it is not yet clear how it fulfils its role within these policies. In the Danish context the evaluation centre has been operating for some four years, and completed its first evaluations only two years ago.

This makes it difficult to assess the real political and administrative significance of external quality control. And it makes it equally difficult to assess the impact on the institutions of higher education. Especially when we are talking about impact on areas like social status and institutional culture, which often change relatively slowly. Nevertheless, the two internal case studies point to some different kinds of impact of the activities of the evaluation centre.

Preparation of the self-assessment reports seems to have a positive internal effect. It confronts teaching staff with their own educational practices, and provokes reflection on change. There is no doubt, however, that it involves considerable work, and that this is a burden for the heads of study programmes and core staff members. This workload is exactly the reason why staff and study boards seldom start such self-assessment procedures on their own initiative; they have to be forced or motivated from the outside. So although self-assessment might be done as an independent and internal procedure, it could be hard to motivate the teaching staff for this without the context of an external evaluation.

Self-assessment has positive impacts, but mostly for persons involved directly in the work. It has proved difficult to involve the majority of teaching staff in work and discussions, both during the evaluation procedure and after the publication of the report. The effect on the everyday culture of teaching staff seems to be uneven.

It should be mentioned that in most institutions one or two students are included in the self-assessment work and the discussions with external evaluators. These students gain considerable insight into the constraints and potentials of the study programmes, and this can be a positive contribution to the study culture (provided, of course, that the insights are communicated to wider groups of students).

The focusing of evaluations on subject-defined study programmes seems to limit the perceived relevance of conclusions and recommendations. Both the history and the social work staff at Aalborg University complain that the recommendations in the reports have little relevance for the Aalborg study programmes, and reflect limited knowledge of the character of studies and research at Aalborg University. The university does have some special features related to study structure and pedagogy, but there is a more general problem involved. All educational institutions and study programs are special; they have their own 'life histories' and their own problems. When external evaluations take as their object the subject-defined study programmes across institutions, their assessment and recommendations will focus on a 'mainstream' or an 'average', which may in fact not exist, and with which individual institutions will have difficulty identifying. In this way criticisms and recommendations may lose much of their potential impact at the decentral and institutional level.

The evaluations seem to have some impact on policy decisions at the central administrative level, but the impact is hard to predict, as shown by both cases.

The central role given to the steering committees, which are to be composed of credible and authoritative persons outside the usual disciplinary circles, and who do not act as peer review groups, seems in at least one of the cases discussed above to have undermined the neutrality of the evaluation. The focus on subject areas across institutions also means that evaluations invariably become involved with the balance of power and status between institutions. This is demonstrated in both internal case studies. It may be that the agencies commissioning evaluations (especially the educational councils) implicitly endorse this, because settlements concerning the role of individual institutions have to be made and adjusted from time to time, but it is not a part of the explicit mission of the evaluation centre, so it creates a situation of uncertainty in the institutions.

This uncertainty characterises not only the policy consequences, but also the follow-up procedures. In the cases discussed, follow-up has been a formal demand that institutions should describe how they had implemented recommendations which they felt had little to do with their situation and problems.

From the perspective of study programmes in a Danish university, and the persons teaching and studying in these programmes, external quality assessment has some positive but also some negative and ambiguous effects. In my view some of the ambiguities result from the role given to external quality assessment in Danish higher education, and from problems in the model of evaluation chosen by the evaluation centre. I must emphasise, however, that the two cases reported in this paper should not be generalised. For instance, the history evaluation was done at a time when the evaluation centre still had little experience with the role of steering groups, and the centre was probably not happy with the political bias of the steering group's conclusions. And clear policy intervention, which has been part of the impact of both evaluations discussed here, has actually not occurred very often.

References

Bache, P. and Maassen, P. (eds) (1994) 'Higher education policy in Denmark.' In L. Goedegebuure *et al.* (eds) *Higher Education Policy: An International Comparative Perspective*. Oxford: Pergamon Press.

Danish Centre for Quality Assurance and Evaluation of Higher Education (1994a) *History Study Programmes within Higher Education: Evaluation Report*. Copenhagen: Danish Centre for Quality Assurance and Evaluation of Higher Education.

Danish Centre for Quality Assurance and Evaluation of Higher Education (1994b) *Social Work Study Programmes: Evaluation Report*. Copenhagen: Danish Centre for Quality Assurance and Evaluation of Higher Education.

Kjersdam, F. and Enemark, S. (1994) *The Aalborg Experiment: Project Innovation in University Education*. Aalborg: Aalborg University Press.

Neave, G. (1988) 'On the cultivation of quality, efficiency and enterprise: an overview of recent trends in higher education in western Europe, 1986–88.' *European Journal of Education* 23, 1–2.

Rasmussen, P. (1991) 'The role of the first year in the educational structure and pedagogy of Aalborg University.' In A. Lorentsen and A. Kolmos (eds) *Quality by the Theory and Practice of Higher Education*, Technology and New Pedagogy series 6. Aalborg: Aalborg University Press.

Thune, C. (1995) *Evaluation and Quality Assurance of Higher Education in Denmark: Background, Methods, and Experiences*. Copenhagen: Danish Centre for Quality Assurance and Evaluation of Higher Education.

Chapter 17

An Australian Approach to Quality in Higher Education
The Case of Monash University

Gay Baldwin

Introduction: the context for quality assessment

In the Australian higher education system, a concern with quality assurance has been growing over at least the last decade. However, what can be described as 'the quality movement' – with its theoretical models and specialised discourse – has impinged on the mainstream consciousness only since the issuing of a brief by the Commonwealth Government Minister to the Higher Education Council in 1991, for an investigation of issues relating to quality in higher education and recommendations for policy initiatives. There is no doubt that developments in European countries, especially Great Britain, had a strong influence on Australian policy trends in this area. Very quickly, 'quality' became the catch-cry of the moment, taking over from the language of 'standards', 'excellence', 'efficiency and effectiveness'.

Whether the new language represents a quite new concern is a matter for debate. Enthusiasts for quality systems tend to alienate many by implying that universities have never before been concerned with 'quality'. Opponents contest the appropriateness of language, concepts and systems drawn from the culture of manufacturing. There can be no doubt, however, that the quality movement, assisted by some very skilful manipulation of carrots and sticks by the Commonwealth government, has penetrated the culture of higher education in significant ways. The last few years have seen a remarkable flurry of activity in setting up systematic procedures designed to assess and improve the quality of university operations, particularly in the area of teaching and learning. How deep and enduring these changes are remains to be seen. This paper offers some tentative judgments about effects in one institution.

National system/government policy

In the Commonwealth of Australia, the six states have constitutional responsibility for higher education; universities are established, and operate, under state legislation. However, the Commonwealth government has taken over funding responsibility, and therefore controls planning. Until recently, the states acted as 'post-boxes' for the direction of funds, but now even that role has disappeared. From time to time, they present positions on policy matters (particularly the always-contentious issue of allocation of places) but, on the whole, seem quite content for the Commonwealth to steer the system through a time of rapid change.

Higher education is almost entirely a public system. Several small private institutions have been established in recent years, but the spectacular and widely-reported financial and political problems of one of these universities may have retarded the growth of this sector. In 1989, the government introduced a 'user-pays' element into the funding of higher education (known as the Higher Education Contribution Scheme). Under this scheme, students pay approximately one-quarter of the average cost of their education, but can defer repayment until they are earning above a designated threshold, and repay through instalments as part of the taxation system. They can also pay 'up-front' and receive a discount for doing so (approximately one-quarter take this option). In this system, no-one is denied access to higher education because of an inability to pay fees; this feature seems to have ensured general acceptance from a citizenry which had become accustomed to 'free' university education.

The university sector has traditionally been based on the assumption of uniform standards across all institutions. With some qualifications, this was largely true of the 'old universities' which comprised the degree-granting sector until the 1950s. Each state had one university – of the ivy-covered-stone variety – and the Australian National University was established in Canberra in

1946. They catered for a very small proportion of the population, largely from elite private secondary schools and a small number of selective public schools. There were separate systems of technical colleges and teachers' colleges, which did not grant degrees, conducted little research and were generally regarded as lower in status than universities.

The 1950s saw the start of a remarkable transformation of Australian higher education, a shift from an elite to a mass system that has much in common with similar movements in other countries, but is arguably the most rapid and far-reaching of all. In 1946, there were 25,600 students in Australian universities, 'plus an unknown but much smaller number in other tertiary institutions' (Universities Commission 1975, p.71). In 1995, there are 622,000 tertiary students. Demand for higher education has exploded, so that, even with this extraordinary expansion of places, there is still a politically uncomfortable level of unmet demand.

The expansion of the university system came in several stages. The first saw the establishment of two new large institutions (the University of New South Wales and Monash) which developed along lines very similar to those of the traditional universities and which were quickly able to compete with them for students and establish strong research records. A second wave produced universities with different profiles and approaches: they did not offer the full range of professional courses, they experimented with interdisciplinary studies and catered for somewhat different groups of people – students from less privileged backgrounds and mature students returning to study. Although attracting staff of high calibre (many of them Australians returning from higher degree studies overseas), these universities found it difficult to build up a research profile comparable with the 'Big Eight'. Some clear status differences emerged in the public mind and these were reflected in measures like intake scores of students.

At the same time, the technical and teachers' colleges were growing and the former were expanding their range of offerings. In 1965, the Commonwealth government, acting on the principal recommendations of a committee it had set up to investigate the future of tertiary education in Australia, known as the Martin Committee, established a binary system, with a university sector and an advanced education sector. The latter was to be different from, but complementary to, the university system, with a stronger vocational emphasis, and was to cost significantly less. A major part of the cost difference was that these colleges were not to be funded for research. A strong theme in the discussions surrounding this inquiry and the government's response was a desire to protect the nature and quality of university education in the expansion that was obviously necessary (Davies 1989). The system perpetuated the clear status differences between universities and colleges, although this was complicated by the perceived excellence of some of the courses offered at the technological institutes (in engineering, for example) which, with their stronger practical orientation, were believed by some to offer better value to employers than more theoretical university courses.

The rapid growth in the system was generally welcomed by the Australian public which, in hindsight, can be seen to have demonstrated a strong belief in the value of higher education and a willingness to fund it generously from the public purse. Amid the confidence and optimism associated with the expansion, there was a muted note of concern about standards, which occasionally broke into public debate. This concern tended to focus on questions of basic skills, particularly literacy. Some employers complained that graduates could not write sentences (a complaint not limited to Australia) and a few maverick academics supported them with outbursts about the poor quality of students, usually coupled with complaints about the secondary schools which had produced them, rather than any consideration of the possibility that there might be room for improvement in universities.

In 1988, another wave of change hit the higher education sector and its effects were so far-reaching that it is often referred to as 'the Dawkins revolution' (after the Minister for Education who initiated it). The famous White Paper (Australian Government 1988) which announced the new agenda offered what was really a re-conceptualisation of higher education and its place in society. The full implications of this are beyond the scope of this paper; for the present purposes, it is enough to point out that, despite the careful gestures towards traditional university values, the paper attempted to re-position higher education as an essential part of the economy of the country and to call it to account in these terms. The re-positioning was signalled neatly – and provocatively – by the reorganisation of government departments and names to produce the super-department of Employment, Education and Training.

The most immediate effect of the shift in government policy was the abolition of the binary divide and the amalgamation of many institutions into a smaller number of larger universities (some amalgamations of colleges had already taken place, but the pressure intensified after the White Paper). Some of these amalgamations involved the joining of colleges with existing universities, others involved several colleges. In some cases, the model was a federation; in others, the institutions aimed for a thorough integration of activities. In the new Unified National System, all institutions were placed on the same funding base, but a 'research quantum' was introduced to fund the bulk of research competitively, on the basis of productivity.

The rhetoric of the Dawkins revolution paid homage to the value of diversity within the system, but beneath the rhetoric could be read a concern for consistency of standards and a desire to set limits on institutional autonomy. Australia now found itself with 38 universities, where a few short decades before there had been seven. Although the growth of the system was politically popular, it was also very expensive. There was a clear need to demonstrate that taxpayers' money was being used efficiently and that the 'gold standard' of university degrees had not been devalued. The pressure for accountability did not start with the Dawkins era; it had been building up steadily for some time, as evidenced by several reports commissioned by the Commonwealth Tertiary Education Commission (Bourke 1986; CTEC 1986). However, the Dawkins changes did add considerable impetus to these developments and coincided with the rise of the quality assurance movement in European university systems. When 'quality' hit Australia several years later, it was an ideal tool for the Commonwealth government to use.

Officially, the Commonwealth government allows and encourages the autonomy of individual universities. It takes a 'hands off' approach to academic matters – issues relating to curriculum, assessment, etc. However, it cannot rely on the operation of market forces to ensure quality, since these forces are constrained within the Australian system by government-determined quotas on places, the reluctance of Australian students to move interstate and the weakness of the private sector. Further, there has been little information available to the public about the quality of educational programmes. Universities have traditions of internal reviews, but the results of these are not published. Beginning in 1988, the Australian Vice-Chancellors' Committee commissioned a number of discipline reviews, with a focus on comparison of standards at the fourth-year honours level of undergraduate degrees. Although these were valuable, the findings were not widely disseminated to the public.

The notion of 'quality audit' seemed to offer the government a way of directing institutions to pay more attention to their own procedures for ensuring and demonstrating quality, while respecting institutional autonomy since, in theory, the universities would retain control over those procedures. Quality assurance measures were not to be prescribed from Canberra. The government would ask institutions to demonstrate that they had a systematic and coherent system for evaluation and improvement. This was the genesis of the Committee for Quality Assurance in Higher Education (CQAHE).

External quality assurance requirements

In 1993, on the advice of its Higher Education Council (1992) and after extensive consultation with the university sector, the Commonwealth government established a system of quality audit, to be administered by the CQAHE. The system is based on annual preparation of portfolios by participating institutions, following guidelines prepared by the committee. It is not discipline-based, but operates at the level of whole institutions, with a particular emphasis on the need for coherent policy direction and systematic monitoring by central administration. The first year, 1993, involved a general overview of all university functions; in 1994 the focus was on teaching and learning and in 1995 on research and community service. The portfolios are studied by a panel appointed by CQAHE, which then visits the universities for one day to investigate the claims made in the documentation. It is a voluntary system, with a 'prize pool' of funds to be allocated according to the judgments of performance. In the first year, the pool was $77 million, in the second, $71 million and in the third $50 million. These are not large sums when set beside the annual higher education budget of $4,783 million (1995/96) Some commentators have commended the political astuteness of the government in being able to produce so much activity for such a small amount of reward money.

Given the voluntary nature of the system, the relatively small incentives and the doubts of many institutions about the process (which have been repeated frequently in the national press), it is surprising that none has refused to participate – although several have considered this option, initially or as a response to the first round and its results. Some senior academic leaders have suggested that it is more the fear of the negative repercussions of not competing than the positive rewards that have ensured their (reluctant) involvement.

One of the main sources of discontent has been a shift from an initial focus on *quality audit* to a concern with *quality assessment*. This is partly attributable to a change of Minister half-way through the first year of the system. The new minister wanted to be able to identify 'half-a-dozen world-class universities' and so directed the CQAHE to place an emphasis on outcomes. The final result of the first 'round' was an uneasy mixture of the two processes: a good deal of attention was given to procedures and systems during the visits, but the ranking of performance seemed to many to reflect long-established status hierarchies, privileging the old universities. The justifications for the rankings reflected an attempt to balance these different considerations. So, those universities in the top band were said to have excellent outcomes and excellent procedures, while those in the second band had excellence in one of these areas but not in the other. Monash, placed in the second band, was judged to have first-rate outcomes, but some problems with its procedures. (It was difficult to understand exactly how the panels had come to their conclusions about outcomes, given the problematic nature of performance indicators in the teaching area.)

When this quality assurance scheme was established, the Opposition parties in the federal parliament were critical of its basic approach. They defined it as centralist, bureaucratic, even 'socialist' in its attempt to impose regulatory systems on institutions. They argued that the market should determine quality; at the time, they were proposing that the mechanism for this would be a voucher system, but have since moved away from this proposal. The Commonwealth government changed in March, 1996, with the Coalition of Liberal and National parties winning office in a landslide victory. The new Minister has announced that there will be significant cuts in funding to the higher education sector. The existing quality audit system is being scrapped.

Institutional characteristics

Monash is the biggest university in Australia, with 40,000 students and 7,000 staff on six main campuses. It has embarked enthusiastically on the most ambitious amalgamations in the national system, involving a research-based university, an institute of technology, a college which had developed from a teacher training institution, a mixed-discipline regional college, and a single-discipline professional college. It has the biggest population of international students in the country.

Because of these mixed antecedents, it has great diversity in its courses, its campus and discipline cultures, student populations, and approaches to teaching and research. It also has a particularly strong tradition of faculty autonomy, stemming from the appointment of full-time deans in its early days, at a time when this was not the norm in the Australian system. This characteristic has been strengthened by the amalgamations; the institution is simply too big to be governed tightly from the centre. So, to quote a university document, the Deans are 'effectively the Chief Executives of devolved "business units"' (Monash University 1995, p.2).

The amalgamations are generally regarded by Monash people as very successful; so too is the operation of the devolved system. However, these features do present the institution with a challenge when it comes to the institution's responsibility for assuring quality across the whole range of operations. This difficulty was the focus of the quality panel's first judgement of the university's procedures in 1993. It identified weaknesses in two areas: there was not enough central direction, in the form of overarching principles and guidelines, and not enough systematic monitoring and evaluation, with feedback loops from the departments and faculties to central administration.

Internal quality assurance systems

The university had already recognised the need for more systematic development of its own procedures before the first quality audit in 1993. The series of amalgamations had only been finalised in July 1992. A lot of work had gone into developing procedures which would allow for the smooth integration of the new campuses into Monash structures. The academic leaders of the institution knew that the next stage involved attention to quality assurance mechanisms that would ensure a reasonable consistency across the university in its academic operations. Some of the measures outlined below were being developed before the first quality audit, but there is no doubt that they were 'pushed along' by that national exercise.

Teaching

The foundation for quality assurance in the area of teaching and learning was the process of course approval. The university found itself with a huge number of educational programmes and more being proposed every day, in response to changes in disciplines and in the workplace. (To give a rough indication of the scope of its offerings: in 1994, Monash had approximately 5,000 separate subjects on its books.) Proposals for new courses came from Faculty Boards to Academic Board, but the volume (given the other responsibilities of Academic Board) meant that they were not receiving detailed scrutiny. Further, the procedures for course approval in the faculties varied considerably. In 1992, an Education Committee was established as a Committee of the Academic Board, with a brief to examine proposals for new courses and subjects, and significant amendments to old ones, in a systematic and rigorous way.

The Committee developed *pro formas* for course and subject proposals which require far more information than previously and which ask proposers to demonstrate that the programmes are based on sound educational principles – in particular, that the teaching methods and forms of assessment are directly related to the objectives. These *pro formas* are now used throughout the institution, and so govern the faculty processes as well as the deliberations of the Education Committee. Each faculty has a representative on the Education Committee; in each case, this person has a major responsibility for the faculty's course approval procedures, so a consistent approach is ensured across the nine faculties. The committee has played a tough role, sending back many proposals for further work. It has been a difficult process, particularly for some academics from the 'old university' part of

Monash, who were not used to preparing extensive documentation for their courses. One of the strange anomalies of the binary system was that, while colleges had to go through demanding accreditation procedures for new courses, universities did not. It is one way in which the old Monash has benefited from the experience of its ex-college members.

These formal approval procedures were only a start. The assumption underlying the establishment of the Education Committee was that it is particularly important in a time of rapid change for the university as a whole to deliberate about whether new courses are appropriate. (For example, ten years ago, many Monash academics would mock 'mickey-mouse' American universities which offered courses in areas like tourism; now tourism is a rapidly-growing area in the University.) In its deliberations, the committee has to keep in mind the fundamental question, 'What is a university education?' Another way of asking this question is 'What are the attributes we aim to develop in all our graduates, regardless of discipline?' It also has to ask whether courses have been designed effectively to develop the core attributes of university graduates. The committee decided early in its life that it needed to develop a set of policies and guidelines to give clear direction to the university community on fundamental educational principles and to establish broad criteria for course approval. This was the genesis of the Monash Education Policy, which is really an integrated set of policies covering teaching activities. It is the first time in the university's history that such principles have been articulated and drawn together in a single statement of educational philosophy.

The Policy starts with a detailed definition of effective teaching, then covers a range of areas such as Course and Subject Objectives, Assessment, Codes of Practice for Staff and Students, Student Workload, Student Representation, and Review of Outcomes. As can be seen from this list, it goes considerably beyond matters relating to course approval, to cover many aspects of course presentation, evaluation and continuous improvement. It also goes beyond a philosophy of education to establish some quite specific requirements of staff and students. It incorporates a 'Teaching and Learning Support Plan' which offers assistance and support for their activities. This includes provision for extended professional development programmes, mentoring schemes, teaching awards, amended promotion procedures to recognise teaching excellence, funds for teaching innovation and the establishment of a network of Associate Deans (Teaching) to balance the existing network of Associate Deans (Research).

The Policy establishes, for the first time, a system of regular, compulsory student evaluation of subjects, based on a question-naire which comprises ten 'core' items and allows individuals and/or departments to select other items from a large item bank. This model attempts to establish some broad, common measures across the institution, while allowing for disciplinary and individ-ual differences. The Policy stresses that this is only one form of evidence of teaching effectiveness and requires groups of staff to consider other evidence, such as the quality of students' written work, patterns of results and their own impressions, in regular meetings at the end of term. The emphasis is on self-evaluation, conducted by staff actually involved in the teaching. However, there is a requirement that the conclusions from their deliberations, including decisions about change and improvement, are reported back through the system in summary form, to heads of depart-ments, deans and the Education Committee. Another feature of the Policy is a more systematic approach to reviews, which are now to be conducted on a cycle (seven years for faculties and the faculties to decide for departments, with five years a common choice). Guidelines are to be more specific and there is to be more attention to following up the recommendations.

Throughout the document, there is a consistent emphasis on improved communication with students – communication to them about expectations, requirements and assumptions (what is being called more explicit teaching) and communication from them about their expectations and needs, and how effectively they are learning.

The Education Policy attempts to strike a balance between central direction and faculty/department/individual autonomy. The basic strategy is to outline a broad requirement and then direct faculties to determine the details according to their circumstances, requiring that they report back on their decisions. A lot of the activity which has taken place since the approval of the Policy in early 1994 has been at the faculty and department levels, with some faculties elaborating aspects in considerable detail. Inevitably the emphases vary, so certain faculties have put more work into developing structures for consulting with external stakeholders (through course advisory committees, for instance) than others. Some have been particularly concerned with achieving greater consistency in assessment procedures, and so on.

The Deputy Vice-Chancellor who carried responsibility for the Education Policy also assumed some responsibility for overseeing faculty implementation. His office developed a 'checklist' of the requirements set out in the policy and members visited the deans for long interviews based on this checklist. Deans reported on how they were interpreting the policies and what steps they had taken to implement them. They raised problems and issues that had arisen during this process, which were conveyed back to the Deputy Vice-Chancellor. Although the exercise looked rather draconian when the responses were registered in the form of a detailed table with ticks and dates for planned initiatives, the deans were generally very supportive and indicated that the visits had been very useful for improving communication with 'the centre'.

Another area which deserves mention is the work done by the PhD and Scholarships Committee. This work actually began several years before the establishment of the Education Committee and the development of the Education Policy, partly because the area of postgraduate supervision has been the focus of national concern since the mid-1980s, as it has in other countries, because of unacceptable completion rates and times. This committee has been responsible for the development of detailed guidelines on the responsibilities of institution, department, supervisor and candidate, the establishment of a rigorous reporting system on the progress of students, close monitoring of completion rates and times, the administration of a questionnaire to all research students in the university and some concerted follow-up activity on the basis of the results.

The examination procedures for postgraduate theses at Monash rely heavily on external examiners, as they do in all Australian universities. However there is little interest in the use of external examiners at the undergraduate level. Even for honours theses, it is comparatively rare. The possibility of extending the practice has been raised during discussions of quality assurance in the last few years, but there is almost no support for it. The argument is usually that it is impractical, given the numbers involved and the tightness of examining schedules, especially in a semesterised system. It is also clear that Australian academics consider it unnecessary for undergraduate programmes.

Research

In general, quality assurance in the research area has been less problematical than in teaching. There has certainly been a good deal of debate about performance indicators, and this debate is still going on. However, there seems to be widespread acceptance of the argument that research performance can be measured and compared. Critics still argue that to measure quantity is not to measure – or assure – quality, but most academics seem to accept the fact that peer judgments of quality are built into the processes of refereeing publications and applications for research grants. Certainly, the production of league tables of institutions based on competitive grants has been well established for some years. League tables based on output measures are more contentious, since they vary considerably according to the definitions and weightings used.

Another issue which is still hotly debated is the prioritising of research areas. The Commonwealth government has attempted to direct research to some extent, by establishing priority areas (related to the nation's needs) for its research funding schemes, such as the Australian Research Council scheme and the National Priority (Reserve) Fund. However, these are not rigidly enforced and have not created significant opposition. It has also tried to encourage institutions to establish priorities for themselves.

Monash has taken a strong stand on this issue. An internal review of the management of research in the university in 1992 resulted in a strong affirmation of the principle of 'parity of esteem' for all areas of research and of the right of all academics to conduct interest-driven research. Further, it has insisted on the appropriateness of the devolved model in research management. Since research is highly discipline-specific, the management and fostering of research activities must be located close to those disciplines. The university has steadfastly refused to prepare the kind of centralist, directive research management plan that has been produced by some other universities, even though it has been subjected to some pressure from the government bureaucracy to do so. Instead, it has developed a set of *Research and Research Training Guidelines*, which outline broad principles and establish the faculty responsibilities for management. It has also established a network across the university of Associate Deans (Research) who meet regularly with the Deputy Vice-Chancellor (Research and Development). This committee has worked well to improve communication across the faculties and between the faculties and the centre. It engages the faculties in the shaping of policy rather than imposing it on them.

In taking this stand, the university has, to some extent, rejected the criticism of the first quality audit team that there was not enough central direction and planning in the research area. It made its arguments strongly in its quality portfolio for 1995, when the focus was on research and community service. These arguments were accepted by the visiting team, on the basis that central administration had established effective reporting mechanisms to ensure that the faculties did indeed develop policies and systematic plans for their research activities. So, for instance, there is no central directive on the contentious issue of prioritising research areas. The university will not establish priorities itself, nor will it insist that the faculties take a particular stance on the issue, but it will ensure that the matter is addressed and debated in appropriate faculty forums.

Central administration does take an active role in monitoring performance. The Research Services Division has done a lot of research on performance indicators, has introduced streamlined processes for gathering information and has engaged in systematic checking of returns for accuracy, the appropriateness of claims, etc. The results are conveyed regularly to faculties for their use in self-evaluation, planning and improvement.

All faculties have prepared research management plans. They differ in approach and degree of specificity, but all have coherent, focused programmes for ongoing monitoring and enhancement of research activity, with clear goals and some numerical targets. Another significant quality assurance mechanism is the close scrutiny of applications for outside studies programmes (formerly sabbatical leave). This scrutiny is conducted in the faculties and is based on the principle that individuals should be able to demonstrate tangible outcomes from previous leaves to earn more. This is a significant shift: 20 years ago, sabbatical leave was regarded as an automatic right.

Community service

Although this is defined by the Commonwealth government as the third major role of universities, it has received much less attention than the others. In making it a joint focus of the 1995 quality audit, the CQAHE was obviously trying to encourage institutions to look at ways of approaching this whole area more systematically. Everyone agrees that academics in Australian universities do a lot of work for the community, as advisers, consultants, expert commentators, performers etc. There have been very few attempts to quantify these activities, let alone establish guidelines for quality in these areas. Last year at Monash, sustained attention was paid to this area, resulting in: the development of a taxonomy for community service activities; the establishment of a register of expertise and interest, to be made available to the public; a survey of all academic staff on their activities in this area; the development of a Community Service Policy.

Impacts on management and decision-making processes

It should be pointed out that the 'quality' movement is only one of a number of developments affecting management and decision-making processes in Australian universities. There has been much talk in recent years of the 'corporatisation' of these institutions, seen by critics as an attack on traditional collegiate values and by proponents as a necessary injection of hard-headed business thinking into organisations which have been hamstrung in their response to change by cumbersome and reactionary procedures. A major review of the management of universities was commissioned in 1995 by the Commonwealth government, as part of its broader agenda of a national strategy for enhancing competitiveness and efficiency.

Planning and resourcing

At Monash, quality assurance concepts and programmes have resulted in the more systematic incorporation of evaluation and monitoring into planning exercises. The 'feedback loops' of responses from stakeholders are not complete, but the framework has been established in relation to students and a number of areas of the university have regular input from employers and the professions. Stronger links with schools have been established, and these will continue to develop through several innovative programmes designed to enhance communication between the sectors (one involving senior secondary teachers spending time at Monash, the other taking Monash students into the schools to act as tutor/mentors). In many areas, planning starts in more rigorous self-evaluation, informed by more data about effectiveness.

The university has devoted significant sums to the development of evaluation mechanisms (such as the student evaluation questionnaire systems, the research data collection systems, etc.) and to support for new positions with significant responsibilities for planning and quality assurance (particularly the Associate Deans for Teaching and Research).

Incentives

In the research area, Monash has operated an incentive scheme, based on performance, for some years. It allocates 12.25 per cent of the operating grant to faculties for academic activities as a Research Quantum; faculty share is determined by a formula incorporating both research grants and publications. This mirrors the Commonwealth government's Research Quantum, but Monash included a publications measure from the start – the Commonwealth has done so only since 1995.

The university has accepted that this principle should be extended to the teaching area, though on a much smaller scale. The Education Policy includes a commitment to allocate 2 per cent of the operating grant to faculties on the basis of demonstrated excellence in teaching. This has been approved but not implemented, and some doubts have surfaced recently about the feasibility of the strategy, given the difficulties with performance indicators of teaching.

Monash has received a total of $14 million dollars from the Commonwealth's Quality Fund in the last three years. The sums are not huge, in relation to the whole budget, but are certainly seen as very useful. They have been allocated according to proposals from faculties, the Computer Centre and other support units, student associations, etc. A major commitment has been to the provision of computer equipment to staff and students throughout the university. It has been possible to spend this money on areas which, in other circumstances, might have been difficult to fund.

Not that computers can be defined as a 'luxury' in the current environment, but in an institution where so much of the budget is spent on fixed salaries, it can be hard to find funds for a large-scale equipment programme. Some faculties were able to offer departments relatively small amounts for staff 'retreats', which could be defined as 'extras' but have proved to be very valuable for group reflection and planning.

As already noted, the staff promotion procedures have been revised to place more emphasis on the systematic demonstration of performance, with supporting evidence, particularly in the teaching area. The university is attempting to tie annual increments more closely to performance in a staff appraisal system. For academic staff, increments within categories have been virtually automatic until now. The National Tertiary Education Union is fighting this very hard. Generally, the whole situation in relation to academic staff appraisal in Australian universities is a mess, for complicated reasons going back a number of years, which are beyond the scope of this paper.

Structural/governance

The pressure for accountability intensified at a time when Monash was devolving more responsibilities to faculties and departments. The policy of devolution is based on a commitment to this model as the most efficient form of management, perhaps accompanied by a recognition that it is now the only workable model in an institution of this size and complexity. There has been some tension involved in responding to the Commonwealth's quality agenda in these circumstances, since that agenda presupposes a significant element of centralised control, direction and scrutiny. A strong theme in the first quality audit visit was the question, 'How do you in central administration know what is going on out there in the faculties?'

The establishment of the Education Committee was an important statement to the university that course approval is a matter for the *whole* institution. In the first two years of its operations, the workload and paperwork were almost overwhelming, raising the question of whether this kind of detailed central scrutiny can be maintained. The intention is that, after an initial learning period, the committee should be able to act as a watchdog, ensuring that the detailed work is handled adequately at faculty level, but not having to immerse itself in the minutiae of proposals. It seems likely that this strategy will be successful. Indications are that faculty procedures and scrutiny have become more rigorous. The faculty committees on undergraduate and postgraduate programmes have grown in importance, and regularly engage in debates about significant educational issues, such as entry standards, assessment principles, fairness of workload, proper management of Recognition of Prior Learning, and so on.

The establishment of the Committee of Associate Deans (Teaching) has provided a forum for cross-faculty discussion of educational issues and the dissemination of good practice. The hope is that it will ensure consistent attention to the quality of teaching across the different faculty cultures, without imposing a single model of 'good teaching'.

The Committee of Associate Deans (Research) has played a similar role, both in providing a cross-faculty forum and in encouraging more activity at the faculty level. All faculties now have research committees and they too are assuming increasing significance in the direction of research activities. The Arts Faculty Research Committee provides a good example of a change in approach. In this faculty perhaps more than any others, research has been regarded as, in some ways, the private concern of individual academics. While affirming the individual's right to pursue whatever research he or she is interested in, this committee has become more interventionist. In 1995, for the first time, it established a faculty research fund to support specific projects and to provide seeding money for the development of large-scale collaborative projects. It has also established a performance indicators system appropriate to the faculty for internal distribution of the Research Quantum.

Heads of departments have assumed an increasingly managerial role, a phenomenon which is by no means confined to Monash. As in other institutions, this development is resented by some, welcomed by others. It is likely that, in the near future, their role will include a more active engagement in staff appraisal, linked to the power to grant or withhold salary increments. This will certainly affect their relationship with staff and may well undermine collegial decision-making procedures at the department level.

The University's Education Policy establishes a basis for more systematic consultation with students and for wider representation of students on decision-making bodies. Faculties have been asked to review their arrangements for representation and report back to the Education Committee.

Curriculum development

As mentioned earlier, this is an area of rapid change in Australian universities and Monash is no exception. Generally, there has been a dramatic burst of creativity in the development of many new courses in areas which have not previously been taught in traditional universities. Ten years ago, Monash offered a handful of undergraduate degrees (B.A., B.Ec., B.Sc., etc.). Now, it offers hundreds, many with specific titles aimed at 'niche markets'. There has also been considerable growth in the provision of combined degrees and a recent development has been the offering of combined degree/diploma programmes, in collaboration with colleges from the Technical and Further Education sector (institutions outside higher education). These developments have been welcomed by many, but are also a source of concern. There is obviously a shift in the balance of general and vocational education in the university sector. It is not clear yet whether this is a radical re-orientation or an adjustment.

The higher education sector is faced with fundamental questions about the nature of university education, the 'gatekeeping' role of institutions and the importance of stakeholders. To what extent should stakeholders determine educational programmes and approaches? What weight should be given to the views and interests of different stakeholders? How should we balance the immediate needs of, say, employers against obligations to society as a whole and to future generations? How does the university's traditional role of critic accord with the imperative to provide 'customised products' for consumers? It is no exaggeration to state that the system is in a state of intellectual turmoil about these issues. It is in this context that the insistence on more rigorous scrutiny of curriculum developments must be understood. The strategy taken at Monash has been to insist on what are essentially traditional academic procedures – the examination of proposals by academic peers, guided by overarching statements of principle.

What is not traditional (in terms of Australian university practice) is the new emphasis on a structured, 'explicit' approach to curriculum development, with a strong focus on student learning and the articulation of principles underlying courses and their internal relationships.

University culture(s)

The forces transforming university cultures in Australia and elsewhere are certainly deeper than the quality assurance movement, which can be regarded as a manifestation of change rather than a cause. The 'corporatisation' of universities which has been taking place over the last decade has parallels in many other areas of social life, which are beyond the scope of this paper. Certainly the conceptualisation of tertiary institutions as business organisations has been particularly shocking to many members of those institutions, because of the traditions and myths surrounding them, which have been just as powerful in Australia as in older countries. The quality debate has focused some of these wider issues on the concept of students as 'customers'. Many academics see this metaphor as offensive and a challenge to fundamental values, while some senior managers claim that it is the only way to force attention to students' interests and needs. (It must be noted that academics in some areas have embraced the new concepts enthusiastically – in business and computing faculties, for example.)

A further source of contention is that a significant number of academics see the new managerial prerogatives associated with the demand for greater accountability as undermining traditions of collegiate decision-making and staff autonomy. At Monash, a concerted attempt has been made to work through the established systems of governance and to build on faculty and department procedures in the construction of a quality assurance system. Certainly, the system depends on responsible oversight from central administration, but it attempts to allow as much room as possible for local interpretation and control. The views of Monash staff on the effectiveness of this strategy would vary widely.

There can be no doubt that, in the system as a whole and at Monash in particular, there is a new emphasis on the importance of teaching and a growing recognition that teaching should be the subject of analysis and reflection. Again, this development probably pre-dates the quality assurance movement, but it is clear that the audit system has worked as an effective catalyst.

Interpretation of outcomes

It is still too early to make a confident judgment about the outcomes of the national quality audit exercises. We need time for the dust to settle. As indicated earlier, the existing system will not continue under the new government. However, the former Labour government had already announced an intention to cut it back significantly, on the basis that the ground-breaking work had been done, institutions had their mechanisms and procedures in place and these would continue to operate without the need for incentive funds.

There has been much criticism of the exercise. Critics – including several Vice-Chancellors – have identified problems with the conceptual approach, values and methodology. However, there is widespread, if somewhat grudging, agreement that it has produced a lot of activity in universities, in the development of policies and the establishment of evaluation and monitoring systems. The crucial question which remains is: 'How deep does all of this go? How much of it will turn out to be window-dressing?'

At Monash, there have been some clear benefits. These include:

- a stronger culture of self-evaluation on the basis of evidence
- the articulation of many things formerly taken for granted – policies, values, educational principles, etc. – which has stirred debate and encouraged reflection
- a re-examination of fundamental questions about the nature of university education
- creativity in curriculum development, in response to concern for the interests and needs of stakeholders
- more sustained attention to the presentation of mission and achievements to the tax-paying public
- a more systematic approach to many aspects of university operations, such as course approval, management training, consultation with students
- better communication between faculties and departments and between these units and central administration
- a shift towards a more student-centred approach in teaching.

On the other side of the ledger must be recorded the following disadvantages, as perceived by many staff:

- excessive bureaucratic demands, resulting in overwhelming volumes of paperwork and increased time spent in meetings
- a perceived loss of autonomy for academic staff
- the alienation of some staff from university management and a climate of cynicism about 'going through the motions'.

As well, there is widespread concern about possible dangers associated with the adoption of quality assurance concepts and systems. The most important of these are as follows:

- excessive responsiveness to stakeholders could threaten the independence of the university and its role as critic
- the conceptualisation of students as customers could undermine the traditional teacher/student relationship
- management models imported from the business culture could prove to be inappropriate and destructive of collegiate relationships and procedures.

Whether all of the activity described in this chapter has made an appreciable difference to the everyday educational experiences of students is still an open question. The university, faculties and departments would hope to get data from student evaluation systems which allow them to chart improvement over time, but since these are still not fully implemented across the whole institution, it is too early to tell whether they will be able to fulfil this function. There is still a lot of scepticism about the validity of student questionnaires and even most supporters argue that they are most useful for formative purposes – to give feedback to teachers on how they can improve particular courses. For summative, comparative purposes, they are rather blunt instruments, able to throw up obvious problems and outstanding successes, but probably not able to discriminate fine differences between courses or over time. The judgements about improvement probably cannot be made globally, but must remain the responsibility of individual teachers and groups of teachers on the basis of a range of evidence, including the quality of student work. The most important role of the institution is probably to ensure that such self-evaluation is conducted as a regular part of academic operations, and to encourage a climate of evaluation and improvement.

Certainly, the student representatives involved in the development of the Education Policy and the work of the Education Committee have been enthusiastic supporters of these developments. They believe that setting out sound educational principles and establishing structures for consultation and monitoring must improve the quality of educational experiences and outcomes.

The immediate future at Monash is likely to be a time of consolidation. Some of the developments of the last few years still need to be worked out in detail and embedded in routine practices throughout the institution. The university is trying to steer a middle course in this period of turbulent change. It has been one of the most active institutions in the country in embracing certain aspects of that change – in extending into new areas, both geographically and academically. It has seen the opportunities created by the 'stirring up' of the higher education system outlined in this paper, but has also tried to protect core university values, working through traditional academic procedures and building on its history of faculty autonomy. It is likely that this juggling act will need to continue for some time.

References

Australian Government (1988) *Higher Education: A Policy Statement*. The Hon J.S. Dawkins MP, Minister for Employment, Education and Training. Canberra: Australian Government Publishing Service.

Bourke, P. (1986) *Quality Measures in Universities*. Canberra: Commonwealth Tertiary Education Commission.

Commonwealth Tertiary Education Commission (1986) *Review of Efficiency and Effectiveness in Higher Education: Report of the Committee of Enquiry*. Canberra: Australian Government Publishing Service.

Davies, S. (1989) *The Martin Committee and the Binary Policy of Higher Education in Australia*. Melbourne: Ashwood House.

Higher Education Council (1992) *Achieving Quality*. Canberra: Australian Government Publishing Service.

Martin, Sir L. (Committee Chairman) (1964–65) *Tertiary Education in Australia*. Report of the Committee on the Future of Tertiary Education in Australia (The Martin Report). Canberra: Australian Publishing Service.

Monash University (1995) *Higher Education Management Review: Submission from Monash University*. Monash: Monash University.

Universities Commission (1975) *Sixth Report of the Australian Universities Commission*. Canberra: Australian Government Publishing Service.

Glossary

AAU	Academic Audit Unit (New Zealand and UK)
CATS	Credit Accumulation and Transfer Schemes (UK)
CEPES	European Centre for Higher Education
CHEA	Council for Higher Education Accreditation (US)
CHEPS	Centre for Higher Education Policy Studies
CNAA	Council for National Academic Awards (UK)
CNE	Comité National d'Évaluation des Éstablissements Publics à Caractére Scientifique, Culturel et Professionnel (France)
CQAHE	Committee for Quality Assurance in Higher Education (Australian)
CRE	Association of European Rectors
CVCP	Committee of Vice-Chancellors and Principals (UK)
CVE	Continuing Vocational Education
COPA	Council on Postsecondary Accreditation (US)
DfE	Department for Education (UK)
EC	European Commission
GSP	Graduate Studies Programme (UK)
HEFCE	Higher Education Funding Council for England (UK)
HEI	Higher Education Institution
HEQC	Higher Education Quality Council (UK)
HMI	Her Majesty's Inspectorate (UK)
IMHE	Institutional Management in Higher Education (Europe)
INQAAHE	International Network for Quality Assurance in Higher Education
ITO	Industry Training Organisation (New Zealand)
JPG	Joint Planning Group (of HEQC and HEFCE)
NPB	National Policy Board on Higher Education Institutional Accreditation (US)
NQF	National Qualifications Framework (New Zealand)
NSB	National Standards Body (New Zealand)
NZCTE	New Zealand Council for Teacher Education (New Zealand)
NZVCC	New Zealand Polytechnic Programmes Committee (New Zealand)
NZQA	New Zealand Qualifications Authority (New Zealand)
OECD	Organisation for Economic Cooperation and Development
QEG	Quality Enhancement Group (UK)
RAE	Research Assessment Exercise
SCOP	Standing Committee of Principals (of higher education institutions)
SPREs	State Postsecondary Review Entities (USA)
TTA	Teacher Training Agency
UNESCO	United Nations Educational, Social and Cultural Organisation
VSNU	Vereniging van Samenwerkende Nederlands Universiteiten

The Contributors

Gay Baldwin is a Senior Research Fellow in the Faculty of Arts at Monash University, working in the area of educational policy and planning. She taught in English departments at several Australian universities before moving into academic staff development and higher education policy. She played a significant role in the development of quality assurance systems at Monash.

Andris Barblan has been since 1976 Secretary General of the Association of European Universities (CRE), the non-governmental organisation for inter-university co-operation in Europe whose headquarters are located in Geneva. *Licencié ès lettres* of the University of Lausanne, he acquired the title of *Docteur ès Sciences Politiques* from the Graduate Institute of International Studies in Geneva for a thesis on the *Image of the English in France during the Colonial Quarrels in the late 19th Century*. He also worked as Youth Secretary for Europe and Asia at the World Council of Churches from 1968 to 1971, and as assistant to Denis de Rougemont at the European Cultural Centre in Geneva from 1973 to 1976.

Tony Becher is a Research Professor of Education at the University of Sussex. Between 1990 and 1996 he was responsible, as Head of Academic Audit, for the University's quality support system. His research interests include academic cultures, postgraduate education and continuing education in the professions. His *Academic Tribes and Territories* (1989) is the most widely cited of his numerous books and articles.

John Brennan is Head of the Quality Support Centre at the Open University. He is co-author of *Higher Education and Work* (1995), *Students, Courses and Jobs* (1993) and *Graduates at Work* (1988).

Roger Brown has been Chief Executive of the Higher Education Quality Council since July 1993. He was previously Head of Research and Strategy at the Committee of Vice-Chancellors and Principals; Chief Executive of the Committee of Directors of Polytechnics; and Secretary of the Polytechnics and Colleges Funding Council (from June 1990). He has also worked at the Department of Trade and Industry, the Cabinet Office, the Department of the Environment, and the Office of Fair Trading. Between 1969 and 1976 he was an officer of the Inner London Education Authority. He has taught and has published a book and a number of articles on the post-war planning of further and higher education in London. He obtained his PhD at the University of London Institute of Education, where is now a Visiting Professor.

Peter de Vries is Projects and Development Officer in the Quality Support Centre of the Open University.

David D. Dill is Professor of Public Policy Analysis and Education at the University of North Carolina at Chapel Hill. His interests include higher education policy and management. He is currently engaged in a cross-national analysis of the impact of public policies on quality assurance in higher education. His most recent books include *Emerging Social Demands and University Reform: Through A Glass Darkly* (1995) with B. Sporn, and *Planning and Management for a Changing Environment: A Handbook on Redesigning Postsecondary Education* with M. Peterson and L. Mets. Dill has served as President of the Society for College and University Planning and has been a Research Associate at the University of Manchester, a Visiting Fellow at Wolfson College, Cambridge, and a Visiting Professor at the University of Twente in the Netherlands.

Lars Engwall is Professor of Business Administration and Chairman of the Quality Committee at the University of Uppsala, Sweden. He is a member of several Swedish academies, among them the Royal Swedish Academy of Sciences. His publications include Models of Industrial Structure (Lexington Books, 1973), Newspapers as Organizations (Saxon House, 1978), and Mercury Meets Minerva (Pergamon, 1992). He is currently doing research on the creation and diffusion of modern management models.

Janet Finch is Vice-Chancellor of Keele University, a post which she took up in September 1995. She has also been involved at national level in a range of policy-making bodies related to higher education. She has been involved in issues of quality and accountability in higher education in a variety of roles, and in 1997 she was appointed as a Board member of the newly created Quality Assurance Agency for Higher Education.

Vin Massaro is Director of Administration and Registrar of Flinders University. He has written extensively on higher education policy and management and is founding editor of the Journal of Higher Education Policy and Management. In the past nine years he has worked and written on quality assessment methods and the development of performance indicators for higher education in Australia, Sweden and with the OECD.

Marie-Odile Ottenwaelter, Professor Agrégé in Classics, has taught for fifteen years, particularly in teachers' education. As a staff member at the Comité National d'Évaluation since 1990, she is responsible for the co-ordination of institutional and discipline-based evaluations. She has participated in several evaluation programmes abroad as well as in a variety of seminars on evaluation of higher education and training workshops of experts. She played an active role both in the implementation of the European Pilot Project for Evaluating Higher Education and in the creation of a European network of quality assurance agencies in higher education.

Palle Rasmussen is Associate Professor in the Sociology of Education at the Department of Social Studies and Organisation, Aalborg University, Denmark. He has done empirical and theoretical research in many areas of the educational system and many aspects of the relationship between education and society. He recently published *Theoretical Issues in Adult Education – Danish Research and Experiences* together with Henning Salling Olesen (Roskilde University Press, 1996). He teaches mainly in Aalborg University's social studies and sociology programmes, and in Open University courses in adult education.

Tarla Shah is the Administrator and Projects and Development Officer in the Quality Support Centre of the Open University. She has been involved in projects on European quality assessment and international peer review and has published several reports and articles on these topics. She is currently involved in an OECD funded project on *Quality Management, Quality Assessment and the Decision-Making Process* and the development of an interantional postgraduate course in higher education studies. She is managing an HEFCE funded project analysing the extent to which recommendations made by subject peers are being acted upon by institutions. She also edits the *Higher Education Digest*. Her previous posts were with the Council for National Academic Awards and the former Polytechnics and Colleges Funding Council.

Andre Staropoli is Secretary General of the Comité National d'Évaluation, Paris.

Christian Thune was a professor at the University of Copenhagen until 1992. From 1984 until 1989 he was dean of the Faculty of Social Sciences. From 1989 until 1992 he was Chairman of the Committee of Chairmen of the National Educational Councils. Since 1992 he has been Director of the Centre for Quality Assurance and Evaluation of Higher Education. In 1993 he became Chairman of the National Council for Educational and Vocational Guidance. Since 1993 he has been a member of the Working Group of Experts and the Management Group for the EC-pilot projects for evaluation in the EC-member countries. He participates in evaluations of universities and institutes in Finland, Ireland, Sweden and Hong Kong.

David Watson is a historian and has been Director of the University of Brighton since 1990. He was formerly a member of the CNAA, the PCFC, the HEFCE (and chair of its Quality Assessment Committee), the Paul Hamlyn Foundation National Committee on Education, and the Joint Planning Group on quality assurance. He has published widely on the history of American and British philosophy and on developments within higher education. He is a member of the National Committee of Inquiry into Higher Education chaired by Sir Ron Dearing.

Ruth Williams is a member of the Open University's Quality Support Centre. She is an experienced researcher and has undertaken considerable work on the UK's external examiner system. She has also worked on a number of projects in the field of systems and methods of quality assurance in higher education both in the UK and internationally. Before joining the Quality Support Centre, she worked at the former Council for National Academic Awards.

David Woodhouse is Director of the New Zealand Universities Academic Audit Unit, and was previously Deputy Director of the Hong Kong Council for Academic Accreditation. He is active internationally in quality assurance, providing advice and training on educational quality assurance in a number of countries. He is on the Board of an international organisation dealing with the quality of education offered across national boundaries and is Secretary and Newsletter Editor of the International Network of Quality Assurance Agencies in Higher Education and an editor of its journal.

Subject Index

Author Index